"This is a great new book on church planting tha[t] theological, cultural, and technical. Church plai
Tim Keller, Redeemer Presbyterian C

"Now here is a clever idea—ask an experienced church-planting pa..... .t-
ing should be done. In *Church Planter: The Man, the Message, the Mission* by Darrin Patrick, an experienced church planter speaks from deep theological conviction, pastoral experience, and missiological vision. Church planting is one of the most important movements of our era—and one that follows the pattern set by the apostles. This book will be welcomed by all who celebrate the renaissance of church planting in this generation."
R. Albert Mohler, Jr., President, The Southern Baptist Theological Seminary

"Darrin Patrick is a friend to church planters. He is widely known as a strong leader and good thinker in church planting today. In this book, Darrin brings together his biblical understanding, theological insight, and pastoral wisdom on what it takes to plant a missional church. For those who are planting or thinking about it, this book will help you to see if you are prepared with the message and for the mission."
Ed Stetzer, www.edstetzer.com; coauthor, *Viral Churches: Helping Church Planters become Movement Makers*

"We have all read books on church planting, planting churches, and church-planting movements. This book is about the church planter . . . his qualifications, his theology and his character. Make no mistake about it, Darrin Patrick covers all the bases on what it takes to be a successful church planter in the twenty-first century. Get the right man, going in the right direction, with the right message and you have impactful combination for the kingdom of God." This is a Christ-centered and gospel-centered approach to launching new churches."
Billy Hornsby, President, Association of Related Churches, Birmingham, AL

"*Church Planter: The Man, the Message, the Mission* is a superb work. Darrin Patrick combines the mind of a careful theologian, the heart of a compassionate pastor, and the passion of a missional Christian. As someone heavily invested in training church planters in a seminary, this will be a must read for those we teach and send out to penetrate lostness in the unreached and underserved cities of our nation and the world. Thank you, Darrin, for this labor of love. You have rendered a valuable service to the body of Christ."
Daniel L. Akin, President, Southeastern Baptist Theological Seminary, Wake Forest, NC

"*Church Planter* comes from the heart of a real man sharing the real gospel from real experience leading Christ's church. Powerful, helpful, hopeful!"
Bryan Chapell, President, Covenant Seminary; author, *Christ-Centered Preaching* and *Christ-Centered Worship*

"If you are called to church planting, Darrin Patrick gets you. More importantly, he understands what it takes to connect you to the gospel, the gospel to the church, and the church to the mission. This book is packed with insight; it's a boot-camp-in-print. If God has enlisted you, then read it and let the training begin!"
Dave Harvey, author, *Rescuing Ambition*; Church Planting & Church Care, Sovereign Grace Ministries

"My new friend, Darrin Patrick, offers an insightful look at the privilege and calling of being a church planter. As one who is passionate about growing God's church, I recommend this book for every pastor and church planter. If you hope to plant a church for the fame of the name of Jesus Christ, be sure to read this book before you do."
James MacDonald, Senior Pastor of Harvest Bible Chapel and Founder of Harvest Bible Fellowship

"I like being pushed, and Darrin Patrick is a careful thinker and a hard-working pastor. Here he has written a clear, carefully considered, well-illustrated introduction to the pastor and his ministry. In reading it, I've been challenged, provoked, and encouraged. I disagree with some things, like Darrin's correlation between the resurrection of Christ and the transformation of cities, but this book has been exciting and helpful and I appreciate it a great deal. I happily commend this book to you, and pray that God will use it to help establish churches that take the gospel of Christ to the end of the world."

Mark Dever, Pastor, Capitol Hill Baptist Church, Washington, DC

"I love this book because I love church planters and I know this book will help them fulfill their calling. I also love that Darrin writes in such a raw way. This isn't an ivory tower book. It's written by someone who has some battle scars because he's been in the trenches of church planting."

Mark Batterson, Lead Pastor, National Community Church, Washington, DC

"Darrin slices through the clutter to give us insight on what is most important in launching a new work—a clear understanding of a Biblically functioning community led by one passionately committed to Jesus. This is a strong, excellent work that goes beyond pragmatic strategies and gives principles that will serve in any context. I'm fired up about a movement of leaders who will live out the core principles of *Church Planter* and launch churches that honor God and share his fame!"

Jud Wilhite, author, *Eyes Wide Open*; Senior Pastor of Central Christian Church, Las Vegas, NV

"Darrin Patrick gets ministry. He understands it's not a career for those of us trying to do something for God. It's a calling that can only be fulfilled faithfully when built upon the foundation of scriptural norms. This is not only a great book for anyone involved in church planting—it's also a great book for anyone involved in pastoral ministry. It will help you (and your team) keep your life, message, and mission aligned with God's vision and calling."

Larry Osborne, North Coast Church, Vista, CA

"*Church Planter: The Man, the Message, the Mission* by Darrin Patrick is a must read for anyone thinking about planting a church or who works with church-planting leaders. While I don't hold to all of Darrin's theology of leadership, I still highly recommend *Church Planter*. When it comes to church planting, Darrin is a guy that absolutely 'gets it' because he has done it! And you will 'get it' too if you read this book!"

Dave Ferguson, Lead Pastor, Community Christian Church, Naperville, IL; Visionary Leader for NewThing

"This book is a weapon. *Church Planter* is one of the more important pieces of equipment that a church planter (or a man aspiring to any level of church leadership) can own. Darrin Patrick writes out of biblical conviction and proven experience, not preference or pragmatics. I trust Darrin. I trust what he's written here. I hope this book is placed in the hands of men all over the world."

Justin Buzzard, church planter, Phoenix, AZ; blogger, BuzzardBlog

"Darrin Patrick has done an amazing job detailing out what we are called to not only as church planters but as pastors and men of God. Whether you are considering planting a church or have been a pastor for decades, I couldn't more highly recommend this book to you."

Matt Chandler, Lead Pastor, The Village Church, Texas

CHURCH PLANTER
THE MAN, THE MESSAGE, THE MISSION

DARRIN PATRICK

Foreword by Mark Driscoll

WHEATON, ILLINOIS

ISBN-13: 978-1-4335-1576-7

ISBN-10: 1-4335-1576-8

PDF ISBN: 978-1-4335-1577-4

Mobipocket ISBN: 978-1-4335-1578-1

ePub ISBN: 978-1-4335-1579-8

Library of Congress Cataloging-in-Publication Data
Patrick, Darrin, 1970–
    Church planter : the man, the message, the mission / Darrin Patrick
    p. cm.
Includes index.
    ISBN 978-1-4335-1576-7 (tpb)
    1. Church development, New. 2. Evangelistic work. 3. Missions—Theory.
I. Title.
BV652.24.P38   2010
254'.1—dc22   2010006580

Crossway is a publishing ministry of Good News Publishers.

VP		19	18	17	16	15	14	13	12	11	10
14	13	12	11	10	9	8	7	6	5	4	3	2	1

CONTENTS

Foreword

I met Darrin Patrick at the first Acts 29 boot camp we ever held to assess and train potential church planters. That was a providential and pivotal moment for me and many other church planters.

Since that day, Patrick has become, by God's grace, a successful church planter with a thriving ministry in St. Louis, Missouri, and a magnet for young church planters around the nation and world. In large part due to his leadership, Acts 29 has seen over three hundred churches planted in the U.S. and in many other nations.

Through it all, Darrin has become a dear friend. I have seen him love his wife deeply, serve his children faithfully, pastor his church dutifully, and preach the gospel passionately, and I have come to love him greatly. There are few great leaders, and even fewer great leaders of leaders. Darrin is both.

He has battled illness, miscarriage, and the fiercest of religious critics, only to become more desirous to repent of his sin, serve humbly, and help others. In short, he's a pastor to pastors with the scars of battle and spoils of victory that earn him the right to be listened to on the issues he speaks about in this book.

When it came time to write the first book on church planting by one of our Acts 29 church planters, it made sense for Darrin to write it because so many leaders from so many denominations and networks look to him for wise, gospel-centered, Bible-rooted, Jesus-focused counsel. Subsequently, I am thrilled to see his book finally published. I believe God will use it to throw a few more logs on the fire of church planting, to call forth many more church planters, to save some church planters from their own folly, and, with the Holy Spirit's empowering, to see more transformed people worship Jesus, which is what church planting is all about.

Mark Driscoll
Preaching and Theology Pastor,
Mars Hill Church
Founder and Lead Visionary of Acts 29

Acknowledgments

I want to thank my dad for being the first man in my life and my godly mother who I wish were alive to read this book.

I also want to thank the board and members of the Acts 29 Network whose courage and faith inspired the words that are written here.

Thanks to the elders and staff of The Journey who served and suffered for our local church so I could write.

Also, without the support of my godly wife, Amie, and our four children this wouldn't have been close to possible.

Finally, glory to Jesus who saved me and called me to himself and to his mission through the local church for the sake of the world.

Preface
Why Focus on Men?

I realize that I have lost many of you before we have even started by using the word "Man" in the subtitle of this book. Why would I rule out more than half the population with such a narrow focus? Why would I be so patriarchal and chauvinistic? How could I reinforce stereotypes about who does or doesn't belong in full-time ministry? Before you put the book down and chalk it up as yet another promotion of testosterone Christianity, read this preface. There is a method to my madness. There is a reason that this book is written from a man to men and is written about the kind of men who are needed to proclaim the gospel and lead the church of God into a broken world. In short, I take this focus because we have a cultural crisis and a theological one that must be addressed.

The Cultural Crisis

We live in a world full of males who have prolonged their adolescence. They are neither boys nor men. They live, suspended as it were, between childhood and adulthood, between growing up and being grown-ups. Let's call this kind of male *Ban*, a hybrid of both boy and man. Ban is juvenile because there has been an entire niche created for him to live in the lusts of youth. The accompanying culture not only tolerates this behavior but encourages it and endorses it. (Consider magazines like *Maxim* or movies like *Wedding Crashers.*) This kind of male is everywhere, including the church and even, frighteningly, vocational ministry.

Ban may be a frightening reality in the church, but he is the best thing that ever happened to the video game industry. Almost half (about 48 percent) of American males between the ages of eighteen to thirty-four play video games every day—*for almost three hours.*[1] The average video

---

[1]Cf. Kay S. Hymowitz, "Child-Man in the Promised Land." This article, which I have used throughout this chapter, can be accessed at http://www.city-journal.org/2008/18_1_single_young_men.html.

After noting that the average gaming time for the eighteen- to thirty-four-year-old is two hours and forty-three minutes per day, Hymowitz wryly adds, "That's 13 minutes longer than 12- to 17-year-olds, who evidently have more responsibilities than today's twentysomethings."

game buyer is thirty-seven years old. In 2005, 95 percent of computer game buyers and 84 percent of console game buyers were over the age of eighteen.[2] *Halo 3* grossed over three hundred million dollars in the U.S. in its first week,[3] and more than one million people played *Halo 3* on Xbox Live in the first twenty hours.[4] Astonishingly, 75 percent of American heads-of-households play computer and video games.[5]

It may be troubling to look at how Ban spends his money, but it is appalling to see how he relates to women. One needs only to follow Ban to "da club" to see what he thinks of and wants from the opposite sex. Again the stats tell the story.

There are 9.7 million Americans living with an unmarried different-sex partner and 1.2 million Americans living with a same-sex partner.[6] Every *second* $3,075.64 is being spent on pornography,[7] 28,258 Internet users view pornography,[8] and 372 Internet users type adult search terms into search engines.[9] Every thirty-nine minutes a new pornographic video is created in the United States.[10]

In the United States, 1.3 women are raped every minute. That results in seventy-eight rapes each hour, 1,872 rapes each day, 56,160 rapes each month, and 683,280 rapes each year.[11] One out of every three American women will be sexually assaulted in her lifetime.[12] The United States has the world's highest rape rate of the countries that publish such statistics. It's four times higher than Germany, thirteen times higher than England, and *twenty times higher* than Japan.[13]

Unfortunately, many young women today have given up trying to find Mr. Right. They are coming to the stark reality that they are probably going to have to settle for Mr. So-So. Ban is good at selling himself as a man, but the reality is that he is just a "man wannabe." Ban typi-

[2]See http://www.seriousgameseurope.com/index.php?option=com_frontpage&Itemid=1&limitstart=44.
[3]Scott Hillis, "Microsoft says 'Halo' 1st-week sales were $300 mln," Reuters, October 4, 2007.
[4]Paul McDougall, "*Halo 3* Sales Smash Game Industry Records," *Information Week*, September 27, 2007.
[5]See http://www.seriousgameseurope.com/index.php?option=com_frontpage&Itemid=1&limitstart=44.
[6]U.S. Census Bureau, 2000; http://usattorneylegalservices.com/divorce-statistics.html.
[7]See http://www.familysafemedia.com/pornography_statistics.html.
[8]Ibid.
[9]Ibid.
[10]Ibid.
[11]See http://oak.cats.ohiou.edu/~ad361896/anne/cease/rapestatisticspage.html.
[12]Ibid.
[13]Ibid.

cally doesn't like absolute truth, but he proves its existence through his continual devolution into junior-high behavior and its accompanying consequences. It is a transcultural reality that assuming the responsibilities of husband and father makes a boy into a man, but Ban doesn't like responsibility, so he extends his adolescence as long as humanly possible.[14] And by delaying having a family, which is the rite of many cultures' progress into manhood, Ban is able to set his focus squarely and supremely on himself.[15]

As Ban puts off adulthood, he also puts off marriage. Why bother with a wife and a mortgage when you can live in your parents' basement, play video games all day, participate in adult sports leagues at night, and barhop every weekend? Hymowitz notes that in 1970, 69 percent of twenty-five-year-old and 85 percent of thirty-year-old white men were married; in 2000 only 33 percent and 58 percent were, respectively.[16] And the data suggests this trend is not slowing. I think this is one of the reasons young men love watching mixed martial arts. They project themselves onto these "superheroes," men who are everything they are not: incredibly disciplined, courageous risk-takers who have the genuine respect of their peers. It's as if watching real men in danger taps into the brain chemistry responsible for what we call masculinity. Curiously, the testosterone and adrenaline that encourage men to seek danger and risk are rarely tapped into for honorable purposes like lifelong marriage and parenting. Instead Ban settles for virtual reality and virtual relationships.

Some men cease fondling themselves,[17] the game controller, or the TV remote and actually participate in adult sports leagues, including the child playground game kickball.[18] Perhaps one major catalyst for young men's love for recreational sports is that it replicates the kind of challenge and competitiveness sorely lacking from their own personal, professional, and spiritual lives. One author called team sports a "civi-

---

[14]Hymowitz, "Child-Man in the Promised Land."

[15]See David Gilmore, *Manhood in the Making: Cultural Concepts of Masculinity* (Binghamton, NY: Vail-Ballou Press, 1990), 41–42, 64.

[16]Hymowitz, "Child-Man in the Promised Land."

[17]According to a Kinsey Institute study on American sexual practices conducted nearly sixty years ago, 92 percent of American men of all post-pubescent ages reported they masturbated regularly. See http://www.teenhealthfx.com/answers/Sexuality/1056.html.

[18]According to the World Adult Kickball Association (WAKA), sanctioned adult kickball has grown to more than seven hundred teams in eighteen states, with more than seventeen thousand registered players. WAKA has more than thirty full-time paid employees and is a million-dollar-a-year business. See http://www.kickball.com.

lized substitute for war,"[19] which would explain why so many men only seem to come alive emotionally on the inside and feel connected socially on the outside to their fellow "weekend warriors." It has become mainstream to be an adult boy.[20]

The masculine journey from boyhood to manhood lies largely in the transition from engaging physically by inflicting pain to engaging emotionally by absorbing emotional pain and persevering through it.[21] Boys must learn how to use their physical strength more passively than actively as they progress to manhood and become what David Gilmore calls "real men." Real men "give more than they take . . . are generous, even to the point of sacrifice."[22] Being a man is about being tough *and* tender.

I have three beautiful daughters who have not only stolen my heart but seem to walk around with it and toss it back and forth between them like a plaything, all the while taunting me with the fact that I'll never be able to get it back from them! But I also have a son, Drew, and because of my keen awareness of and pastoral interaction with the cultural influence of Bans, I know that my work is cut out for me when it comes to raising a godly man. As with all of us dads with similar aspirations, my only hope is the Holy Spirit. So I recently wrote a little prayer that reflects the kind of men we need. Drew and I pray this prayer together almost every night. It is a prayer for him and for me:

> God, make me a man with thick skin and a soft heart. Make me a man who is tough and tender. Make me tough so I can handle life. Make me tender so I can love people. God, make me a man.

All of this is to say that we have a couple of generations of males who were not raised by men, and the result is a prolonged male adolescence. In a culture where the influence of godly men is desperately needed, this void results in a legitimate cultural crisis. We are not going to solve it by ignoring Ban and hoping that he eventually grows up. We are not going to solve the problem by simply telling women that they should take up the slack. We might solve the problem by modeling bibli-

---

[19]John Carroll, quoted in Leon J. Podles, *The Church Impotent* (Dallas: Spence Publishing, 1999), 168.
[20]For evidence of this, see http://www.rejuvenile.com.
[21]Podles, *The Church Impotent*, 43.
[22]Gilmore, *Manhood in the Making*, 229.

cal manhood and calling adult boys to forsake their youthful lusts and become the men that God is calling them to be in the context of the local church. This call should come from godly men and women sitting in the pews and, specifically, from the pulpit of God's church. The models should be men of God.

Theological Crisis

Our world is jacked up in a myriad of ways. Obvious problems abound: sex crimes against children, violence committed by unjust governments, unethical business practices that drain the honest incomes of decent, regular folk—the list goes on and on. But one of the more subtle areas of unhealthy confusion and conflict I've seen involves gender. Definitions are important here.

Our *sex* is defined by our body: we are male or we are female, tangibly, because of our genitalia. *Gender*, though, is a little less tangible. Our gender is a mixture of our actions, our mentality, and our characteristics.[23] And since, according to the Bible, God made both males and females in his image and likeness, gender is inextricably linked with spirituality. Being a male has to do with biology; being a man has to do with how one relates to, thinks about, and serves God.

Males and females are reflections of God's character, and men in general are not doing so well at bearing God's image with integrity. Because the issue is at its heart a spiritual issue, correction must come in the form of theological redress. Just as God singled out Adam though both he and his wife sinned,[24] I think it wholly appropriate to take the opportunity this book affords to directly address men, to "call them out" for their sin and "call them up" to be more than just males.

I didn't grow up going to church, and as a young man I didn't understand all the seemingly nitpicky Christian arguments when I did begin attending. One of these theological issues was the debate about whether both men and women could hold the office of elder. The church I started attending (where I eventually became a Christian) was very passionate about this particular debate. Because my church

---

[23]Podles, *The Church Impotent*, 37.
[24]Genesis 3:9.

believed that only men could serve in the office of elder, I believed the same thing. It wasn't until seminary that I actually engaged the debate and began to consider the reasoning on each side. The church where I served during seminary believed that both men and women could be elders.[25] This view is called egalitarianism.[26] For a few years I embraced this view—largely because, once again, my church believed it. I read a couple of books supporting the egalitarian position and began to share my views with my classmates and professors. Since my personal passion and focus was in starting new churches, I decided to write a paper I titled "Starting New Churches in the 21st Century." One of the main arguments of the paper was that the church needed to embrace egalitarianism or run the risk of becoming irrelevant to the modern world. I remember being so passionate about the issue that I began to devour every book I could find on the topic.

Along the course of my research, however, an odd thing happened—I became convinced that the complementarian position was the biblical position. I came to believe that God has reserved the office of elder for men, and I came to this conclusion not because of what my church taught or because of cultural trends but because of intense personal study of Scripture and the work of biblical scholars and linguists much wiser and more skilled than I.

As I worked my way through the material on this issue,[27] I was stunned at how clear the Bible was on it.[28] When I say clear, I do not mean to imply that those who hold to an egalitarian interpretation are not godly or that God is not using them in mighty and effective ways. Many of my friends and several of my mentors hold to the egalitarian position. In fact, one of my most impactful mentors was an unmarried

---

[25]I owe much of my development as a teacher and leader to Rick McGinniss who founded and pastors North Heartland Community Church in Kansas City. See http://www.northheartland.org.

[26]Egalitarianism is contrasted with complementarianism and holds that men and women can and should serve equal roles in the church and home. Complementarianism, by contrast, holds that men and women are equal in worth but are called to complementary roles in certain church offices and in the home. The best defense of the egalitarian position, in my opinion, is Sarah Summer's *Men and Women in the Church: Building Consensus on Christian Leadership* (Downers Grove, IL: InterVarsity, 2003).

[27]Some helpful books on this subject are Dan Doriani, *Women and Ministry* (Wheaton: Crossway, 2003); Jerram Barrs, *Through His Eyes: God's Perspective on Women in the Bible* (Wheaton: Crossway, 2009); and *Recovering Biblical Manhood and Womanhood: A Response to Evangelical Feminism*, ed. John Piper and Wayne Grudem (Wheaton: Crossway, 1991).

[28]Some of the most relevant texts include 1 Timothy 2:11–15, 1 Timothy 3:2, Titus 1:6, Ephesians 5:22–33, and 1 Corinthians 11:1–16 and 14:33b–35.

adult woman. Also, I actively serve with pastoral leaders of other networks[29] who disagree with Acts 29's complementarian stance. I do think, however, that the clarity and weight of Scripture points to the office of elder being reserved for men. This view, which is mainly derived from the epistles in the New Testament, is consistent with the rest of the Bible. Though both men and women were called prophets in both the Old[30] and New[31] Testaments, only men were priests and apostles.

Women, according to Scripture, are coequal with men in worth, dignity, and value and are able to serve in full-time ministry. They serve as deacons and worship leaders, teaching and using their spiritual gifts in service to God in his church. I can say without hesitation that our church would not be in existence without key women, both on staff and in the pew, who use their God-given spiritual gifts to build up the body of Christ. Our female worship leaders take our church to God's throne in powerful ways. Our deaconesses serve the needs of our church in ways that male deacons could not. Our elders' wives offer wisdom and insight that has proven absolutely essential for our church's survival and effectiveness.

There is absolutely no indication in Scripture that gender plays any role in God's sovereign distribution of spiritual gifts. It is troubling that those who love the Bible tend to focus on what women can't do instead of what they can do. The focus, unfortunately, is on the restriction rather than on empowerment.[32] In general, complementarian churches have done a deplorable job of equipping and empowering women to use their God-given gifts in the church. I believe women can use any gift that God has given them in the church and that only the office of elder is reserved for men. This may seem paradoxical, but I think it is biblical.

I believe that Scripture consistently teaches the principle of male leadership, not only in the church but in the home as well,[33] tying this principle to the created order, not to a cultural context.[34] Therefore, men should serve as "first among equals" in both the home (as husbands and fathers) and in the church (as elders and pastors). Alexander Strauch

---

[29]For instance, Dan Kimball and Erwin McManus's network http://theoriginsproject.org, as well as Dave and Jon Ferguson's network http://www.newthing.org.
[30]For example, Deborah in Judges 4:4.
[31]For example, Philip's daughters in Acts 21:9.
[32]This was the main catalyst for Jerram Barrs's book *Through His Eyes: God's Perspective on Women in the Bible.*
[33]Ephesians 5:21–33; 1 Peter 3:1–7; Colossians 3:18–19.
[34]1 Corinthians 11; 1 Timothy 2:11–15.

rightly articulates, however, that "the principle of male headship . . . does not in any way diminish the significance and necessity of active female involvement in the home or church."[35] Husbands in the home and pastors in the church are not more valued or more gifted, but they are charged with more responsibility and will be accountable to God for the way they lead. We see this clearly in Paul's letter to the church at Ephesus where husbands are called to love their wives as Christ loved the church, being the head of their homes like Christ is the head of the church.[36] This means that husbands, like Jesus, are to lead their home by being first to love, first to forgive, and first to suffer and to be accountable for sin regardless of whether it is their "fault." We see this principle in Genesis 3:9, where God addresses Adam for Eve's sin, and in Romans 5, where Adam is held accountable for Eve's sin.

We also see this charge for the leaders and pastors of God's church in Hebrews 13:17 (the most terrifying verse in the Bible for pastors!).[37] Elders and non-elders are equal in the church, but they have differing roles, which is analogous to the relationships within the Trinity—Father, Son, and Spirit. The persons of the Trinity are equal, but there is, nevertheless, submission within the Godhead by the Son and by the Spirit to the Father. My interpretation of this divine deference is that submission is a characteristic of a healthy relationship. Submission indicates a pervasive humility and mutual trust that orients the partners in relationship. Submission is good and requires not only that one person submits but that one assumes the leadership role. God, in his wisdom, has placed the man in the leadership role, both in the family and in the church. And the character-shaping work that God wants to do in husbands, pastors, and fathers will be done in the context of the leadership role.

It is my conviction that when the home and the church are rightly ordered—when husbands and elders accept that God's beloved people have been placed under their care and that he holds them accountable for the spiritual health of his children—families and churches will begin

---

[35]Alexander Strauch, *Biblical Eldership: An Urgent Call to Restore Biblical Church Leadership* (Littleton, CO: Lewis and Roth, 1995), 58.

[36]Ephesians 5:25.

[37]Hebrews 13:17 says, "Obey your leaders and submit to them, for they are keeping watch over your souls, as *those who will have to give an account.* Let them do this with joy and not with groaning, for that would be of no advantage to you." In the home, God has ordained husbands and fathers to take the lead in love, service, and suffering. In the church God has called elders/pastors to do the same.

to resemble the perfect community we see in the Trinity. When this begins to happen, men will actually be attracted to taking responsibility in the home and the church because they will sense the call to follow Christ in leadership as an inspiring and uniquely masculine one.

What is needed in the church is not dominance —abuse of power by abusive, self-centered men—we have had enough of that. What we really need is a resurgence—a healthy infusion of godly men to serve the church by the power of God's Spirit.[38]

Consider these revealing statistics gleaned from David Murrow, author of *Why Men Hate Going to Church* and director of Church for Men:[39]

- The typical U.S. church congregation draws an adult crowd that's 61% female, 39% male. This gender gap shows up in all age categories.[40]
- On any given Sunday there are 13 million more adult women than men in America's churches. This statistic comes from Barna's figures on male/female worship attendance, overlaid upon the Census 2000 numbers for adult men and women in the U.S. population.
- This Sunday almost 25% of married, churchgoing women will worship without their husbands. I came up with this figure by taking the U.S. Census 2000 numbers for total married adults and overlaying Barna Research's year 2000 percentages of male vs. female attendance at weekly worship services. The figures suggest at least 24.5 million married women attend church on a given weekend, but only 19 million married men attend. That's 5.5 million more women, or 22.5%. The actual number may be even higher, because married people attend church in much greater numbers than singles.
- Over 70% of the boys who are being raised in church will abandon it during their teens and twenties. Many of these boys will never return.[41]
- More than 90% of American men believe in God, and five out of six call themselves Christians. But only two out of six attend church on a given Sunday. The average man accepts the reality of Jesus Christ, but fails to see any value in going to church.[42]

---

[38]I got this "dominance vs. resurgence" language from http://www.churchformen.com.
[39]All of the stats that follow are taken directly from http://www.churchformen.com/allmen.php.
[40]"U.S. Congregational Life Survey—Key Findings," October 29, 2003; www.uscongregations.org/key.htm.
[41]"LifeWay Research Uncovers Reasons 18 to 22 Year Olds Drop Out of Church," available at the LifeWay Web site, http://www.lifeway.com/lwc/article_main_page/0,1703,A=165949&M=200906,00.html. Accessed September 12, 2007.
[42]Barna Research Online, "Women Are the Backbone of Christian Congregations in America," March 6, 2000; http://www.barna.org.

Former Major League Baseball manager Leo Durocher's quip that "baseball is like church. Many attend, few understand" is most true for men.

Though this issue of gender roles is one of the hottest debates in our current cultural climate, complementarianism has been the dominant position of the church for two thousand years and has only been challenged in the last hundred years or so. Certainly we complementarians have much work to do while living out the implications of our position. Growth must come by strongly correcting the abuses of power of some ungodly male leaders, as well as learning to honorably and respectfully disagree with those who don't hold our view. I believe that churches, denominations, and networks—especially the ones attempting to plant gospel-centered churches—can work together despite disagreements on this issue. We must learn to disagree well. Why? Because the gospel must go forward. And the gospel will not likely prevail in a given city with only Reformed, male-led churches.[43] We therefore want to partner with all kinds of churches that stay within the Apostles' Creed.[44]

I hope our theological differences don't keep you from reading this book. I believe many of the principles found here can translate despite our theological differences. One day we will all sit before Jesus, and he can correct our doctrinal errors. We all "see in a mirror dimly."[45] Until all truth is manifested in the light of God's glory, let's work toward building healthier churches, which is the supreme aim of this book.

We have a spiritual crisis and live in a world full of Bans. We have Bans in our city, our neighborhoods, our churches, and our families. Ban needs godly men and women to show him there is more to life than what he is currently experiencing. Ban needs to be more than just a male. He needs to be becoming God's man who is being transformed by God's gospel message and is wholeheartedly pursuing God's mission.

---

[43]See http://www.acts29network.org/about/doctrine.
[44]This is what I love about Redeemer Church's Planting Center (RCPC). They plant all kinds of churches that hold to orthodox Christianity so they can reach world cities; see http://www.redeemer.com/about_us/church_planting.
[45]1 Corinthians 13:12.

The Man

A good minister that has the presence of God with him in his work is the very greatest blessing that ever God bestows upon a people, next to himself. (Jonathan Edwards)[1]

A man must himself be cleansed, before cleansing others: himself become wise, that he may make others wise; become light, and then give light: draw near to God, and so bring others near; be hallowed, then hallow them. (Gregory of Nazianzus)[2]

Take heed to yourselves, lest you be void of that saving grace of God which you offer to others, and be strangers to the effectual working of that gospel which you preach; and lest, while you proclaim to the world the necessity of a Savior, your own hearts should neglect him, and you should miss of an interest in him and his saving benefits. Take heed to yourselves, lest you perish, while you call upon others to take heed of perishing; and lest you famish yourselves while you prepare food for them. (Richard Baxter)[3]

Conversion is the *sine qua non* in a minister. Ye aspirants to our pulpits, "ye must be born again." Nor is the possession of this first qualification a thing to be taken for granted by any man, for there is very great possibility of our being mistaken as to whether we are converted or not. Believe me, it is no child's play to "make your calling and election sure." (Charles Spurgeon)[4]

---

[1]Jonathan Edwards, *The Salvation of Souls* (Wheaton, IL: Crossway, 2002), 140.
[2]Gregory of Nazianzus, *Oratorian* 2.71, quoted in Andrew Purves, *Pastoral Theology in the Classical Tradition* (Louisville: Westminster John Knox Press, 2001), 9.
[3]Richard Baxter, *The Reformed Pastor* (Edinburgh: The Banner of Truth Trust, 2001), 53.
[4]Charles Spurgeon, *Lectures to My Students* (Grand Rapids: Zondervan, 1972), 9. *Sin qua non* is a Latin phrase that means "without which not"; i.e., that which is a necessary precondition.

1

A Rescued Man

No one, no matter how skilled an orator, how gifted a leader, or how extensive the theological pedigree, should endeavor to shepherd the church of Jesus without first having experienced the saving power of the Shepherd who is full of grace. While a pastor/church planter may be a good man or a talented man or a clever man, he must be, first and foremost, a rescued man. He must be a man who has been rescued from the slavery and foolishness of his own sin and saved by the freedom and "foolishness" of a God who displayed his perfect justice and love by laying down his life on behalf of the very ones who wronged him. The mandatory requirement and primary qualification for a man who desires to serve and lead in the name of Jesus is to have personally experienced forgiveness and acceptance from Jesus.

Unfortunately, you don't need extraordinary discernment to realize that many churches have a pastor who is trying to lead people to a Savior he has yet to personally encounter.

Many people make a tragic assumption that pastors and church planters must certainly be Christians. This assumption, however, over-looks the fact that it is possible, and for some remarkably easy, to fake the requisite gifts for ministry. A person can be a very gifted communicator, counselor, and leader without ever truly knowing Christ. In fact, Christ addressed this issue in Matthew 7:21–23 when he said:

> Not everyone who says to me, "Lord, Lord," will enter the kingdom of heaven, but the one who does the will of my Father who is in heaven. On that day many will say to me, "Lord, Lord, did we not prophesy in your name, and cast out demons in your name, and do many mighty works in your name?" And then will I declare to them, "I never knew you; depart from me, you workers of lawlessness."

This is an amazing declaration. If it is possible to prophesy, cast out demons, and do *many miracles* in Christ's name without ever truly knowing him, then certainly it is possible to plant or lead a church without a saving relationship with him. If spiritual gifting is no proof of authentic faith, then certainly a job title isn't either. The Puritan pastor and theologian Richard Baxter writes about this reality very vividly:

> O sirs, how many have preached Christ, and yet have perished for want of a saving interest in Him! How many, who are now in hell, have told their people of the torments of hell, and warned them to escape from it! How many have preached of the wrath of God against sinners, who are now enduring it! O what sadder case can there be in the world, than for a man, who made it his very trade and calling to proclaim salvation, and to help others to heaven, yet after all to be himself shut out![5]

"Examine yourselves, to see whether you are in the faith. Test yourselves" (2 Corinthians 13:5).

Over the years, I have known several pastors who seemed to lack saving faith.[6] I remember how one youth pastor with whom I was friends in college disclosed to me that he was in ministry primarily because he belonged to a great youth ministry in high school. He said that even though he doubted his own salvation, he was already "committed to professional ministry." Another guy I know planted a church largely, in his own words, to impress his dad. In a coaching appointment with me, he confessed that he was concerned that the counselor he was seeing was going to unearth the stunning reality that he had planted the church to gain not only his dad's favor but God's favor as well.

I could tell many similar stories. The point, for now, is that many people who involve themselves in helping professions (social work, counseling, and others) do so in order to solve some of their own problems. Such people use their service to others to gain healing for themselves. Many men do the same with the pastorate. This may sound noble in some regard; the more we serve others, the more we realize that they

---

[5]Baxter, *The Reformed Pastor*, 72.
[6]Since only God knows a person's heart, we can never be the final judge of another person's salvation. At the same time, Scripture calls us to be discerning about the character of those around us. Warning about false prophets, Jesus says, "you will recognize them by their fruits" (Matthew 7:20).

are actually serving us. I get it. The major difference in the pastorate, however, is that such men are seeking not only to help themselves but to *save* themselves.

One of my first mentors, Wayne Barber, whom God used to confirm my sense of calling into ministry, confessed in one of his sermons that he was not a Christian during the first few years of his ministry. He said that he became a pastor so he could earn God's favor. Wayne, like many others, was using ministry as a way to cover and atone for his own sin. He was trusting in what he was doing for God instead of trusting in what Christ had done for him.

Unfortunately, churches are often so desperate for leadership that they are willing to overlook character flaws in a leader, especially in a gifted one. People may think, *He may not exhibit godly character, but he can preach the paint off of the wall . . . he is a wonderful counselor . . . he can inspire people to follow him!* With the vast majority of churches declining or in plateau, gifted but unregenerate men become a prized commodity in the professional Christian economy.

Other churches simply aren't equipped to discern between a regenerate and an unregenerate leader. Sometimes a church's view of the pastorate has been so influenced by the bottom-line, grow-at-all-costs American business model that there is little or no emphasis on finding someone who has been called by God. In the past few years I have been asked to consult for several evangelical denominations and networks, as well as a few mainline denominations, regarding hiring, firing, and recruiting decisions. I have found that the main question both liberals and conservatives often start with is not, *Is this man a Christian?* but rather, *Can this man grow the church?* This lead question is revealing and alerts us to one reason why there are so many men who are planting and leading churches, yet who do not have a saving relationship with Jesus Christ.

Certainly there is an ethical concern when a man deceives the church about his own "credentials" for ministry. But it is more than just an ethical issue. The well-being of the church (and its pastor) is at stake. Consider what happens to a man who tries to lead or plant a church without first having been rescued from his sins. He will either feel *beat up* (condemned, insecure, and inadequate) or *blown up* (puffed up, arrogant, and proud), depending on whether the church is declining or growing. In either case the pastor/church planter who seeks to lead the church without first being rescued from his sins sets himself up for idolatry, heartache, and ultimate failure because he is using the church and his ministry as a means to save himself. Only the rescued man can truly serve Christ's church, because only the rescued man has an identity and motive for ministry outside of ministry itself.

However sad the final state of an unregenerate[7] pastor may be, the final state of a church led by such a man is even worse. Though God sometimes mercifully uses preachers with false motives,[8] the church under such a pastor generally suffers spiritually, communally, and missionally, and it eventually withers and dies. Most churches do not grow beyond the spiritual health of their leadership. Spurgeon's metaphors are helpful:

> A graceless pastor is a blind man elected to a professorship of optics, philosophizing upon light and vision, discoursing upon and distinguishing to others the nice shades and delicate blendings of the prismatic colours, while he himself is absolutely in the dark! He is a dumb man elevated to the chair of music; a deaf man fluent upon symphonies and harmonies! He is a mole professing to educate eaglets; a limpet elected to preside over angels.[9]

Simply put, a man who is a stranger to the things of God will be totally unable to teach them to others. Yet many pastors enter the ministry with serious doubts about their own salvation! Could this be one reason why thousands of churches will close their doors this year in North America and why the vast majority of North American churches are in plateau or decline?

Since being a rescued man is the foundational qualification for any aspiring pastor/church planter, and since no man can succeed in minis-

---

[7]As Wayne Grudem notes, the word *unregenerate* literally means "one who is not renewed in heart and mind or reborn in spirit." It is contrasted with one who is regenerate. It is important to remember that a regenerated spirit is not something a person can achieve. Rather it is like being born—it is something that happens to a person outside of his power. See Grudem's *Systematic Theology: An Introduction to Biblical Doctrine* (Grand Rapids: Zondervan, 1994), 699–700. See also Ezekiel 36:26–27; John 3:3–8; James 1:18; 1 Peter 1:3.
[8]See Philippians 1:15–18.
[9]Charles Spurgeon, *Lectures to My Students* (Grand Rapids: Zondervan, 1972), 9–10.

try without it, it is necessary to carefully consider what it means to be a rescued man before we rush on to discuss other qualifications.

What does it mean to be *rescued?* The Bible uses many words to describe the miracle of salvation: adoption, justification, redemption, reconciliation, etc. One picture that the Bible uses to describe this reality is that of *new birth.* Jesus said, "Truly, truly, I say to you, unless one is born again he cannot see the kingdom of God" (John 3:3). The term theologians often use to describe this new birth is *regeneration.* Regeneration refers to the in-planting of new spiritual life into the heart of a sinner, causing him or her to love God and others. J. I. Packer describes regeneration in this way: "The new birth or regeneration is an inner recreating of fallen human nature by the Holy Spirit. It changes the disposition from lawless, godless self-seeking into one of trust and love, of repentance for past rebelliousness and unbelief, and loving compliance with God's law henceforth. It enlightens the blinded mind to discern spiritual realities and liberates and energizes the enslaved will for free obedience to God."[10] A rescued man has been reborn into this new spiritual life, which enables him to repent of his sin and trust in Christ's work on his behalf. "Therefore, if anyone is in Christ, he is a new creation. The old has passed away; behold, the new has come."[11]

It is also possible to describe what it means to be rescued by looking at what God does in the life of someone who has been truly rescued from his or her sins. In Matthew 22:37–40 Jesus taught that the entire Old Testament hangs on two short commandments: "You shall love the Lord your God with all your heart and with all your soul and with all your mind. This is the great and first commandment. And a second is like it: You shall love your neighbor as yourself. On these two commandments depend all the Law and the Prophets." A rescued man not only *believes* this truth at the heart and core of Christianity, but actually *does* love God with all his heart, soul, mind, and strength, and as a result he seeks to love his neighbor as himself. A rescued man is a man whose love for God is growing holistically—in his affections, in his thoughts, in his motives, in his passions, in his duties, and in every area of his life. He is also a man

---

[10]James Packer, *Your Father Loves You: Daily Insights for Knowing God* (Wheaton, IL: Harold Shaw Publishers, 1986), January 22.
[11]2 Corinthians 5:17.

who demonstrates a growing love for other people by sacrificing himself for others and laying down his life for their good. In short, a rescued man is growing in genuine love for God and neighbor.[12]

A rescued man is also a man in whom the Holy Spirit is at work, producing the fruit of righteousness. In Galatians 5:22–24 the apostle Paul wrote, "The fruit of the Spirit is love, joy, peace, patience, kindness, goodness, faithfulness, gentleness, self-control; against such things there is no law. And those who belong to Christ Jesus have crucified the flesh with its passions and desires." In the original Greek, the word "fruit" in verse 22 is singular. Paul is not listing a kind of spiritual menu by which some people choose love, others choose peace, others choose patience, and so on. Rather, all these qualities together constitute the fruit that a Christian man produces. A rescued man is a man who increasingly displays all of these qualities in his life—love, joy, peace, patience, kindness, goodness, faithfulness, gentleness, and self-control.[13]

If you aspire to pastoral ministry, you must begin with an honest examination of your own salvation, your own rescue. Do not assume that you are a Christian just because you are or want to be a pastor. Jesus said that *"many"* who cast out demons in his name will not be saved (Matthew 7:22). Make sure you know for yourself the salvation you are proclaiming to others. Be willing to question your motives for ministry, and make sure you are not trying to earn God's favor. Salvation is the first and most important qualification for Christian ministry. Without it, nothing else is possible, and if you go into ministry without it, you will ruin yourself and those you seek to serve.

In the next chapter we will examine what a man who is qualified to lead the church looks like. Before that, however, please consider the following questions designed to help readers revisit their belief in the life, death, and resurrection of Jesus and the ministry of the Holy Spirit.

> 1) Are you genuinely and currently trusting Christ to be both the forgiver of your sins and your only hope for eternal relationship with God?

---

[12]First John 2:9–10 says, "Whoever says he is in the light and hates his brother is still in darkness. Whoever loves his brother abides in the light, and in him there is no cause for stumbling."

[13]First John 2:3 states, "And by this we know that we have come to know him, if we keep his commandments."

2) Imagine standing before God, the righteous Judge of all people. In your mind, are you tempted to list your good deeds in defense of your salvation or are you aware that you are dependent on the work of Christ—his obedient life, sacrificial death, and powerful resurrection—for salvation?

3) Is there evidence of the Holy Spirit's work in your life and character?

a. Do you have a general sense that you are a true child of God? (See Romans 8:15–16; 1 John 4:13.)

b. Read Galatians 5:22–23. Are "love, joy, peace, patience, kindness, goodness, faithfulness, gentleness, self-control" characteristics that are being developed in you? Would those closest to you say they regularly see these traits in your life?

c. Read Matthew 7:16–20. Does your ministry bear good fruit? Are people and the church being built up, or is dissension and divisiveness a characteristic of your ministry?

4) If you are currently a pastor or church planter secure in your "rescued man" status, are you confident that those leading with you are believers in the true gospel of grace?

Ministry is not a profession. It is a vocation. . . . One must be called in order to do it. Although pastors may struggle with exactly what it means to be called by God to lead a church, they must have some sense that they are in ministry because God wants them to be. Time and again, amid the challenges of pastoral ministry, this divine, more-than-subjective authorization is a major means of pastoral perseverance.
(William H. Willimon)[1]

Do not enter the ministry if you can help it. If any student in this room could be content to be a newspaper editor, a grocer, a farmer, or a doctor, or a lawyer, or a senator, or a king, in the name of heaven and earth, let him go his way.
(Charles Spurgeon)[2]

I believe God made me for a purpose . . . but he also made me fast. And when I run, I feel His pleasure. (Eric Liddell)[3]

---

[1]William H. Willimon, *Pastor: The Theology and Practice of Ordained Ministry* (Nashville: Abingdon Press, 2002), 141–145.
[2]Charles Spurgeon, *Lectures to My Students* (Grand Rapids: Zondervan, 1972), 262–67.
[3]From the movie *Chariots of Fire*, screenplay by Colin Welland, Warner Brothers, 1981.

2

A Called Man

Over 2,500 years ago God called a man named Jeremiah to be a prophet with these words: "Before I formed you in the womb I knew you, and before you were born I consecrated you; I appointed you a prophet to the nations."[4] Yet the more Jeremiah followed God's call, the more he was mocked, ostracized, and persecuted by those to whom he spoke. He is often called "the weeping prophet" because of the depth of his struggle as a called man.[5] Consider the calling of Jeremiah. Jeremiah was called to be a prophet. Most people think of a prophet as something like a fortune-teller—predicting the future, reading minds, and the like. And there is definitely evidence of forecasting and even seeing the future in visions throughout the Bible. But more often than not, a biblical prophet was one who spent as much time looking at the past and the present as they did looking into the future. A prophet was, and still is, one who examined the past and present in order to rebuke God's people for their sins and call them to covenant faithfulness to their God.

Jeremiah was that kind of a prophet. As he looked at the past and present condition of God's people, the future didn't look so good. What he saw was a rebellious, ungrateful, stubborn, completely sinful people, and God called Jeremiah to hold up a mirror to this "stiff-necked" people.[6] Jeremiah's primary vocation was to criticize and pick apart every aspect of the culture to which he was called to "minister." And he was particularly good at his job, which made his life a target for his culture.

Jeremiah was an equal opportunity critic: from the common Israelite and the religious professionals, to the king and his entourage, no one emerged unscathed. He condemned casual sex and orgies,

---

[4] Jeremiah 1:5.
[5] Someone once told me that to agree to serve God in vocational ministry is accepting a call to lifelong suffering.
[6] As seen in Exodus 32:9 and a number of other passages.

denounced the rich for oppressing the poor, rebuked the poor for not aspiring to a better life, and blasted the whole lot for worshipping every dime-store idol that grabbed their eye. He was a ruthless offender of God's people and a first-rate prophet, which left him friendless.

You feel Jeremiah's pain in one of the most vulnerable moments captured in Scripture, when Jeremiah said, "Whenever I speak, I cry out, I shout, 'Violence and destruction!' For the word of the LORD has become for me a reproach and derision all day long" (Jeremiah 20:8). Being a called man is a lonely job, and many times you feel like God has abandoned you in your ministry.

But the God who called Jeremiah burned deep within the prophet. And in the same breath Jeremiah could accuse God of not blessing his ministry and also exclaim, "If I say, 'I will not mention him, or speak any more in his name,' there is in my heart as it were a burning fire shut up in my bones, and I am weary with holding it in, and I cannot" (Jeremiah 20:9).

Jeremiah's call brought him nothing but heartache, and yet he could not give it up. Why? *Because God's Word was like a fire in his bones.* Translation: *because God had called him.*

Jeremiah is a picture of what it is like to be called into pastoral ministry. Ministry is more than hard. Ministry is impossible. And unless we have a fire inside our bones compelling us, we simply will not survive. Pastoral ministry is a calling, not a career. It is not a job you pursue just because you like attention, or because your mom thinks you'd be good at it, or because it does not involve heavy lifting. I am continually shocked at how many men are trying to do ministry without a clear sense of calling. Please hear this: If you don't feel a sense of calling to ministry, then please, find another vocation! Only those like Jeremiah who have a strong, fiery calling from God should pursue pastoral ministry.

What Is the Call?

One of the most important things to do when assessing your calling is to study the calling of other men and what other men have had to say about calling.

Martin Luther, the sixteenth-century church reformer and theologian who sparked the Protestant Reformation, taught that "calling is two-fold . . . divine, which is done by the highest power, which is of faith . . . [and] a calling of love . . . as when one is desired by friends to preach a sermon. Both vocations are necessary to secure the conscience."[7] Luther listed eight qualities that a minister must have:

1. Able to teach systematically
2. Eloquence
3. A good voice
4. A good memory
5. Knows how to make an end
6. Sure of his doctrine
7. Willing to venture body and blood, wealth and honor in the work
8. Suffers himself to be mocked and jeered by everyone.[8]

John Calvin, the Reformer and theologian who followed in Luther's footsteps, also distinguished between two aspects of calling. He wrote, "The secret call means the good testimony of our heart, that we undertake the offered office [not] from . . . any selfish feeling but from a sincere fear of God. . . . The external call has the church as a witness. . . . None are to be chosen save those who are of sound doctrine, holy lives . . . and provided with the means necessary to fulfill their office."[9]

John Newton, the eighteenth-century Anglican clergyman and writer of the famous hymn "Amazing Grace," noted three indications of a call. First, a call to ministry is accompanied by "a warm and earnest desire to be employed in this service." Second, a call to ministry is accompanied by "some competent sufficiency as to gifts, knowledge, and utterance." And third, a call to ministry is accompanied by "a correspondent opening in Providence, by a gradual train of circumstances pointing out the means, the time, the place, of actually entering upon the work."[10] George Whitefield, the eighteenth-century evangelist, gives this advice for those considering a call: "Ask yourselves again and again whether you would preach for Christ if you were sure to lay down

---

[7] *The Table Talk Theology of Martin Luther*, edited and introduced by Thomas S. Kepler (Grand Rapids: Baker, 1952), 234.
[8] Ibid., 23–89.
[9] John Calvin, *Institutes*, Book IV, Chap. 3, 111–112.
[10] *Letters of John Newton* (London: Banner of Truth Trust), 545–546.

your life for so doing? If you fear the displeasure of a man for doing your duty now, assure yourselves you are not yet thus minded."[11]

Charles Hodge, the nineteenth-century Reformed theologian, distinguished between intellectual qualifications, spiritual qualifications, and bodily qualifications, all of which must be present in a genuine call. Intellectual qualifications are "ability, knowledge, orthodoxy." His spiritual qualifications are "a high appreciation of the office, strong desire for it from proper motives, willingness to go anywhere and to submit to everything in the discharge of the duties, [and] a sense of obligation—so we say, 'woe is me if I preach not the gospel!'" His bodily qualifications are "good health and the necessary gifts of utterance."[12]

Robert L. Dabney, another nineteenth-century Presbyterian theologian, wrote that God calls a man into ministry "by enlightening and influencing the man's conscience and understanding, and those of his Christian brethren, to understand . . . the qualifications in himself which reasonably point out preaching as his work."[13] The qualifications he lists include: (1) a healthy and hearty piety, (2) a fair reputation for holiness of life, (3) a respectable force of character, (4) some Christian experience, and (5) an aptness to teach.[14]

Let me pull us out of the distant past and share with you from the recent past about how I was called into ministry. I was sitting in my very first Christian summer camp worship service, and to be honest, I was a little creeped out by the sheer volume of youth group kids in the chapel of this small, denominational Christian college. The college was located on a mountain, and half of its facilities were in Tennessee and half were in Georgia. We were in the South with a capital S. I had never been in the South before. Where I grew up, there was a strange combination of Midwestern and Southern culture, which meant that some people were friendly, but most were not. Well, in the South *everyone* is nice, or at least they are to your face. The only saving grace of all the "niceness" was that the "Southern ladies" were very friendly, which was good news—not like the gospel is good news, but good news nonetheless.

[11] *Letters of George Whitefield: For the Period 1734–1742* (Edinburgh: The Banner of Truth Trust, 1976), 81–82.

[12] Charles Hodge, *Princeton Sermons: Outlines of Discourses, Doctrinal and Practical* (London: The Banner of Truth Trust, 1958), 311.

[13] Robert L. Dabney, *Discussions: Evangelical and Theological*, Vol. 2 (London: The Banner of Truth Trust, 1967), 27.

[14] Ibid., 31.

The strangest thing about being in this place was that it seemed that all of these kids around me had grown up in church. This was totally bizarre for me because I had not grown up in the church, which meant that I was not versed in the nuances of Christian subculture. I didn't know most of the "choruses" or the ridiculous hand motions that seemed to accompany about 80 percent of the "praise songs." I didn't understand how to only *appear* to be intently listening to the speaker. I wasn't proficient in the skill of "fake feverish note-taking," which is a necessary skill when you want to appear like you are paying attention but really need to write a love note to your third girlfriend of your weeklong summer church camp experience. Nevertheless, I was doing my best to ignore a lot of the "youth groupness" of the camp in order to focus on what God was saying to me.

This particular Christian camp had a camp pastor. I liked the guy the first time I saw him. First, he was funny. He didn't seem to take himself that seriously. Secondly, he was 6'7", well north of 300 pounds, and had played college basketball. I liked the thought of listening to a preacher who could probably give me a run for my money in a fight.

This camp pastor got up and did something that was very unusual for a youth camp (and sadly for many churches, as I now realize). He opened up a Bible. Now this was a strange thing in and of itself, but he took it to a new level. This humorous, extra-large camp pastor didn't just use the Bible as a jumping-off point for some teenage felt-needs talk (don't drink, smoke, chew, or date those who do). He actually taught the Bible verse by verse to teenagers! He had a knack for using sermon illustrations that connected with the dudes in the room, mostly because they always involved sports, hunting, or fishing, which was what most of the guys at this camp were picking as a major in college. He did well at blending good biblical teaching with appropriate contextualization.

I remember he was teaching through this wonderful book called Philippians, which was penned by the hand of the apostle Paul when he was suffering for Jesus in a rat-infested prison with Roman guards. Toward the end of camp, he was preaching from Philippians 3:12–17, and it was at that point that I knew God was calling me to serve him in vocational ministry. God internally spoke to me from this passage, saying that I should not only strain forward to what lies ahead, pressing toward the goal and forgetting what lies behind like every other Christian, but that I must also imitate Paul by spending the rest of my life suffering for and serving the church. I had no idea what that looked like, nor any idea what it would require of me, but I accepted God's call that day.

Discerning the Call

Your call to ministry does not have to be like my call, or anybody else's call for that matter. In fact, one of the most interesting features of calling is that whether you look in the pages of the Bible or the annals of church history, God rarely calls two people in the exact same way. It is very important not to standardize the calling experience. Sometimes it is a dramatic Damascus Road experience. Other times it is more of an inward pull. But however your sense of calling has developed, it is imperative to recognize that *you must have a clear sense of calling before you enter ministry*. Let's examine the nature of the call to ministry a little more intently.

An aspiring pastor/church planter who is seeking to test his sense of calling should look for confirmation in at least three areas: heart confirmation, head confirmation, and skill confirmation.[15]

Heart Confirmation

There is nothing like going to a rock concert and getting hammered. By the music, I mean. If the sound is right at a show, you can feel the bass on your chest, seemingly disrupting your heart rhythm. There is a pressure, a force that you cannot escape until you leave the venue. This pressure is similar to the heart confirmation of a call to ministry. You feel it in you. You feel it on you. It is a pressure on your heart and soul. An inescapable pressure. An unavoidable pressure. A pressure that evokes deep longing to be a pastor.

First Timothy 3:1 refers to the one who "desires the office" of elder-ship. In fact, this desire could be considered the first qualification of an elder. The man who is truly called to ministry *desires* it. He does not

---

[15]I am speaking on the popular level with this terminology; it is also legitimate to use the term *heart* to refer to the whole person. Cf. the helpful discussion in Bruce K. Waltke, *The Book of Proverbs: Chapters 1–15* (Grand Rapids: Eerdmans, 2004), 909–902.

enter the ministry grudgingly, dolefully, reluctantly, dragging his feet. He enters ministry because he wants to and feels joy in pursuing this desire. This doesn't mean there isn't appropriate caution because of the high calling of the office, but it means that there is an excitement, a joy, and a sense of privilege to be able to serve God in this way.[16]

A true call often comes with an insatiable desire to, at all costs, serve God and his people. There is a strong sense in the heart that it is ministry or nothing else. Consider the call of Nehemiah. The book bearing his name begins by describing a heart-call to serve God by leading the people of God. In chapter 1 Nehemiah inquires about the state of those who survived the exile and the physical condition of the great city, Jerusalem. The report he receives is not encouraging. "The remnant there in the province who had survived the exile is in great trouble and shame. The wall of Jerusalem is broken down, and its gates are destroyed by fire" (Nehemiah 1:3). This news cut right through to Nehemiah's heart. We know this because of the following verse:

> As soon as I heard these words I sat down and wept and mourned for days, and I continued fasting and praying before the God of heaven. (Nehemiah 1:4)

This is the essence of Nehemiah's call, literally the *heart* behind his call to ministry. Nehemiah didn't take the news home and think about it for a few days. Nehemiah didn't immediately start problem-solving and strategizing, though later he certainly would do these things and do them very well. No, when Nehemiah heard the news, it broke his heart. The text emphasizes the urgency, angst, and heartache of Nehemiah, saying he responded immediately with deep sorrow and that he actually mourned for days. Mourning is what we do when someone dies, and it is one of the most profound, painful human experiences. And here we see that Nehemiah is mourning because God's people and God's city are in ruins. His heart is cut by the news, and Nehemiah had no choice but to alter the course of his life in order to serve God and his people with his very best gifts. This is the heart-call.

In a heart-call, a deep inclination in the soul says, *I must do this or I*

---

[16]This also does not mean there isn't a little "humble reluctance" on the part of the called.

will die. The called man cannot imagine going into another vocation: he daydreams about ministry, he talks about ministry, and he cannot wait to be in ministry. There is an abiding, relentless desire for the work of ministry that the called man cannot shake off or ignore—even amidst hardship, persecution, and fear.

This strong desire in the heart can sometimes result in anxiety and apprehension. Questions are forced to the surface, like *Can I really do this? Can God really use me? What if I fail?* Nothing provokes insecurity like signing up to follow God's call and do God's work. A man who is truly called may doubt and struggle with his calling at times, but ultimately he will not be able to walk away from it. His doubts may *test* his desire for ministry, but they will not *destroy* his desire to minister. It is important to recognize that doubts and feelings of insecurity are not signs that you aren't called. People who are genuinely called often go through seasons of doubt and uncertainty. But over time the sense of calling grows stronger, not weaker.

This heart confirmation goes beyond a mere passing whim or initial excitement at the prospect of going into ministry. It is what Spurgeon refers to as "an intense, all-absorbing desire for the work."[17] It is what Newton calls "a warm and earnest desire to be employed in this service . . . he cannot give it up . . . the desire to preach is most fervent."[18] To put it simply, the man who is *called* to ministry *desires* to be in ministry so strongly that he cannot hold back: it is fire in his bones, just as in the case of Jeremiah. It is a deep desire to protect and provide for the people of God, as Nehemiah did. This heart confirmation is an essential component of the call. However, it is not enough to indicate a genuine call to ministry. A man who is truly called by God also experiences a head confirmation.

Head Confirmation

Head confirmation is an important aspect of discerning a call to ministry, but it is often overlooked because of how easy it is to focus on the heart confirmation. It is easy to allow the emotions of a perceived call to outweigh everything else. But a genuine call to ministry goes beyond

---

[17]Spurgeon, *Lectures to my Students*, 26.
[18]John Newton, *Memoirs of the Rev. John Newton*, in *The Works of the Rev. John Newton*, Vol. 1 (Edinburgh: The Banner of Truth Trust, 1985).

desire and emotions into thoughtfulness and planning. The head confirmation is an evaluation by the person who feels called to ministry as to what specifically he is called to do. Whereas the heart confirmation is more general and ethereal, the head confirmation is specific and practical. The heart confirmation rises up through your passions and cries out, *I want to give my life to the church!* The head confirmation follows up on these passions and asks, *How specifically can I serve* this *church?*

Many men have surrendered to ministry in general without any clue as to *which* ministry in particular they are called to serve. Christian history shows us that a call to ministry is generally accompanied by a specific ministry burden. This does not mean that the first ministry assignment is the final assignment, but it does mean that a call to ministry originates in a specific setting.

One of the common errors of young men who surrender to ministry is to simply adopt the model of a church that they have experienced or idolized. A similar mistake is to blindly adopt the ministry philosophy and practice of a ministry hero. The man who is experiencing head confirmation is thoughtful about his *own* philosophy of ministry, his own ministry style, his own theological beliefs, his own unique gifts, abilities, and desires. In short, there is uniqueness to the way he wants to do ministry. Unlike many young men who know much about what they are *against* and little about what they are *for*, the man who is experiencing head confirmation thinks through very carefully and deliberately, *What am I for with my life and ministry? What are my specific burdens for the church? How can I best serve the church in these areas?*

One of our church's former interns, Gavin, has a heritage of ministry in his family. His grandfather was a pastor, his dad is a pastor, and both of his older brothers are in ministry. Gavin feels the desire himself to be a pastor, but he also desires to pursue further study. Right now he is thinking through questions like, *Do I want to do ministry simply because those closest to me have done it? How is God calling me specifically to serve in ministry? Is God calling me to earn a PhD and teach or to serve in the local church?* These kinds of questions and the struggles that accompany them are in the category of head confirmation. The ultimate test of head confirmation is when a young man can say, *God is confirming, through my thoughts, my specific ministry calling.*

Head and heart confirmation are both important. They both fit into the category of what many pastors and theologians have described as the *internal call*. But by themselves they are incomplete. A genuine call to ministry manifests itself not only in the thoughts and desires of the called person but also in his gifts, abilities, and skills. This last aspect of confirmation fits into the category of what theologians name the *external call* because it is the one that is most easily recognizable to other people.

Skill Confirmation

I did not grow up going to church as a kid, so when I became a Christian and began to experience the heart and head aspects of the call, I didn't have a paradigm for what to do with God's call on my life. The tradition of the church I was attending was to walk forward at the end of the service to signify spiritual commitment. You walked forward if you wanted to become a Christian. You walked forward if you wanted to join the church. You walked the aisle if you wanted to be baptized. And, as strange as it may sound, you walked forward to make your sense of God's call for vocational ministry public.

My church had a process for helping young men as they explored a call to ministry. First, the church confirmed that we were indeed called. There was an examination of character as the church asked, *Is this young man qualified in his character?* (We will deal with this examination in greater depth in the next chapter.) The church also examined the skills of the man who claimed to be called by asking, *Does this man have the gifts required to perform ministry?* These two examinations of character and skill are paramount for the one who is called because he is able to check his subjective prompting objectively against the church's evaluation.

Inevitably as the church examines the skill of the man, that man's call is refined. The church not only helps answer the question, *Am I called?* but also the question, *To what am I called?* In this way the church serves as both a valuable filter for distinguishing between a true and false calling as well as a guide for pursuing a true calling. In short, the church helps the man discern specifically what ministry to pursue.

There are two ditches that church leaders can fall into as they help confirm a man's calling to gospel ministry. First, they can make it too easy to be affirmed in gospel ministry. A church can accept uncritically a man's *internal call*—the man's subjective sense of calling—as God's affirmation. Churches who fall into this ditch have the attitude, *Just let the boy preach!* Many times this approach produces a man who relies on his gifts and fails to develop his character, which all but ensures future disqualification.

The other ditch is when the church makes it too hard to be affirmed in gospel ministry. Such churches set the bar too high with regard to skill development (being a great preacher) or with regard to education (a candidate must have finished seminary). Many gifted pastors started successful ministries even though they had never been to seminary, like Mark Driscoll or Matt Chandler, two pastors whom I serve with on the board of Acts 29 and who have had great pastoral influence. We need to be careful not to set the bar so high that we exclude from ministry men whom God is genuinely calling.

How should the church test whether or not a man is called into pastoral ministry from a skill perspective? There are at least two tests a church should consider. The first test involves the man's understanding of Scripture. Questions that should be answered might include:

1. Does he have a working knowledge of the whole of Scripture?
2. Can he articulate the gospel story throughout the Scripture?
3. Does he understand the controversial verses that have caused division in church history (Calvinism vs. Arminianism, method and mode of baptism, and so on)?
4. Can he explain the Christ-centered nature of Christian theology?

The second test involves inspecting the fruit of his ministry. Questions that should be answered here might include:

1. Can he inspire the church for mission?
2. Can he cast vision for the church and inspire people to pursue that vision with him?
3. Can he organize the church to reach its goals?
4. Can he set up systems and structures that run apart from his direct influence?

Jim Collins's famous analogy of "the bus" speaks to the job of the skilled leader. He says that the job of a leader is "to get the right people on the bus, wrong people off the bus, and the right people in the right seats."[19] The church should discern if the candidate can build something that runs itself instead of depending on himself to make it run.

All three of these confirmations—heart, head, and skill—must be present in a genuine call. The Pentecostal/charismatic camp tends to focus on heart and the supernatural calling from God. The Reformed/evangelical camp tends to focus on the head. The mainline churches often focus on skills. But in a genuine call all three are present.

We will conclude this chapter with some questions for aspiring pastors and church planters to ask themselves to test and discern their calling:

1. Do I strongly desire pastoral ministry? Is the thought of doing something else with my life unimaginable?

2. Has God given me specific convictions and thoughts about how I can best serve the church with my life?

3. Do I want to go into ministry in order to make a name for myself, to prove that I am somebody, or to atone for past failures? Am I testing my motives for ministry and asking God to refine my desires and thoughts?

4. Do I love people? Do I want to help people? Is my desire to go into ministry mainly about me or mainly about helping other people by pointing them toward Christ?

5. Do I enjoy learning and communicating the truth about God to people from Scripture? Am I willing to be disciplined in my study habits as a pastor?

6. Am I able to lead people effectively toward a goal? Are people able to follow me? Am I willing to take some hits for decisions that I make?

---

[19]Jim Collins, *Good to Great: Why Some Companies Make the Leap and Others Don't* (New York: HarperCollins, 2001), 13.

Should we as a nation be called to defend our hearths and homes, we should not send out our boys and girls with swords and guns to meet the foe, neither may the church send out every fluent novice or inexperienced zealot to plead for the faith. (Charles Spurgeon)[1]

The conduct of the prelate should so far surpass the conduct of the people as the life of a pastor sets him apart from the flock. . . . It is necessary, therefore, that one should be pure in thought, exemplary in conduct, discreet in keeping silence, profitable in speech, in sympathy a near neighbor to everyone, in contemplation exalted above all others, a humble companion to those who lead good lives, erect in zeal for righteousness against the vices of sinners. (Cyprian)[2]

Better have no elders than the wrong ones. (Jon Zens)[3]

---

[1]Charles Spurgeon, *Lectures to My Students* (Grand Rapids: Zondervan, 1972), 13.
[2]Quoted in William H. Willimon, *Pastor: The Theology and Practice of Ordained Ministry* (Nashville: Abingdon Press, 2002), 301.
[3]Jon Zens, "The Major Concepts of Eldership in the New Testament," *Baptism Reformation Review* 7 (Summer 1978), 29, quoted in Alexander Strauch, *Biblical Eldership: An Urgent Call to Restore Biblical Church Leadership* (Littleton, CO: Lewis and Roth, 1995), 83.

3

A Qualified Man

Many people wonder why it is necessary to have qualifications for a pastor. They might think, "If someone wants to be a pastor, should he not have that right, regardless of whether he meets a list of criteria? And who decides what the criteria are anyway?" The Acts 29 network is often criticized for being "too focused" on assessing the qualifications of prospective church planters.

The truth, however, is that all of us see the need for criteria in other professions. No one would board a plane if they knew that the "pilot" loved planes but didn't have a pilot's license. No one would want to be operated on by a "surgeon" whose primary credential was that his father was a doctor. A young couple would not entrust the design of their dream home to an "architect" whose portfolio was the back of a Lincoln Logs box. Qualifications are important in every job, and the more important the job, the more important the need for stringent qualifications.

The New Testament places a very strong emphasis on the importance of appointing qualified elders in the church.[4] As Alexander Strauch notes, "The New Testament offers more instruction regarding elders than on other important church subjects such as the Lord's Supper, the Lord's Day, baptism, or spiritual gifts."[5] Moreover, there is more teaching in the New Testament about the *qualifications* for eldership than about any other aspect of biblical leadership.[6]

The reason for this strong emphasis is that elders are charged with the sacred task of caring for the eternal souls for whom Christ died. Since a pastor has the extremely important job of teaching and caring for eternal souls, it is important to make sure that the wrong men

---

[4] 1 Timothy 3:1–7; Titus 1:5–9; 1 Peter 5:1–4.
[5] Strauch, *Biblical Eldership*, 103.
[6] Cf. ibid., 68–72.

are not appointed to this office. When an unqualified doctor performs surgery, or an unqualified pilot flies planes, or an unqualified architect builds a house, people get hurt and things fall apart. It is no different in the church: people usually end up getting hurt when they are under unqualified leaders, and everything from marriages to the church itself is likely to fall apart.

The New Testament allows a lot of flexibility with regard to exactly how elders are to function in the church. We are told to have elders, but we are not told everything about elders. The pattern for leadership that the New Testament has set, however, is *a plurality of elders.*[7] Elders serve as the lead overseers of the church, teach and preach the Word, protect the church from false teachers, exhort and admonish the saints in sound doctrine, pray for the sick, and judge doctrinal issues.[8] Elders are men who are well known by the community, have tested character and proven integrity, and are doctrinally sound. Elders must be men who can pastor themselves as well as others, having personal self-discipline and maturity, as well as the ability to relate well to others and to teach and care for them. In plurality there is accountability and a strength that one man alone lacks. "Woe to him who is alone when he falls and has not another to lift him up!" (Ecclesiastes 4:10).

The Qualifications of Eldership in the New Testament

There are a few different lists of qualifications for eldership in the New Testament, but the most extensive is 1 Timothy 3:1–7:

> The saying is trustworthy: If anyone aspires to the office of overseer, he desires a noble task. Therefore an overseer must be above reproach, the husband of one wife, sober-minded, self-controlled, respectable, hospitable, able to teach, not a drunkard, not violent but gentle, not quarrelsome, not a lover of money. He must manage his own household well, with all dignity keeping his children submissive, for if someone does not know how to manage his own household, how will he care for God's church? He must not be a recent convert, or he may become puffed up with conceit and fall into the condemnation of the

---

[7]Acts 14:23; 15; 20:17, 28; 1 Timothy 5:17; Philippians 1:1; Titus 1:5; James 5:14; 1 Peter 1:1; 5:1.
[8]Cf. Strauch, *Biblical Eldership*, 16.

devil. Moreover, he must be well thought of by outsiders, so that he may not fall into disgrace, into a snare of the devil.

In one regard this list of qualifications is noteworthy because it is so un-noteworthy. Almost all of what is required here of elders (or overseers) is required of any believer elsewhere in Scripture. For example, the stipulation that an elder not be a drunkard does not imply that other believers are allowed to imitate frat boys and be binge drinkers. Likewise, the fact that an elder must not be a lover of money does not suggest that non-elders in the church can make money their functional savior. Anyone who serves Christ is required to not be a drunkard or a lover of money. So what sets elders apart?

Elders are not a higher class of Christians. Rather, as D. A. Carson notes, "what is required in some sense of all believers is *peculiarly required of the leaders* of believers."[9] Carson couldn't be more right. Elders are called to uniquely focus on and live out the virtues to which all Christians aspire.

The term *overseer* comes from the Greek *episcope*, which is used interchangeably with the term *elder* (Titus 1:5, 7). *Episcope* describes one who looks after, considers, examines, and provides covering for someone or something. In ancient Greek society, an overseer was a guardian, controller, ruler, or manager.

What does an elder oversee? Elders oversee *people*—people who are made in the image of God, people for whom Christ died, people deeply loved by God. One of the reasons it is essential for elders to be godly men is that when elders are not godly, it is very difficult for the people to become godly. As John MacArthur has written, "whatever the leaders are, the people become. As Hosea said, 'Like people, like priest' (4:9). Jesus said, 'Everyone, after he has been fully trained, will be like his teacher' (Luke 6:40). Biblical history demonstrates that people will seldom rise above the spiritual level of their leadership."[10]

Although Paul's list is not exhaustive and was written to address a particular set of circumstances in a particular context, the list is very helpful for discerning what *type* of person Paul thinks will make a good

[9]D. A. Carson, *The Cross and Christian Ministry* (Grand Rapids: Baker, 1993), 95, emphasis mine.
[10]Quoted in Strauch, *Biblical Eldership*, 70.

elder. Let's look over Paul's list of qualifications and see what kind of people he has in mind for this office.

Anepileptos, "Above Reproach"

This term describes a man who is free from any serious character blights, is respected by those who know him, and is widely known to live a godly life. Chrysostom notes, "Every virtue is implied in this word."[11] William Mounce argues that "above reproach" is really the fountain from which all the others flow: "the first stands as the title over all these qualities: the overseer must be above reproach; all that follows spells out what this entails."[12] The most basic and most fundamental qualification of an elder, therefore, is that he be beyond reproach; this is the all-encompassing title of all that Paul describes here in 1 Timothy 3. Mark Driscoll calls "above reproach" the "junk drawer" term that Paul applies to what it means to be qualified.

Mias Gunaikos Andra, "Husband of One Wife"

His mind and heart are devoted to his wife. He is a "one-woman man."

At first glance, Paul might appear to be prohibiting a divorced man from being an elder.[13] But it is more likely that he is speaking of a man's devotion for and connection to his wife. To be qualified, a man must be exclusively devoted to his wife, having a deep emotional, social, and sexual connection to her.

Practically, this means that a pastor's marriage must be sound. More than that, it seems to indicate that a lack of emotional or physical intimacy in a marriage would keep a pastor from ministry. In other words, it suggests that an unspectacular sex life would keep a man from being a qualified pastor. Pastors are to take the lead in emotional, social, and sexual connection with their wives. As in all the qualifications, this does not mean that the pastor, or his marriage, is perfect. It means that the marriage is worth imitating. It means that other single and married men

---

[11]Quoted in William D. Mounce, *Word Biblical Commentary*, Vol. 46, *Pastoral Epistles* (Nashville: Nelson Reference and Electronic, 2000), 169.
[12]Ibid., 152.
[13]Cf. the discussion in ibid., 170ff.

look at how the pastor loves and serves his wife as a model for their own devotion to their wife or future wife.

Nephalios, "Sober-minded" or Temperate

The pastor is to be self-controlled (not led by emotions or lusts). He has freedom from debilitating excesses or rash behavior.

This qualification speaks to the emotional life of a man. A qualified pastor must be a man who is able to control his desires and emotions through submission to the power and authority of the Holy Spirit. The issue Paul seems to be addressing here is that a qualified man is led by the Spirit, not by his emotions. This doesn't mean that a pastor must become dead inside, unable to feel and emote at all. It does mean, however, that a man who submits to the Spirit emotionally will likely avoid sins like marital infidelity, financial impropriety, and unrighteous anger. The hope is that he will lead the church he pastors to avoid the same.

Consider Pastor Bruce Wesley's struggle to control his emotions.[14] Bruce says,

Church planting really exposed my emotional dysfunction. Looking back at that time in my life, I was angry all the time. I lived just below the boiling point every waking hour of every day. I justified my anger by telling myself I was just driven to champion the gospel in my little area of responsibility. But the day-to-day reality at home was that my wife and children walked on eggshells because of my unpredictability.

Two years after we planted Clear Creek, I began to recognize a very distinct emotional detachment from my wife and kids. Worse, I realized that I was probably the last member of the family to figure this out. My wife and kids were already feeling disconnected.

I remember asking myself one day, "What if I planted a successful church, but did not know how to love, cherish, protect and connect with my own wife and kids? What if I reached the end of my one and only life and my wife and children wanted nothing to do with me?"

A wise and godly friend helped me realize a couple of things. First, he helped me see that angry outbursts are like doing a cannonball into a pool—you don't really know how far the splash reaches because

---

[14]For more information about Bruce and his church visit http://www.clearcreek.org.

you're just jumping in with your eyes closed. My anger was splashing on people I never intended to reach.

Secondly, he helped me realize that I was leveraging my emotional energy to help me stay engaged in a process or to fight through tough situations, which can be a very good thing. But my emotion was anger, and the anger was pointed squarely at people, especially those closest to me. I realized that my anger was connected to my over-desire to be successful. Anybody who stood in the way of me and my goals was met with my wrath.

Lo and behold, it was the gospel that changed me. One day my friend said to me, "There is nothing you can do that will make God love you more and nothing you can do that will make God love you less." Now, I had said about as much hundreds of times over the course of my ministry life. But when my friend said it in that particular moment, God's Spirit opened my heart to see again the vastness of his grace.

I realized that I was trying to earn God's love through hard work and success. I was angry because that is an unending, unproductive, and utterly futile task. The result of my idolatry and self-righteousness was anger. And the result of my anger was a growing distance between me and the people who loved me. It's when I learned to preach the gospel to myself that my emotional world changed. Under grace, in light of the gospel, I became a self-controlled man. I'm grateful . . . and so are my wife and kids.

Sophron, "Self-controlled"

He must have a sound mind (he is able to focus and not be distracted easily). He has good judgment and common sense.

Paul teaches in Galatians 5:22–23 that self-control is a result of the Spirit's work in our lives. In the context of that passage, Paul seems to indicate that self-control is not a result of willpower but is the fruit of God's power as we walk in and are led by the Holy Spirit. So it seems that Paul is saying here that a pastor should be a man whose life is characterized by the Spirit's controlling him with the result that his "self" is controlled.

Kosmios, "Respectable"

This means to have a well-ordered life (a life that is not characterized by chaos).

This qualification seems to deal with the general character of a pastor's life, something of a decibel meter for the life of a pastor. One of my pastor friends was a man who didn't have his life together. His car was never clean on the outside, and the inside was worse. His yard was landscaped by nature, which means it was full of weeds (he told his young children they were flowers). Not only were his car, house, and lawn disheveled, but *he* was disheveled. There was a general franticness about the way he carried himself. He was always in a hurry, his conversations were always rushed, and chaos permeated any environment in which he found himself. The result of all of this was that he was not respected, and that's because he wasn't respectable. To be respectable means that a pastor has a good handle on the responsibilities of his life, to the point that others view him not necessarily as a man who has it all together, but as one who can bear the weight and complexity of his life, which then qualifies him to lead the various complexities of the church.

Philoxenos, "Hospitable"

He loves strangers. He is not cliquish.

Contrary to popular belief, this qualification doesn't mean that the pastor and his wife should have potlucks at their house for all the people in the church. Nor does it mean that pastors' homes should be a revolving door for people in the church to come and hang out, watch network television, and "do community." The word "hospitable" refers to the way the pastor and his family welcome those outside the faith. In other words, to be hospitable is to be a friend of sinners and thus to be like Jesus.

An excellent example of community-centered hospitality is found in Alex Early's story of how he planted Four Corners Church in what he calls "a gay-friendly Americana rock 'n' roll bar."[15]

> In January of 2007, I left a cushy church job for something more radical. I had continued to read the Gospels over and over again and continued to see Jesus as a "friend of sinners." I scrolled through my phone and looked at my calendar. I was appalled. I had no unbelieving friends. Everyone in my life was a Christian, white, upper-middle-class, Republican. I knew no "sinners." I started to think, "Who in

---

[15]For more information about Four Corners Church visit http://fourcornersnewnan.org.

the Bible belt doesn't know Jesus and why?" I thought of the local bar scene. I thought of the homosexual community.

God told me to quit my church job and go downtown to a gay-friendly bar called the Alamo and get a job there. The clientele is unique, and staff are covered in sleeve tats and are quite open about their atheism. I thought to myself, "Perfect."

I got a job as a bar-back. My job was to stock fridges and clean the place up. I would substitute teach from 7:45 A.M.-3:15 P.M. and then go to the Alamo from 4:00 P.M.-2:00 A.M. four days a week. I started having conversations with Alamo coworkers and patrons, getting to know them, and slowly having opportunities to share about the person and work of Christ.

Eventually I won the ear of the owner of the Alamo, Amy Murphy. Amy, a thirty-seven-year-old lesbian and self-proclaimed atheist, found out I was planting a church. She asked me about it one day, and when I told her I was hosting a meeting in my living room for people who were interested in the church, she asked if she could come. "Of course," I said. To my surprise, she actually came.

After the meeting, Amy approached me, saying, "You need a bigger place for church." I laughed and said, "Yeah, why don't you give me the Alamo." In a grace-filled moment of utter surprise, Amy said, "OK. Done." And it was. She told me we could have it rent-free, and we started meeting at the Alamo the following Sunday.

Months later, Amy and I were sitting in her backyard on a summer day eating BBQ, and she said, "I feel like I have a new heart. I pray all the time and ask Jesus to forgive me for my sins and help me live for him at work because it's such a crazy job. I mean I've known over the past few months that God was with me, but now I feel like God is actually inside of me. Is that normal?"

It was my immense pleasure in that moment to tell Amy that Jesus had saved her, that what she was feeling and experiencing was one of the primary benefits of salvation, the indwelling of God's Spirit.

Since then, Amy has opened several other bars in and around Atlanta, and she wants to help other churches plant in her spaces so that more people can meet Jesus.

Didaktikos, "Able to Teach"

This indicates skill in teaching.

Though we will delve into this in detail in another chapter, we must note here that it is required that a pastor be able to teach. A qualified pastor is able to take the Scripture and help people understand what it means in its original context and in its contemporary application.

"Not a Drunkard"

He has no known idolatry (addiction). In the King James Version, this reads, "not given to wine."

This qualification seems to speak to the release valve of the pastor. Working out is a legitimate way to blow off the pressure of the day. Playing with your kids is an acceptable manner of relieving stress. Making love to your wife is a biblically encouraged way of distracting yourself from the difficulties of ministry. Hitting the bottle is not. As Mark Driscoll has often said, "You know you are in trouble as a pastor when your accountability group is Jim Beam, Jack Daniels, and Jose Cuervo."

This qualification seems to be speaking to addiction to substances generally and is not limited to wine. As I coach and mentor church planters and pastors, I am shocked at the number of them who are either addicted or headed toward addiction to alcohol. Increasingly, the same is true with prescription drugs. One pastor I know could not relax without several beers after work and could not sleep without the aid of a sleeping pill. Not only is this physically, mentally, and emotionally dangerous, it is a sign of deep distrust in God's ability to meet our needs and provide our strength.

Plektes, "Not Violent"

In the King James Version of the Bible, *plektes* is translated "striker." Simply put, you can't be a pastor if you are getting into fistfights with church members or lost people in your city. I remember meeting one pastor who was in the process of being disqualified because he was a brawler. I was doing ministry in the French Quarter of New Orleans during the Mardi Gras festival. If you are not familiar with the street party known as Mardi Gras, it is one of the most decadent events in North America. Mardi Gras makes a frat party look like Sunday dinner at Great-grammas's house. At Mardi Gras I personally witnessed people having sex in the street, people vomiting on the street, more than a smattering of people getting drunk on the street, and many of those people then relieving themselves on said street. Of course (surprise, surprise), this was no ordinary street; it was the infamous Bourbon Street.[16] As shocking as it was to witness this kind of debauchery, it was even more of a shock to see one of the local pastors literally knock out a Mardi Gras reveler with a single right hook. Good fighter, bad pastor. In short, you can't be a pastor if you tend to handle conflict like Mike Tyson "handled" Evander Holyfield. Suffice it to say that tending the flock with brass knuckles is roundly frowned upon in Scripture.

Epiekes, "Gentle"

The word "gentle" here does not refer to soft, passive, dead-fish hand-shake guys who need rearview mirrors implanted in their heads because they back down so much. Gentleness in this context means to be lenient, willing to yield when yielding is possible. It describes a man who does not always have to have his own way. This qualification speaks to the stubbornness quotient of a man. Qualified men do not always have to have their way. They are willing to not be right for the sake of the church.

Amachos, "Not Quarrelsome"

He must not be quarrelsome (cf. 2 Timothy 2:24–25).

You can't be a pastor if your "pastoral counseling" produces more heat than light. In other words, you are not a qualified man if you turn most discussions into arguments. There are men who love nothing more than to "take the other side" and play "the devil's advocate." This kind of behavior might make you a successful seminary student, but it will disqualify you from being a pastor.

Aischrokeredes, "Not a Lover of Money"

He must not desire money more than God (Hebrews 13:5; 1 Timothy 6:7–9).

A man who understands the challenges and rewards of being free from the love of money is Jason Martin, who pastors the Journey Church in Atlanta, Georgia.[17] In the course of his vocational ministry life, Jason

---

[16]Bourbon Street in particular and the French Quarter in general had a unique smell—a combination of alcohol, urine, and vomit, which I imagined as the smell of sin.

[17]For more information about Jason and the Journey Church visit their Web site, http://discoverthejourney.net.

has served churches that made up for a lack of gospel focus by offering a nice salary and cushy benefits to pastors. The Holy Spirit convicted Jason of settling for the temporary monetary comforts the church provided instead of challenging people to promote the everlasting benefits the gospel alone can bring.

When Jason took the bold risk of replanting his church, putting all their resources into the formation of a gospel-centered presence on the west side of Atlanta, it came with financial disadvantages.

Jason says of that time, "Committing to unifying people and replanting was, from a financial perspective, a terrible move. I went from a very comfortable, full-time salary to not receiving anything from the church for almost three years." He adds, "I guess I'm like most men. I've always wanted to give my family the security and comforts that many other families have. But bringing gospel transformation into churches has often meant my family has to learn to live with less, not more."

While the tangible benefits might not be as plentiful, Jason admits he wouldn't change a thing.

"In the last couple of years of replanting, we have witnessed God do extraordinary things that are well worth the financial strain we've experienced. Temporary satisfaction with money and the pleasure it offers pales in comparison with eternal satisfaction with the gospel and the pleasures that come with forgiveness of sins and right relationship with God," Jason says.

Pastors who love money will eventually put that love before the good of the church. They will make decisions to ensure their own job security and salary increase, decisions that the majority of the time will hinder the forward progress of the gospel. In addition, pastors who love money tend to misappropriate money (using the church credit card for personal purchases, stealing from the offering, and increasing their salary without the elders' approval, to give just a few examples).

Proistemi, "Managing His Own Household Well"

This means to stand before, to rule, to be diligent (to be the spiritual leader in one's family).

The Puritans used to say that you can't pastor the big church (your congregation) if you can't pastor the little church (your family). If you can't teach your kids Scripture, you can't teach the church. If you can't answer your wife's theological questions, you can't be the one who answers the theological questions of the church.

Proistemi also refers to a man who is able to keep his children under control with all dignity—to cause children to obey in a graceful manner because of loving, pastoral parenting. Too many pastors' kids behave like rebellious little demons. It is not their fault. Many pastors discipline their children's rear ends but fail to discipline their kids' attitudes, the real catalyst of misbehavior. This doesn't mean that the kids of a pastor should always be perfect, sweet little angels, but rather that they should be under the loving control of parents whose discipline nurtures within them a healthy fear of God.

Neophutos, "Not . . . a Recent Convert"

He must not be newly sprung up (a baby Christian). This qualification has to do with the spiritual maturity of the pastor, specifically his longevity as a Christian. Obviously this qualification, along with the rest of the qualifications, is subjective, which is why the local church should be intimately involved with regard to this qualification issue.

Marturian kalen, "Well Thought of by Outsiders"

He must have a good reputation with those outside the church, one who knows unbelievers and is respected for his faith. This qualification implies, first and foremost, that elders will have relationships with unbelievers. This qualification makes no sense otherwise. Elders should be men who are respected not just by the church but by non-Christians as well. While elders are called to a biblical standard, which is higher than the world's standard, they should *at least* meet the world's standard for decency. A good reputation with non-Christians also protects against character attacks from those outside the church.

Qualified elders will exhibit integrity in their workplace and will be known as hard workers, in accordance with Colossians 3:22–23. They will also pursue relationships with non-Christians with interest and will allow themselves to be known by others. In such relationships they will be honest about their faith and their life.

Moving on from Here

If you have some "red flag" areas that are surfacing in your thoughts as you read these chapters, please do not foolishly ignore them. If the Holy Spirit is convicting you in an area of qualification, it must be addressed. While some of us who have tender consciences need to be reminded that the only person who is ultimately qualified for ministry is Jesus, others of us need to spend some serious time in prayer about these issues and not just brush them off. These qualifications are not arbitrary: they are designed to protect you, your family, and the church from failure, sin, and pain. It would be much better to take a season off from ministry than to disqualify yourself from ministry.[18] If in reading these qualifications you realize that you are not yet qualified for the pastorate, I want to give you three encouragements.

First, it is important to remember that the biblical qualifications for ministry are not a now-or-never thing. In other words, being disqualified from ministry is not necessarily permanent. If after reading these qualifications you realize that you are not qualified for ministry, it does not mean that you can never be in ministry again. If you are a young aspiring pastor who is struggling with an addiction, for example, it may be that the Lord wants you to make progress in this struggle for a time before you enter ministry in order to help you minister more effectively. But it does not necessarily mean you can never enter ministry. Or if you are currently a pastor guilty of neglecting your family, it may mean you need to take a season away from ministry and circle the wagons in order to invest in your family. But it does not necessarily mean that you can never be in ministry again.

Second, being a pastor is not the most important thing in your life. Your first calling is not to be a pastor but to be a Christian. We must never idolize the ministry by thinking that we are of no value without it. We must look to Christ and his work on the cross on our behalf in order

---

[18]For those in the ministry struggling with sexual sin, a helpful resource is John H. Armstrong, *The Stain That Stays: The Church's Response to the Sexual Misconduct of Its Leaders* (Ross-shire, Scotland: Christian Focus Publications, 2000).

to find our deepest identity and purpose. If you have to make a choice between continuing in the ministry or being a faithful Christian, choose the latter. It will be much better for you, your family, and Christ's church.

Third, being a pastor is not the only way you are valuable to the church. If you take a season away from the pastorate, that does not mean you are prohibited from supporting the church and its leadership, from serving in the church as a layperson, or from using your spiritual gifts to edify the body. Your willingness to step down for a season will be instructive to others about the need for personal holiness and the height and weight of the pastoral office. Ultimately the Lord can use such a scenario for his good.

For all of us, wherever we are in our calling, these qualifications are a challenge to seek holiness and blamelessness in our personal lives, in our relationships, and in our public office. Ultimately none of us are qualified before God to serve his people. As the apostle Paul asks, "Who is sufficient for these things?" (2 Corinthians 2:16). Our hope is not in ourselves but in Christ who calls us, purifies us, equips us, and qualifies us.[19]

---

[19]If you have further questions about your qualification for ministry, the best thing to do is ask for help from the leadership of your church. If this is not an option, you should consider attending an Acts 29 assessment process. You can learn about that at http://www.acts29network.org/plant-a-church/assessment-process.

Men depend on God's blessing and favorable providence for success in all affairs, but the dependence of the success of this affair on God's influence is more manifold and more immediate. It depends on God in every way. It is he that must furnish and qualify a minister for his work. It is he that must give a heart sincerely and earnestly to seek the ends of it. It is he that must assist him in private and in public. It is he that must dispose a minister well to his people, and it is he that must incline their hearts well to him, and so influence both, that good understanding may be kept up between minister and people that may make way for the success of his ministry. (Jonathan Edwards)[1]

[A pastor] must die to all passions of the flesh and by now lead a spiritual life. He must have put aside worldly prosperity; he must fear no adversity, desire only what is interior. . . . He is not led to covet the goods of others, but is bounteous in giving of his own. He is quickly moved of a compassionate heart to forgive. . . . [He] sympathizes with the frailties of others, and so rejoices in the good. . . . He so studies to live as to be able to water the dry hearts of others. . . . By his practice and experience of prayer he has learned already that he can obtain from the Lord what he asks for. (Gregory the Great)[2]

[1]Jonathan Edwards, *The Salvation of Souls* (Wheaton, IL: Crossway, 2002), 14–23.
[2]Gregory the Great, *Pastoral Care*, I.10, 38, quoted in Andrew Purves, *Pastoral Theology in the Classical Tradition* (Louisville: Westminster John Knox Press, 2001), 67.

4

A Dependent Man

I noticed something recently at the gym. It seems there are basically two kinds of guys who go to the gym. Near the free weights and on bench presses, you find the huge no-neck guys who spend most of their time doing heavy lifting. These guys are huge. However, most of them are not in great shape, and you hardly ever see them on the treadmill or doing sit-ups. Then, on the treadmill, you find skinny, zero-body-fat guys who can run like gazelles but hardly ever hit the weights. Both groups tend to stay in the area where they are most comfortable and avoid their areas of weakness. One day after a great workout I sensed the Spirit telling me: *it is the same with pastors.* Pastors tend to stay in their strengths and avoid their weaknesses. "Theology guys" tend to spend a lot of time reading and discussing dead theologians. "Missional guys" tend to spend a lot of time analyzing culture and drinking lattes. "Shepherding guys" tend to spend a lot of time hanging out with people and counseling them. But rarely do we see pastors step out of their strengths into their areas of weakness. Why is this? Because it is uncomfortable. It is difficult. It is flesh-starving.[3]

The reason I mention this at the beginning of this chapter is that one of the greatest spurs to dependence on God is stepping out of your comfort zone and ministry strengths into your weaknesses. You will feel inadequate, but paradoxically you will be more potent for God's kingdom than ever because you will be forced to depend more on God's power than on your own. And ultimately it is only God's power that makes any of us able to accomplish breathing, thinking, and walking, not to mention ministry.[4]

What I essentially want to say in this chapter is that *our effectiveness in ministry depends directly on our dependence on the power of the Holy Spirit.* As

---

[3]Biblically speaking, the flesh is that part of us that has yet to be surrendered to God; cf. Romans 8:7.
[4]"Apart from me you can do nothing," says Jesus in John 15:5.

goes our walk with God, so goes our ministry. Only when we are vitally connected to him can we be vitally helpful to others. Spurgeon said it best years ago: "The labour of the Christian ministry is well performed in exact proportion to the vigour of our renewed nature."[5]

Why Is Dependence Important?

Most of the young men I've encountered who aspire to serve God in vocational ministry gravitate toward the pragmatics of ministry performance: preaching improvement, church growth, cultural engagement, etc. It is good to pursue excellence in these areas. However, the paradox of Christian ministry is that our peak performance in leading, shepherding, and preaching comes fundamentally from a rich spiritual life, and not from ministry skills per se. Becoming a better preacher, leader, shepherd, and cultural exegete depends entirely on the health and vitality of a pastor's spiritual life.

There is little doubt that in order to lead a church well in the twenty-first century, one must read current authors from the realm of the church and from the realm of business.[6] As Mark Driscoll often said, "Acts 29 guys are to believe in *sola* Scriptura but not *solo* Scriptura."[7] Because of common grace, we can glean principles from the business world—all truth is God's truth. However, if we are going to learn dependence upon God and experience personal inner renewal, we must go back a few centuries.

What I have noticed is that much of the writing on contemporary spirituality is shallow and focused on behavior modification (though, of course, you can find exceptions). Much of the devotional literature of previous eras of church history was not as enamored with "success," not as engulfed by entertainment, and was generally more thoughtful about a vital, spiritual inner life. Sadly, most pastors today spend little time reading the classics. We therefore have a truncated, cut-down, impoverished idea of spirituality. We have forgotten that our heads and our

---

[5]Charles Spurgeon, *Lectures to My Students* (Grand Rapids: Zondervan, 1972), 17.
[6]A couple of must reads I recommend are: Jim Collins, *Good to Great: Why Some Companies Make the Leap . . . and Others Don't* (New York: Harper Business, 2001); Michael Gerber, *The E-Myth: Why Most Businesses Don't Work and What to Do About It* (New York: Ballinger, 1985).
[7]*Sola Scriptura* was one of the principles of the Reformers during the Protestant Reformation five hundred years ago. It refers to the belief that the Bible alone is our ultimate authority in matters of theology and life.

hearts are inextricably tied together, and we have forgotten that the most important thing in our ministry is our own walk with Christ.

John Wesley, who made it his regular custom to spend two hours per day in prayer, wrote, "God does nothing except in response to believing prayer." Most people say, "Two whole hours! I am too busy to spend that much time in prayer!" But Martin Luther once famously said, "If I fail to spend two hours in prayer each morning, the devil gets the victory through the day. I have so much business I cannot get on without spending three hours daily in prayer." According to Luther, being busy is *all the more* reason to spend much time wrestling with God in prayer.

Richard Baxter, the Puritan pastor and theologian, counseled those seeking to serve in pastoral ministry with these words: "When your minds are in a holy, heavenly frame, your people are likely to partake of the fruits of it. Your prayers, and praises, and doctrine will be sweet and heavenly to them. They will most likely feel when you have been much with God: that which is most on your hearts, is like to be most in their ears."[8] Baxter is reminding us of something that we often forget but that should be pretty obvious to us: our people can tell when we are close to God—and when we are not. It will come out in our sermons, our prayers, our leadership, and even our conversations. As Moses' face shone to the Israelites after he had been with God, so our lives will radiate his presence when we have been with him.[9] Ultimately pastors talk way too much to keep secrets! Who we are before God seeps out of us constantly.[10]

Baxter continues: "If we forbear taking food ourselves, we shall famish them; it will soon be visible in their leanness, and dull discharge of their several duties. If we let our love decline, we are not like to raise up theirs. If we abate our holy care and fear, it will appear in our preaching: if the matter show it not, the manner will. If we feed on unwholesome food, either errors or fruitless controversies, our hearers are like to fare the worse for it."[11] In other words, not only can our people tell where we are spiritually, but *we are a pattern for them*. They will not likely pursue

---

[8]Richard Baxter, *The Reformed Pastor* (General Books LLC, 2009), 61.
[9]Exodus 34:29–35.
[10]It is wise to heed the words of Matthew 12:34 and pay attention to our words because they reveal our heart.
[11]Baxter, *The Reformed Pastor*, 61–62.

holiness with greater zeal than we do. They will likely not share their faith more often or more effectively than we do. They will not likely labor before God in prayer more than we do.

What Is Dependence?

Sandwiched in the middle of his most famous sermon, the Sermon on the Mount, Jesus challenges his followers with regard to the dependent life. His words have interesting implications for those of us who desire to be in public ministry or are currently in public ministry:

> And when you pray, you must not be like the hypocrites. For they love to stand and pray in the synagogues and at the street corners, that they may be seen by others. Truly, I say to you, they have received their reward. But when you pray, go into your room and shut the door and pray to your Father who is in secret. And your Father who sees in secret will reward you.[12]

Jesus is exposing the tendency of religious leaders to appear to be men of prayer because they often talk to God in public. These verses challenge those of us in public ministry to ask ourselves: *Which do I love more—to pray in public or to pray in private?* To the degree that we value public prayer over private prayer, we are seeking the approval of men, not of God. It is much easier for leaders to pray in public because we are required to do so and because we are often praised for how wonderful and articulate our public prayers are. I have noticed this in my own life as I listen to myself pray in public and in private. My public prayers tend to be articulate, thoughtful, and smooth. My personal prayers are often incoherent, overly emotional, and choppy.

Why is it so easy to be great at public prayer and terrible at private prayer? The logic of Jesus in Matthew 6:5–6 explains this dichotomy: it is an issue of *reward*. Simply put, we are immediately rewarded for praying well in public, but we are not for private prayer. Public prayers are often praised by those around us who are impressed by our oratorical ability. Public prayers are often empowered by the excitement of the moment rather than by the sobering reality of the eternal. Thus public prayers

---

[12]Matthew 6:5–6.

are often more driven by performance than by passion, by people rather than by God.

Private prayer is the revealer of the true spiritual condition of the human heart. Do we pray privately for what God might do for us or for a better understanding of God? Do we pray to get closer to a better (i.e., easier, more comfortable) life, or do we pray to get closer to God?

In addition to prayer, many other practices cultivate dependence on God. One is *fasting*. Jesus calls us to fast in private, and he calls us to pray in private (Matthew 6:16–18). It is interesting that our Lord says *when* you fast, not *if* you fast (v. 16). Implication: you should fast. Fasting is a very helpful way to reduce distractions, focus on God, and cultivate a sense of dependence on him. Most pastors don't fast, which is evident by their constantly expanding waistlines.

Another helpful practice is *meditation*. I define meditation as pondering God's Word, asking questions about the application of its truth, speaking that truth to oneself, and using God's Word in prayer to God himself.[13] Meditation allows the Holy Spirit to speak the truth of Scripture into our lives during our private devotions and reading of the Bible.

There are other practices that can help us cultivate dependence on God, such as memorizing Scripture, private worship, taking a Sabbath rest, and serving others. Our focus, however, should not be on what we are doing but on *getting close to God*. "Do not let your left hand know what your right hand is doing" (Matthew 6:3). When we focus on a list of practices, we can become legalistic, focusing either on how well we are doing or how poorly we are doing, and we miss the whole point. Besides, different people will find different practices helpful. So each one of us needs to learn how *we* best cultivate dependence on the Holy Spirit. There is no formula: our goal should be simply to do whatever we need to do to cultivate more of a sense of dependence on God in our lives. I appreciate Jack Deere's paraphrase of John 17:26: "Father, grant me power from the Holy Spirit to love the Son of God like you love him."[14] This must be our heart's cry.

---

[13]Donald Whitney's book *Spiritual Disciplines* is a helpful resource for learning more about Christian meditation (Colorado Springs: NavPress, 1997).

[14]Jack Deere, *Surprised by the Power of the Spirit: Discovering How God Speaks and Heals Today* (Grand Rapids: Zondervan, 1993), 201.

In the Acts 29 Network we like to say that we are "charismatic with a seat belt." We believe that supernatural spiritual gifts have not ceased and thus should be pursued by all Christians (see, for example, 1 Corinthians 14:1) and used in worship gatherings (1 Corinthians 14:26). For us, though, being open to the supernatural work of the Holy Spirit means more than just making room for certain spiritual gifts. It also means that the *whole* of our ministry as Christian pastors must be characterized by the supernatural—that is, by what is not possible without God's help, by what we are unable to do through our natural abilities. We become more dependent when we recognize the truth of Francis Schaeffer's motto in our own ministries: "what we are doing is not just difficult—it is impossible."

There is also an aspect of spiritual warfare in our ministry that must be acknowledged. If you don't think demons are real, try planting a church! You won't get very far in advancing God's kingdom without feeling resistance from the enemy. As modern westerners we often forget that we have an enemy and that he actively opposes us. Becoming a dependent man means becoming more aware of the spiritual warfare going on all around us, recognizing our part in that unseen reality (Ephesians 6:12; 2 Corinthians 10:3). We are not called to *defeat* the Devil—Christ has already done that at the cross, and the days until his final and complete triumph over Satan are numbered. What we are called to do is *resist* the Enemy (James 4:7) and become firm in our faith (1 Peter 5:9). God will be faithful to protect us and to give us help against Satan's assaults.

Detecting Dependence

For many of us, answering the question, "Am I living in dependence on God?" is a difficult task. Part of the reason for this is that we often do not know whether we are living in dependence on God because we are disengaged from our hearts. Here are some questions we can ask ourselves to help us discern the orientation of our hearts:

> 1) *Which do I want more—to know God or to achieve for God?* Some verses to meditate on: Philippians 3:10; Exodus 33:13; 1 Timothy 4:6–10.

2) *When was the last time I experienced a prompting of the Holy Spirit?* Verses to meditate on: John 4:7–19; Acts 16:6–10.[15]

3) *Am I consistently being convicted of sin in my life?* Verses to meditate on: Hebrews 12:5–11; John 16:7–8; 1 John 3:9.

4) *Am I consistently accepting my acceptance by God through Christ?* Verses to meditate on: 2 Corinthians 5:17, 21.

5) *Where do my thoughts go when I am not forced to think about anything?* Verses to meditate on: Psalm 63:1–4. If your mind goes immediately to your fantasy football team, something is wrong!

There is no neat formula for developing dependence on God.[16] The best way forward is to cultivate a desire to know and experience God more deeply. Blaise Pascal (1623–1662) was a French mathematician and theologian. At the age of thirty-one, he had an intense experience of God's presence. He never spoke of it to anyone, but he did write a short journal entry about it, which he then sewed into his coat so he would always be reminded of it. We will close this chapter by reading Pascal's *memoriam* as an encouragement for us to seek God in this way.

Pascal's *memoriam*:

In the year of grace 1654, Monday 23 November. . . .

From about half-past ten in the evening till about half an hour after midnight.

FIRE

God of Abraham. God of Isaac. God of Jacob.

Not of the philosophers and the learned.

Certainty. Joy. Certainty. Emotion. Sight. Joy.

Forgetfulness of the world and of all outside of God. . . .

The world has not known thee, but I have known thee.

Joy! Joy! Joy! Tears of joy. . . .

My God, will you leave me? Let me not ever be separated from you.[17]

---

[15]The word "concluding" in Acts 16:10 helps us see that although promptings are mystical, they are also connected to strategic thought. Paul had two checks in his spirit and an open vision, but it wasn't until he concluded—put all these things together cognitively—that he knew where the Spirit was leading.

[16]For those of us who are completely burned out, however, the first step is probably to get away and rest. Once a month I get away for the day, once a quarter I try to get out for two days, and once a year I try to get away for a week. The purpose of these times is rest, relaxation, and solitude with God. Some of us are so busy that we are not giving God access to our hearts. By slowing down and spending some unhurried time away from our ministry, we can allow God to speak into our lives. For those of you who are reading this who are totally dry, consider taking a sabbatical, a season off from ministry. One counselor told me that pastors should go on a three-month sabbatical once every seven years, or even a six-month sabbatical if possible. Trust God to maintain the ministry in your absence. You will be better able to serve your people once you are refreshed.

[17]William L. Portier, *Tradition and Incarnation: Foundation of Christian Theology* (Mahwah, NJ: Paulist Press, 1994), 38–39.

Our weakest-minded, most timid, most carnal, and most ill-balanced men are not suitable candidates for the pulpit. There are some works which we should never allot to the invalid or deformed. A man may not be qualified for climbing lofty buildings, his brain may be too weak, and elevated work might place him in great danger; by all means let him keep on the ground and find useful occupation where a steady brain is less important: there are brethren who have analogous spiritual deficiencies, they cannot be called to service which is conspicuous and elevated, because their heads are too weak. (Charles Spurgeon)[1]

---

[1]Charles Spurgeon, *Lectures to My Students* (Grand Rapids: Zondervan, 1972), 13.

5

A Skilled Man

Major League Baseball scouts are constantly on the lookout for the "five-tool player"—the guy who can hit for both average and power, throw, catch, and run on an elite level. These kinds of players come few and far between. They are out there, but they are rare. And with the ability to make a good team into a great team, they are invaluable to owners, managers, teammates, and fans.

The skills requisite to planting a successful church are also invaluable. Being a pastor/church planter requires three basic skills: leading, teaching, and shepherding. And like the five-tool player, a three-tool church planter or pastor with all the necessary skills is rare. Generally speaking, to be an effective pastor/church planter you must have two of the three to be able to lead a prevailing church. Also speaking generally, to effectively plant or grow a church, you must be a strong leader. If you are primarily gifted as a priest, you will tend to gravitate toward ministry contexts where you can be relationally connected to those around you, which often works in a smaller church, an established church, or as the number two guy in a church plant. To be the lead pastor in a church plant, however, you have to be able to lead—to cast vision, to create energy, to motivate, to inspire, and to build systems. While we can grow and change in our ministry skill sets, we don't normally change in who God has made us to be or in how he has wired us to work in ministry. It is therefore very important for a pastor or for a potential or current church planter to think carefully and honestly about his ministry skill set and about where he will best function in the church.

In this chapter we will discuss the three primary ministry skills in terms of the three offices of spiritual leadership in ancient Israel (and the three offices of Christ)—prophet, priest, and king. First, however, it is necessary to say a few words about the office of elder. Holding a New

Testament-sanctioned church office is not the same as participating in ministry. Because of the indwelling presence and power of the Holy Spirit, all believers are called to do ministry. Ministry is possible because the Holy Spirit supplies gifts to all believers to help them serve God for the good of the church.[2] A church office, however, is not a ministry like leading a Bible study, being a greeter at your church, or simply sharing your faith.

The office of elder is the highest office in Christ's church. An elder is unique not because he is specifically called to ministry, but because he shares the authority and responsibility for overseeing the church. It is the elders who have the final responsibility to test the teaching of the church against the deposit received from the apostles. They have the responsibility to see that the congregation is cared for in a manner that befits God's precious people. While they perform many of the ministry roles associated with the care and instruction of the people, those roles are not unique to the elders. Elders are to equip the congregation, but all members of the church are to use their gifts to build up the body.[3] Elders are to care for the church, but everyone is to care for each other.[4] Elders have the responsibility to see that all persons properly use their gifts in ministry.

Teaching is a particularly significant example in which a ministry central to qualified eldership is not limited to elders. Elders must be able to teach (1 Timothy 3:2) and labor diligently in preaching and teaching (1 Timothy 5:17). Paul urges Timothy, an elder, to teach diligently.[5] However, teaching is also a gift that can be given without regard to the office of elder or to gender.[6] Many others along with Paul taught the Word of the Lord in Antioch.[7] Priscilla and Aquila instructed Apollos.[8] The contributions to the church meetings, which include psalms, teachings, revelations, tongues, and interpretations, cannot be limited to elders (1 Corinthians 14:26).[9]

---

[2]1 Corinthians 12:7: "To each is given the manifestation of the Spirit for the common good."
[3]Ephesians 4:11–16.
[4]1 Corinthians 12:25.
[5]1 Timothy 4:11, 13; 5:7; 6:2; etc.
[6]Romans 12:7; 1 Corinthians 12:28.
[7]Acts 15.35.
[8]Acts 18:26.
[9]The Second London Confession (1677) expresses this distinction in relation to preaching: "Although it be incumbent on the Bishops or Pastors of the Churches to be instant in Preaching the Word, by way of Office; yet the work of Preaching the Word is not so peculiarly confined to them, but that others also gifted, and fitted by the Holy Spirit for it, and approved, and called by the Church, may and ought to perform it" (XXVI, Section 11).

The New Testament describes the office of elder, overseer,[10] or pastor as the highest office in a local church. This esteem to the office of elder is obvious when you discern what the New Testament charges elders to do. Functionally, elders in the local church do three main things:

1. Guard the teaching ministry of the church.
2. Ensure the spiritual care of the church.
3. Oversee the direction of the church.

We will examine each of these responsibilities in turn.

Prophets—Guardians of Truth

"Follow the pattern of the sound words that you have heard from me, in the faith and love that are in Christ Jesus. By the Holy Spirit who dwells within us, guard the good deposit entrusted to you" (2 Timothy 1:13–14). Elders are the chief teachers in the local church.

Prophets are those pastors who guide, guard, protect, and proclaim the truths of Scripture. They tend to ask questions like, "What does the text say?" and "Where is the church going?" Prophets are often placed in charge of the teaching ministry of the church, guarding the pulpit from errant doctrine. Prophets can make excellent teachers because they hold a high view of Scripture, enjoy studying God's Word and sharing the insights they find there, and provide clarity on tough theological issues. Elders who are primarily prophets do not merely read Scripture—they expound it and teach it, much like Ezra and the Levites did when they "gave the sense" of the Word.[11] Paul writes this very thing to Timothy: "Until I come, devote yourself to the public reading of Scripture, to exhortation, to teaching" (1 Timothy 4:13). These elders bear the overwhelming burden of responsibility for the correct analysis of Scripture and for the principles derived, the applications given, and the judgments made in the

---

[10]It is generally agreed among Protestants that the Bible uses the terms elders and overseers as different ways of referring to the same office. Pastoring, by contrast, is a ministry that elders and others do. The name *pastor* has come to be associated with the office of elder. The name given the office is not critical, as indicated by Paul's varied terminology. However, this must not be allowed to obscure the difference between office and ministry or to limit pastoring to elders.

[11]Nehemiah 8:8.

assembly. They are also granted the authority necessary to carry out that responsibility, including the authority to appoint or admonish, to encourage or silence.

With that said, we do not see any specific ministry role limited to elders. It is in this sense that elders of The Journey and elders of all Acts 29 churches believe that ministry is not gender-specific, though the office of elder is. We do not believe that any gift or any specific ministry would be closed to a woman on the basis of her gender alone. However, wisdom suggests that some ministry roles in the church ought to be regularly filled by elders. For example, we believe the central teaching position should be held by elders since that aspect is central to the office of elder. Thus the pulpit ministry should be led and guided by the elders. It seems to follow suit that the elders would preach the majority of the time in the local church in which they serve.

The need for elders to guard the teaching ministry of the church is clearly seen in Paul's vivid and compelling final challenge to the Ephesian elders in Acts 20:17–31. The last verse in the passage not only shows us Paul's pastoral heart but also the heart that all local church pastors are to develop: "Therefore be alert, remembering that for three years I did not cease night or day to admonish everyone with tears." Paul says that every single day, with tears, he reminded these elders of the importance of guarding the ministry of their local church. He gives his fellow elders several principles for guarding and protecting the local church through their teaching ministry.

Preaching and Teaching the Whole Counsel (Acts 20:20, 27)

For years the church preached through the Bible because that is what people expected. People came to church because they expected to hear verses read and expounded. Most who attended did not expect to "get much out of it," and they were left to themselves, the Holy Spirit, and their Sunday school class to figure out how to apply the sermons they were hearing.

In the 1970s, the seeker movement brought a much needed course correction in how the teaching ministry of the local church should be done. It focused on applying the message. I will never forget hearing the question, "What do you want them to do?" The problem with almost every course correction is that there is an overcorrection. So in many churches today you get a narrow teaching menu that focuses primarily on developing your "God-given potential" by gaining skills in personal finances, parenting, marriage, and conflict resolution.

While these and many more felt needs should be handled by the preaching ministry of the church, they should be addressed along with the rest of the content of Scripture. The good pastor/teacher gives the church a healthy menu by teaching through the Bible with good exposition of the passages. This is accomplished verse by verse through books of the Bible and also by dealing with pertinent topics that will edify the congregation.

Exposing False Doctrines and Teachers (v. 29)

Paul's burden for the elders of God's church was not only for them to teach all of God's Word to the church, but also to refute and correct false doctrine. Elders must not only passionately and systematically teach truth, they must also consistently and directly refute error. The tendency of human beings is not only to suppress and push down the truth but also to seek out false teachers.[12] I have observed an interesting paradox: sinful human hearts want false teaching, and sinful false teachers seek out people with sinful hearts. Many people are uncomfortable with the idea that pastors are supposed to refute false teachers and expose false teaching. It may help to remember that *false teaching hurts people.* A doctor who did not correct a false idea about how to fight sickness would not be a good doctor because even good patients would be hurt. In the same way, pastors must oppose false teaching because false teaching hurts the precious sheep Christ died to save. "For the time is coming when people will not endure sound teaching, but having itching ears they will accumulate for themselves teachers to suit their own passions, and will turn away from listening to the truth and wander off into myths" (2 Timothy 4:3–4).

---

[12]Romans 1:18: "For the wrath of God is revealed from heaven against all ungodliness and unrighteousness of men, who by their unrighteousness suppress the truth."

Priests—Shepherds of the Flock

"Obey your leaders and submit to them, for they are keeping watch over your souls, as those who will have to give an account. Let them do this with joy and not with groaning, for that would be of no advantage to you" (Hebrews 13:17).

No other verse in the Bible begins so promisingly for a pastor trying to lead a disparate group of sinful people. Nothing in the Bible sounds more authoritative and supportive of pastors than "Obey your leaders and submit to them." If only it ended there. However, few passages in the Bible are scarier for a pastor than the back half of Hebrews 13:17. Elders must make sure the souls of the congregation are watched over, for they will give an account to God for how they care for the congregation.

Priests lead the church by identifying and helping to meet people's needs. They tend to ask questions that start with "who." They are shepherds. Priests tend, guide, and feed the flock,[13] not by lording their positional authority over them, but by being encouragers, affirmers, servants, loving confronters, listeners, truth-tellers, wise counselors, and more.[14] Pastors help the weak.[15] Pastors pray for the sick.[16] Pastors support, encourage, protect, and guide the flock. They train, nourish, and mature the flock.

Those who lead the church in this capacity are most like Christ when functioning in the priestly office. More than prophets and kings, priests emphasize personal, intimate care that strengthens and grows the individual spiritually.

Several years ago I heard Rick Warren say something in a talk on some random sermon tape (remember those?) that really stuck with me. He said he was tired of young pastors telling him how much they loved to preach without talking about how much they loved the people to whom they were preaching. I have never forgotten that admonition. Warren's challenge gets to the heart of what it means to be an elder in the local church. It means that you use your teaching gift not for your own pleasure but for the edification and protection of the church. You don't preach to hear yourself, you preach to heal the church.

---

[13] Acts 20:28.
[14] 1 Peter 5:1–3.
[15] Acts 20:35.
[16] James 5:14.

A pastor must be a great listener. A good priest helps people feel like they are the most important persons in the world when being counseled by that pastor. Pastors must work to help people feel understood. In a real sense we are assuming the role of spiritual director for the members of our church. As we will discuss in our chapter on the shepherding leader, this spiritual direction is not to be done only by the pastor, but the pastor must take the lead for modeling this kind of spiritual care. The pastor is to be the main community-building encourager of the flock.

Kings—Builders of the Vision

"Let the elders who rule well be considered worthy of double honor, especially those who labor in preaching and teaching" (1 Timothy 5:17).

Kings develop strategies for bringing the vision and mission of Christ-centered living to fruition. They tend to ask the question "How?" They function like executives of the church because they spend a great deal of time and energy building and executing plans to sustain and grow a healthy church. Pastors who are more kingly minded add meaning to the New Testament word *overseer* because they "see over" the myriad details of local church ministry. And when functioning like Christ, they do so in order to "oversee" the direction of the church. Especially in new church plants, elders don't just concern themselves with specific ministry departments; they concern themselves with the ministry of the whole church. They are to stand before the church and keep her on mission in fulfillment of her redemptive potential. Elders work with the deacons to equip and serve the members to bring the gospel to the city. Deacons lead the church by serving her; elders serve the church by leading her.

Elders ensure that the church is led well when they are able to reproduce themselves. "Do not neglect the gift you have, which was given you by prophecy when the council of elders laid their hands on you" (1 Timothy 4:14). "And what you have heard from me in the presence of many witnesses entrust to faithful men who will be able to teach others also" (2 Timothy 2:2). Leaders take responsibility for the direction of the church. Though they may delegate some of this responsibility, they do not abdicate it. They lie awake thinking about what the church should be, where the church should go, and how the church should function.

Then, assuming they actually fall asleep, they wake up thinking about how to execute the very same things.

Because the church requires strong leadership, it is only logical that elders have the gift of leadership. All Christians must lead in certain capacities, in their role as parents or members of a community or even as small-group Bible study leaders, for instance. Certainly all Christians must lead in crisis events in the midst of unbelievers, much like the apostle Paul in the midst of a shipwreck.[17] With that said, Scripture seems to indicate that there are those who have a distinct gift of leadership.[18] In 1 Corinthians 12:28 Paul refers to the gift of administration (*kubernesis*), using a Greek word that can be translated "governments" (as in that verse in the King James Version). The word can refer to someone who pilots a ship or to someone who has responsibility for leadership.

C. Peter Wagner writes this about leadership: "The gift of leadership is the special ability that God gives to certain members of the body of Christ to set goals in accordance with God's purposes for the future and to communicate these goals to others in such a way that they voluntarily and harmoniously work together to accomplish those goals for the glory of God."[19] Regarding the gift of leadership Chuck Swindoll writes: "The gift of leadership is defined as this: the ability to organize and lead projects, to see them through from start to finish, while handling people tactfully and providing the vision to keep them at the task."[20]

Mark Daniels writes, "Leadership is the spiritual gift of those Christians empowered by God to lead the Church and its ministries in pursuing its mission."[21] Leadership guru John Maxwell writes, "Leaders have two characteristics: first they are going somewhere, and second they are able to persuade other people to go with them."[22]

It is important to note that the gift of leadership is not relegated to a certain personality type. It appears that Paul, Peter, and James all pos-

---

[17] Acts 27.
[18] Romans 12:8.
[19] C. Peter Wagner, *Finding Your Spiritual Gifts: Wagner-Modified Houts Questionnaire* (Glendale, CA: Regal Books, 1995).
[20] Charles R. Swindoll, "7 Building Blocks for Leaders," *Insights* (February 2007), 1, 3.
[21] Daniels wrote this as an entry on his weblog, *Better Living: Thoughts from Mark Daniels*. This entry, "Opening Your Spiritual Gifts," can be found at http://markdaniels.blogspot.com/2006/12/opening-your-spiritual-gifts-day-19.html.
[22] John C. Maxwell, *Leadership Gold: Lessons I've Learned from a Lifetime of Leading* (Nashville: Thomas Nelson, 2008), 77.

sessed the gift of leadership, yet they had radically different personalities. Leadership gifting is not based on whether or not you are an introvert or an extrovert or whether you are detail-oriented or less than attentive to details.

The gift of leadership is discovered and developed in the same way as other spiritual gifts—that is, through life experience, training, and the maturing process. Even though it is the product of the Spirit's presence and God's grace, this gift requires diligence, faithfulness, hard work, and commitment to God's purposes if it is to be exercised effectively.

Dangers for Prophets, Priests, and Kings

As with any ministry philosophies that nuance and distinguish between people's gifts, there are tendencies to be avoided when considering the prophetic, priestly, and kingly aspects of ministry. While we've examined the positive aspects of these roles, we must also spend some time looking at the pitfalls that mature prophets, priests, and kings will avoid.[23]

First, any church developing a leadership culture that incorporates the prophet, priest, king philosophy must avoid the temptation to view it as a personality test. Since Jesus was the perfect prophet, priest, and king, and since as believers we are becoming more like Christ, we should be growing in all these areas. Leaders, especially pastors, must not lock people (themselves included) so firmly into any of these categories that they limit the usefulness of the gifts God has given to build up the church. For example, as Drew Goodmanson notes, just because someone is emotional does not mean he is a priest.[24] Sticking an emotional person who is not a priest in a counseling scenario could easily do more harm than good. Stereotyping is too simplistic, too limiting to help the church. Maturing leadership teams will avoid this temptation.

Prophets

While prophets make excellent guardians of truth, they can also focus so heavily on doctrine that they neglect to preach grace. Prophets must

---

[23]Pastor Drew Goodmanson at Kaleo, an Acts 29 church in San Diego, has been very influential for me in the positive and negative tendencies of the triperspectival ministry philosophy. More information from Drew can be found at http://www.goodmanson.com.
[24]See http://www.goodmanson.com/20070-7/03/the-dangers-of-triperspectivalism.

avoid influencing *heads* to the exclusion of *hearts*. Prophets must also fight against arrogance, legalism, and contempt for people who do not share their beliefs and passions.

Priests

Christlike priests will avoid influencing *hearts* to the exclusion of *heads*. Where prophets must fight arrogance, many priests must do battle against cowardice. Because priests can often value subjective feelings over objective truth, priests can let sin slide so as not to upset the apple cart of someone's life. Confrontation may not be a preference for a priest, but it must be done when truth is being compromised.

Kings

Kings are excellent leaders. They get things done. They build systems that help other people get things done. And because they focus so much on results, kings must avoid shutting out the gospel of grace by programming the gospel of grace to death. Kings also have a tendency to see what is broken and needs fixing, which can be extremely helpful in the life of the church. But kings must fight to keep morale high and slow down long enough to celebrate ministry wins.

Skilled pastors are overseers, theological guardians, and sound teachers who know their strengths and leverage them to build up the church. Skilled pastors also know their weaknesses and limits, and part of their skill is in bringing other leaders around them to take up the slack. As we have seen in our examination of the prophet, priest, and king leadership perspective, leaders are not bound to one personality type. As we close this chapter, I offer some questions to help you discover your natural leadership tendencies in the context of the triperspectival model. Remember, the most skilled pastors will have an evident blend of these three offices, but all leaders will naturally lean toward one over the others.

1. Are you a theologically motivated leader with a high view of preaching and teaching? Do you tend to be a black-and-white thinker in regard to biblical truth and living? Do you communicate vision primarily through writing and/or the teaching platform? Do you find

yourself asking questions that start with "what" or "where"? If so, you may be a natural prophet.

2. Are you an encourager of people? Are you skilled at discerning the needs of people? When a plan or strategy is implemented, are you most concerned about how people will be impacted? Do you find yourself asking questions that start with "who"? If so, you may be a natural priest.

3. Are you an organizational thinker? Are you a problem-solver? Are you a practical thinker who also enjoys thinking of new ways to solve old problems? Are you helpful at getting the right people in the right places in a ministry context? Do you find yourself asking questions that start with "how"? If so, you may be a natural king.

Shepherds are willing to bear the pain and endure the brunt of the sheep for the sheep. True elders do not command the consciences of their brethren but appeal to their brethren to faithfully follow God's Word. Out of love, true elders suffer and bear the brunt of difficult people and problems so that the lambs are not bruised. The elders bear the misunderstandings and sins of other people so that the assembly may live in peace. They lose sleep so that others may rest. They make great personal sacrifices of time and energy for the welfare of others. They see themselves as men under authority. They depend on God for wisdom and help, not on their own power and cleverness. They face the false teachers' fierce attacks. They guard the community's liberty and freedom in Christ so that the saints are encouraged to develop their gifts, to mature, and to serve one another. (Alexander Strauch)[1]

If Christ so loved the souls of men as to lay out Himself and deny Himself at this rate for the salvation [and happiness of souls], then surely the ministers of Christ should be ready greatly to exert themselves and deny themselves and suffer for the sake of [the salvation and happiness of souls]. For as Christ often said, "the servant is not above his master, nor the disciple above his lord" [Matthew 10:24]. (Jonathan Edwards)[2]

Go to them as soon as they hear you are sick, whether they send for you or not. (Richard Baxter)[3]

[1]Alexander Strauch, *Biblical Eldership: An Urgent Call to Restore Biblical Church Leadership* (Littleton, CO: Lewis and Roth, 1995), 98.
[2]Jonathan Edwards, *The Salvation of Souls* (Wheaton, IL: Crossway, 2002), 170.
[3]Richard Baxter, *The Reformed Pastor* (General Books LLC, 2009), 103.

6

A Shepherding Man

Scripture tells us that during his earthly ministry Jesus had compassion on the crowds that followed him because "they were like sheep without a shepherd" (Mark 6:34). Sheep without a shepherd are extremely vulnerable—they can drift away from food and safety, risking attack by ferocious animals whose very instinct is to kill them. They can get separated from the fold and in their confusion put themselves at great risk for exposure to the elements, starvation, and serious injury. This poignant picture that our Lord uses to describe people in the world should remind us not only of our own vulnerability apart from our Shepherd but should also awaken our compassion and remind us of how desperately people need oversight and aid in their spiritual lives.

The Heart of a Shepherd

Christ still has the same compassion for people today, and he has appointed the leaders of his church to serve as shepherds for his chosen sheep. As shepherds, we must eagerly and diligently care for the people over whom God has set us. We must be like the man who seeks out his one lost sheep and does not rest until he has found it and safely brought it home.[4] We must be like the ultimate Shepherd, who laid down his life for the sheep he loved.[5] Richard Baxter describes the shepherding ministry of pastors:

> The whole of our ministry must be carried on in tender love to our people. We must let them see that nothing pleaseth us but what profiteth them; and that what doeth them good doeth us good; and that nothing troubleth us more than their hurt. We must feel toward our people, as a father toward his children: yea, the tenderest love of a

---

[4]Luke 15:4.
[5]John 10:11.

mother must not surpass ours. We must even travail in birth, till Christ be formed in them. They should see that we care for no outward thing, neither wealth, nor liberty, nor honour, nor life, in comparison of their salvation; but would even be content, with Moses, to have our names blotted out of the book of life, i.e. to be removed from the number of the living: rather than they should not be found in the Lamb's book of life.[6]

Why Pastoral Care?

There are numerous reasons why pastoral care—shepherding—is needed in our churches.

Because the sheep are precious to Jesus, who purchased them with his own blood.[7]

We are not dealing with replaceable objects that can become obsolete like a cell phone but with God's prized creations. Even though sheep often bite, they are still precious. Even though they get filthy and smelly and make dumb choices, they are still precious. Since Christ offered his infinitely valuable life for these sheep, it is a great sin against him when we watch over them with a lazy eye or fail to fight the ravenous wolves or neglect to seek out sheep that have wandered away! What Christ values, we must value. As Christ laid down his life for the sheep, so we must lay down our lives for his sheep.[8]

Because wolves are present and ready to destroy the sheep.[9]

Where there are sheep, you can be sure there are wolves, and when we fail to fend them off, our people are wounded. It does not take a physical assault for a predator's presence to be felt. The fear of attack leads to distrust and risky behavior, which of course leads to increased vulnerability. It is the utmost cruelty to give our people over to wolves. Wolves are a very real and present danger to our flocks. We are the lead protectors and overseers of our people. If we do not protect them from wolves, who will?[10]

---

[6]Baxter, *The Reformed Pastor*, 117.
[7]Acts 20:28: "Pay careful attention to yourselves and to all the flock, in which the Holy Spirit has made you overseers, to care for the church of God, which he obtained with his own blood."
[8]1 John 3:16.
[9]Acts 20:29: "I know that after my departure fierce wolves will come in among you, not sparing the flock."
[10]It is important to distinguish between wolves, who consciously and deliberately attempt to harm the sheep, and spiritually immature Christians, who sometimes harm the sheep without malicious intention. Both kinds of people need to be confronted, but courageous and skillful pastors will be much more severe with wolves.

Because pastors will give an account to God for how they cared for his people.[11]

Pastors will literally stand before Christ one day and give an account for how they treated the sheep for whom he died. If you went out for the evening and hired a babysitter for your children, would you not want an account of how things went upon your return? How upset would you be if your children were harmed by the babysitter's neglect? How much more will we incur the discipline of Christ if we neglect the eternal souls for whom he died! As pastors, we are often tempted to avoid conflict or criticism in order to please the masses by letting dangerous situations just "blow over." But with the knowledge that we will stand in judgment before God Almighty, we are wise to remember that a pastor must always be fearless before his critics and fearful before his God. Let us tremble at the thought of neglecting the sheep. Remember that when Christ judges us, he will judge us with a special degree of strictness.[12] Jonathan Edwards, himself a preacher, warns us: "Those precious souls that were committed to our care lost through our neglect will rise up in judgment against us and shall declare how we neglected their souls."[13]

Because hirelings abound in the church.[14]

Not every church employee with the title "pastor" is actually fit to be one. Increasingly, the people who come into our churches will have wounds, not to mention a whole lot of baggage, from being poorly shepherded by hirelings masquerading as pastors at other churches. I have noticed this at The Journey, the church I pastor. Many of our people, while under the care of their previous church, were hurt by poor to awful leadership. One Journey member saw the elder team at her previous church give in to gossip and hearsay from bitter and ungodly men and women. The result was that half the pastoral staff left the church, virtually killing the church's impact and reputation in the community. In many ways the greater casualty was that this young woman was so disheartened by the experience that it took several years before

---

[11]Hebrews 13:17: "Obey your leaders and submit to them, for they are keeping watch over your souls, as those who will have to give an account."

[12]James 3:1 says, "Not many of you should become teachers, my brothers, for you know that we who teach will be judged with greater strictness."

[13]Edwards, *The Salvation of Souls*, 21.

[14]John 10:12–13: "He who is a hired hand and not a shepherd, who does not own the sheep, sees the wolf coming and leaves the sheep and flees, and the wolf snatches them and scatters them. He flees because he is a hired hand and cares nothing for the sheep."

she felt healthy enough to regularly attend and join another church. Unfortunately, there are a myriad of other stories I could share. The other Journey pastors and I have observed that it usually takes *at least* six months of attending and another six months of relationship before these walking wounded are ready to trust again. Needless to say, it is especially important to provide good shepherding for people who have been hurt.

Throughout history many shepherds have failed to care for God's people. And the Bible is clear that God is none too happy about these careless shepherds. Jeremiah 23:2 tells us that if shepherds fail to tend to the flock, the flock will be cared for by God himself. In Zechariah 11:15–17 God declares that the worthless shepherd who deserts his flock will face the sword and in so doing will lose both his arm and his sight.

No doubt God's priority is to provide excellent shepherding for the precious souls in his church. "I will set shepherds over them who will care for them, and they shall fear no more, nor be dismayed, neither shall any be missing, declares the LORD" (Jeremiah 23:4). It is God's church, not ours. Therefore let us serve faithfully in it and shepherd in a way that reflects the compassionate care of Christ.

The Results of Pastoral Care

Faithful shepherding has tangible benefits, not just for the church but also for the pastor.

Shepherding Prepares the Pastor for Living

When you deal with the sin of others, you become more aware of your own sin. When you shepherd the stubborn, you see your own stubbornness. When you shepherd the selfish, you see your own selfishness. When you shepherd the broken, you inevitably see your own brokenness. Positively, when you see others obey, you want to obey. When you see others use their gifts effectively, you want to use your gifts effectively. This should come as no surprise to us, since it is the Holy Spirit who reveals sin, empowers obedience, and imparts gifts. Both the Greek and Hebrew words for *spirit* mean "air" or "breath." The English word *spirit* comes from the Latin *spiritus*, which also means "air" or "breath." This is where we get words like *respiratory* (breathing) and *expire* (no more breathing). It is also where we get the word *inspire*. It's as if when the Spirit is at work in those whom we counsel, we pastors are, by the same Spirit, *inspired* to repent, believe, and obey with the best gifts we have.[15]

Shepherding Prepares the Pastor for Preaching

The more contact you have with your people and their struggles, the more you will know how to effectively preach to them. How sad it is when a pastor preaches to his church and has no idea what to say to them because he is out of touch with the state of their souls! The more time you spend going deep in pastoral care with people throughout the week, the more you will know about how to contextualize your message, address specific sins, confront resistance to truth, expose cultural idols, and make concrete applications on Sunday. Many of us would be much better preachers if we were better counselors.

Shepherding Helps Your Influence in Preaching

Shepherding humbles you and kills the self-righteousness and pride that prevent people from receiving your delivery of the gospel. When you have spent real time with real people, you gain an emotional connection with your hearers that engages both their minds and their hearts. The truth is that many pastors are like the tin man—a hard outer shell with no heart. Though they preach the truth, they do not connect with their listeners. But when your people know that you are involved not just in the "sweet by and by" but in the "nasty now and now" of their lives, they tend to believe what you are saying. They might even, miracle of miracles, apply what you are preaching. Shepherding gives credibility to the preacher, which gives credibility to the message preached. The more time you spend as an authentic shepherd, the more people will *hear* you and *obey* the Scripture.

Shepherding Helps You Stay Close to Jesus

There is something about dealing with the enormity of people's sin that necessitates staying very, very close to God. In preaching, it is easy to

---

[15] I am indebted to Frederick Buechner for the connection between spirit and inspiration, mentioned in his book *Wishful Thinking* (San Francisco: HarperCollins, 1973), 110.

hide a lack of spiritual connection with God through good preparation and raw ability. But the unpredictability and sheer emotional content of pastoral work confronts you with your own necessity for a Savior. In preaching you can prepare what you will say ahead of time. But in pastoral work there is a lot of room for insecurity and anxiety as you wrestle with the questions, objections, and arguments of your people in real time. It is terrifying! It drives you to dependence on God.

Shepherding Tests the Genuineness of Your Faith

The fiery furnace of pastoral work can burn off the many rough edges of your personality and cause healthy refining and growth. I believe pastoral work, the real brass tacks of dealing with the day-to-day struggles of your people, does more to humble and test a minister's spirituality than study by itself could ever do. I've heard Tim Keller say that preaching is like firing artillery. It is a relatively safe and clean job because artillery men are removed from the actual battle line. But pastoral work is like being in the infantry. It is hand-to-hand, eyeball-to-eyeball combat. Being a good preacher may or may not make you a better shepherd, but being a good shepherd will definitely make you a better preacher.

The Duty of a Shepherd

So far I have been speaking of the importance of spiritual shepherding, but I have not yet defined exactly what it is. Richard Baxter, in his classic book *The Reformed Pastor*, offers a helpful picture of what it means to be a shepherd. He writes, "a minister is not merely a public preacher, but is to be known as a counselor for their souls, as the physician is for their bodies, and the lawyer for their estates: so that each man who is in doubts and straits may bring his case to him for resolution. . . . We must not only be willing to take the trouble, but should draw it upon ourselves, by inviting them to come."[16]

A shepherd is, simply stated, a *spiritual doctor*. Shepherds care for the health of people's souls, just as doctors care for the health of people's bodies. Shepherds, therefore, fight spiritual sickness and encourage spiritual health among their people. They oversee the holistic spiri-

---

[16]Baxter, *The Reformed Pastor*, 96.

tual growth of the flock through preaching and teaching, discipleship, administration of the sacraments, church discipline, admonishment, encouragement, fellowship, and example. They take the lead in fulfilling the commands of 1 Thessalonians 5:14: "admonish the idle, encourage the fainthearted, help the weak, be patient with them all."

The reality, though, is that there are too many sheep to shepherd. The average pastor can shepherd about seventy-five people, which (not coincidentally) is roughly the average size of a church in North America. Therefore, unless you want a church of that size or less, you must learn how to set up systems that promote pastoral care in your local church. Not even Moses was able to judge all of the people of Israel; he had to set up systems and structures to care for the people.[17] We who aspire to the pastorate must consider the words that Jethro spoke to Moses in relation to his calling: "You and the people with you will certainly wear yourselves out, for the thing is too heavy for you. You are not able to do it alone" (Exodus 18:18).

Many of our churches expect the pastor to be the *only* source of pastoral care and counseling. This expectation is not only highly unrealistic (imagine a hospital without a competent nursing staff), but it also has devastating effects on pastors and their families. It also threatens the longevity of a church's vitality because it stunts leadership development. Keeping the medical parallel, imagine a hospital where no interns and residents are training to make sure that care continues, even when long-time doctors retire. Pastors were never designed to be the only caregivers/counselors in the local church. True congregational change occurs not merely as a result of the gifts and services of the pastor but because of the gifts and the services of the entire church. Spiritual care and development is not limited to contact with "God's anointed"—in fact, most growth happens in relationships with "God's ordinary."

All of this means that if we aspire to be effective shepherds over God's people, we will need to do more than *personal, one-on-one shepherding*. We will also need to set up shepherding systems such as small-group Bible studies, community groups, or missional communities. The sad truth is that many churches use such systems—Sunday school, commu-

---

[17]Exodus 18:13–27.

nity groups, and the like—merely as tools for Bible study rather than as a means for pastoral challenge and care (one component of which will certainly be Bible study). People have reduced community to learning about the Bible, singing songs, and exchanging shallow pleasantries. The church has settled for programs that provide cognitive information but lack holistic spiritual formation. My church, The Journey, is a multi-site church, meaning that we are one church with many locations. If you are a pastor, this may or may not be your situation. Regardless, The Journey elders have realized that community groups are an essential ministry for any campus (what we call each location) that we launch. This means that if God brings us an opportunity to begin a new campus, we must have two things in place in order to call that endeavor a Journey campus.

1) We must have a qualified man to serve as campus pastor.

2) We must have at least one community group up and running *before* launch.

Yes, we want worship services. Yes, we want children's ministry. Yes, we want to serve the poor and feed the hungry and engage with artists and creatives in whatever locale we are pursuing. But we believe that if people are not doing life-on-life ministry together, exposing their doubts, struggles, wins, and breakthroughs together under the light of the gospel, that campus will be ineffective in doing all of those important ministries I mentioned above. This philosophy is reflected in The Journey's impact statement: *Love God. Connect people. Transform the world.* We believe those things can only happen in that order.

One of the funniest discussions in the 2008 United States presidential race was the debate about President Obama's former career as a community organizer. He was ripped pretty soundly by conservatives and questioned by legitimate undecided voters because it was hard to understand exactly what Obama did in this role. Does one apply for the job of community organizer? Are there listings on job search Web sites for community organizers? As one insightful pundit put it, you know what a community organizer does when you observe the community. Likewise, you know that a pastor is a good shepherd when you observe the community he is growing and encouraging.

Good shepherds equip church members to shepherd one another in the context of small groups. The early church was made of smaller, missional house churches that we must mimic in the twenty-first century. The church must get smaller as it gets larger.[18] Here are some essential questions for a good shepherd to consider: Are the people under your care loving God both privately and corporately? Are they taking ownership over connecting other people into the church community? Together, are they mobilizing toward the mission of God to transform the world? An effective shepherd will do all he can to answer those questions in the affirmative.

What Should Happen in Such Groups?

Playing off the "one anothers" found throughout the New Testament, I offer the following principles as a way to measure the community quotient in your church:

In biblical community, people teach and encourage each other.[19] In a community group, people can apply and be accountable to live out the points of the sermon in ways that cannot happen in a corporate worship gathering. It is impossible to be as direct and nuanced in a sermon as is possible in a small group. Shepherds who build systems of care and challenge help people live what they profess and contextualize general biblical truths to specific life situations.

In biblical community, people serve and honor each other.[20] One way this happens is by the practicing of spiritual gifts,[21] some of which (words of knowledge, hospitality, mercy, etc.) will inevitably be more effective in a small-group setting than in the corporate worship service.

In biblical community, people share with each other. They share material goods (Acts 2:44–46; 4:32–33), burdens (Galatians 6:2), struggles (Ephesians 4:25; Hebrews 3:13; James 5:16), and visible affection

---

[18]Some would point to Richard Baxter's practice of regularly visiting and catechizing each member of his church as an argument against merely *overseeing* shepherding ministries. It is true that pastors should be engaged in personal shepherding as well as overseeing shepherding systems, but we must remember that Baxter himself also said, "If a captain can get the officers under him to do their duty, he may rule the soldiers with much less trouble, than if all lay upon his own shoulders" (*The Reformed Pastor*, 102). In addition, this approach has biblical warrant in the events of Exodus 18 and is a practical necessity for large churches.
[19]Colossians 3:16 ("teaching and admonishing one another in all wisdom"); Romans 14:19; Galatians 6:1; Ephesians 4:15; Hebrews 10:24.
[20]John 13:14; Romans 12:10; Galatians 5:13; Philippians 2:1–4.
[21]1 Corinthians 12:7, 1 Peter 4:10–11.

(Romans 16:16). They strive to listen to each other more than they speak (James 1:19), they consider each other more important than themselves (Philippians 2:3–4), and they abound in love for each other (1 Thessalonians 3:12).

A shepherd is one who "velcroes" people together, as it were, so that they can pastor one another. The role of the pastor is to connect undisciplined people with disciplined ones so that they learn how to discipline themselves. It is to connect those who are hurting with those who can help them gain healing. It is to help the directionless gain guidance through wise friends. In a real sense the job of the shepherd-pastor is to encourage a family environment where the church can help believers re-parent one another with both love and truth.

The Temptations of a Shepherd

There are many temptations and dangers to beware of as we seek to grow in our shepherding skills.

Shepherding to Hide from Your Own Sins

Many pastors use their shepherding ministry to hide from their own sins, deficiencies, and flaws. I first came on staff at a church when I was only nineteen. I was a youth pastor working under another pastor who took an interest in me. I was really attracted to the possibility of being mentored and challenged in my character by someone in ministry. Unfortunately this is just the opposite of what happened. This was back in the 1980s when many churches had only one phone line, so if you picked up the phone you could hear another person's conversation. One day I picked up the phone and overheard a very inappropriate conversation that this pastor was having with a woman in the church. I began to do some research, and I suspected that the pastor was sexually involved with several women in the congregation. I remember the confrontational meeting that I had with the pastor and the deacons of the church. Without hesitation, all of them said this pastor was there every time they were in the hospital or had a need or had a sick child. They basically said that because this pastor was such a good shepherd, they were going to overlook his sexual immorality. In that moment I began to realize that some pastors use shepherding ministry in order to atone for their sins and deficiencies in other areas.

Shepherding in Order to Manipulate the Church

Some pastors use a shepherding ministry in order to force their pet projects and opinions on the church. Say you have a building program that you really want to push through. You know there is going to be great opposition, so you use your shepherding skills to butter people up so you can get what you want from them. The same thing can happen with a budget item or the hiring or firing of a staff member. Pastors who are gifted at shepherding need to beware of the temptation to use their gift in order to push an agenda.

Shepherding in Order to Cover Your Weaknesses

Another danger for pastors is to shepherd in order to cover their own weaknesses. I know a pastor who refuses to develop his preaching gift but instead uses his shepherding gift to cover up his weakness in preaching. It is not just that he does not have a gift of preaching: he does not even *work* at improving his preaching skills, because he knows that he can rely on his shepherding to keep his people happy. Others may be tempted to avoid strong leadership of the entire flock by staying in the comfort zone of their shepherding role to individual sheep. Many people will avoid a life of mission with God if they are not challenged, and especially if they feel like their needs are being met by a shepherd. A good shepherd is prepared to lead as much through strong preaching and leadership as he is through tender care and counseling.

Shepherding in Order to Conquer Problems

Sometimes we are tempted to use a shepherding ministry in order to achieve a sense of personal achievement. What I mean is that we take the counselee as a challenge to overcome rather than as a person to help. Many pastors stubbornly continue to minister to people who long ago should have been referred to a professional counselor because they want to win. William Willimon says it well: "Without knowing when to refer (to professional counseling), we pastors are in danger of hurting in our misguided attempts at helping. We attempt to do more than we are equipped to do, wasting valuable time, and robbing other pastoral activity of needed focus and energy."[22]

Shepherding in Order to Win Acceptance

Some pastors I know spend an inordinate amount of time around people because their personal identity is wrapped up in their shepherding role. Any ministerial gifting can become an idol, but it is deceptively easy to idolize shepherding because it can feel so holy and loving. Again Willimon informs us, "Manipulation of others can come in many forms. Sometimes the humble servant leader, going about simply serving others, can be a cover for manipulating the laity to serve the servant's needs for adoration, appreciation, and affection."[23] We have to ask ourselves the question, *why* do I spend so much time around people? Am I shepherding them for God's glory and their good or for my own affirmation?

Becoming Godly Shepherds

How can we grow in our shepherding skills and cultivate the kinds of compassion to which Christ calls us? Here are some helpful tips I have learned along the way:

1) *Identify areas that make you feel uncomfortable when you are around hurting people.* It could be that certain types of struggles remind you of your own failings or hurts from your past. It might be appropriate to seek biblical counseling to address some of these wounds. It is often the case that when we have not dealt with our own wounds and received healing from the Lord, our ability to feel deep compassion is stunted. As we receive compassion from the Lord, we are liberated to extend the same compassion to those around us.

2) *Practice listening to people.* Instead of always having an answer, just listen to people who are hurting. Trust the Spirit to do the healing. It is amazing what good listening can do (in both you and them).

3) *Consider your personality.* If you are highly introverted, for example, the problem might be the volume of people you are trying to shepherd.

---

[22]William H. Willimon, *Pastor: The Theology and Practice of Ordained Ministry* (Nashville: Abingdon Press, 2002), 179.
[23]Ibid., 68.

In that case you have to know your limits and bring others along to help you.

4) *Discern your idols.* A lot of people do not have compassion for others because they are gaining their approval from people or using people to further their own ministry goals. The problem with this is that the minister's focus is primarily on himself and not on the people under his care. This idolatry is highly offensive to God and destructive to people.

5) *Look to the cross.* Consider what Christ has done with his unending love for you in hanging on the cross. Remember the thorns on his brow, the stripes upon his back, the spikes in his wrists and feet, the splinters from the rough wood all up his back, the derision of the crowds, the desertion of his closest friends, the shame of the cross, the slow asphyxiating death, and—worst of all—the wrath of the Father. Consider the results of his love: saving you from an eternity in hell to an eternity in his presence. Ultimately, to shepherd well you must apply the gospel you preach to others to your own heart.

The more you understand what Christ, your Shepherd, has done for you, the more you will be formed into a godly and compassionate shepherd for others.

We are seeking to uphold the world, to save it from the curse of God, to perfect the creation, to attain the ends of Christ's death, to save ourselves and others from damnation, to overcome the devil, and demolish his kingdom, to set up the kingdom of Christ, and to attain and help others to the kingdom of glory. And are these works to be done with a careless mind, or a lazy hand? O, see, then, that this work be done with all your might! (Richard Baxter)[1]

Those that are about to undertake this work should do it with the greatest seriousness and consideration of the vast importance of the work, how great a thing it is to have the care of precious souls committed to them, and with a suitable concern upon their minds, considering the great difficulties, dangers, and temptations that do accompany it. It is compared to going to warfare (1 Corinthians 9:7; 1 Timothy 1:18). (Jonathan Edwards)[2]

[1]Richard Baxter, *The Reformed Pastor* (General Books LLC, 2009), 12.
[2]Jonathan Edwards, *The Salvation of Souls* (Wheaton, IL: Crossway, 2002), 51–52.

7

A Determined Man

The apostle Paul wrote to the Corinthians, "Be watchful, stand firm in the faith, act like men, be strong" (1 Corinthians 16:13). Paul knew that the Christian life requires a persevering, dogged determination. If this is a requirement for Christians, how much more so must it be for those who lead local churches, who are held to a higher standard.[3] If the soldier must be tough, how much more the captain or the general!

The Command to Be a Determined Man

Sadly, toughness and determination are often lacking in church planters and pastors. It is staggering to see the number of pastors who end up divorced and the number of seminary graduates who leave the ministry within the first five years. The average tenure for a pastor at a church is about three years (and less than two years for a youth pastor).[4] While there are, of course, wonderful exceptions, the sad truth is that most pastors do not make it for the long haul.

Great damage is done to a church when a pastor is undetermined and leaves it prematurely. Eugene Peterson compares this to *raping* the church: "Impatience, the refusal to endure, is to pastoral character what strip mining is to the land—a greedy rape of what can be gotten at the least cost, and then abandonment in search of another place to loot."[5] Often a pastor has the greatest impact on his church only after he has been there a number of years. When pastors fail to endure in ministry, they drastically cut short their impact. In many ways, your influence in ministry will only be as deep as your grace-empowered determination before God to persevere.

---

[3]James 3:1.
[4]Michael Kowalson, "We're Not Called to Quit," originally published February 15, 2007; http://monday morninginsight.com/index.php/site/comments/were_not_called_to_quit.
[5]Eugene H. Peterson, *The Contemplative Pastor: Returning to the Art of Spiritual Direction* (Grand Rapids: Eerdmans, 1989), 49, italics his.

If you are a pastor or church planter, you will face many moments where you are ready to tap out and give up the good fight. The questions are: *How will you make it? Where will you find the strength to keep going?* If you remain faithful in ministry over the long haul, it will not be because of your ambitions, your strength of will, or your desire not to let others down. Amidst the buffetings of ministry, these motivations will eventually wane. The only way you will endure in ministry is if you determine to do so through the prevailing power of the Holy Spirit. The unsexy reality of the pastorate is that it involves hard work—the heavy-lifting, curse-ridden, unyielding employment of your whole person for the sake of the church. Pastoral ministry requires dogged, unyielding determination, and determination can only come from one source—God himself. In this chapter we are going to consider what it looks like to live as a determined pastor.

The Motivations of a Determined Man

So how do we cultivate determination and toughness to endure in ministry for the duration? We'll start with some motivations from the final verse in 1 Corinthians 15: "Therefore, my beloved brothers, be steadfast, immovable, always abounding in the work of the Lord, knowing that in the Lord your labor is not in vain" (v. 58).

Remember God's Love and God's Promise

It is interesting how many of Paul's commands to the church come from his reminders of the status of the church. In other words, the imperatives (what to do for Christ) flow from the indicatives (what is true for us in Christ). For example, in Colossians 3:1–3 Paul commands the Colossian believers to seek the things above, to set their minds on heavenly things. But he motivates the Colossians to do this because they have been raised with Christ, meaning that their position before God in Christ is secure because they have literally been hidden with Christ in the sight of God. This is also Paul's method in his letter to the Ephesians. In the first three chapters Paul reminds the church of who they are in Christ, and then in the last three chapters Paul challenges them to practically do (apply) the gospel in their actual lives. The imperatives flow from the indicatives.

We see this pattern very clearly in 1 Corinthians 15:58. Read it again: "Therefore, my beloved brothers, be steadfast, immovable, always abounding in the work of the Lord, knowing that in the Lord your labor is not in vain." Paul sounds like a college football coach whose team is behind at halftime. He commands the church to be "steadfast, immovable, always abounding." The word "steadfast" can also be translated as "firm." The image that arises in my mind here is that of a soldier who refuses to stay in the foxhole no matter how many bullets are flying on the outside. Taken by itself, this exhortation might motivate a mere emotional burst of ministry energy or some behavioral modification that would last for a short time. However, Paul isn't trying to be a cheesy self-help guru or a fired-up football coach. He bases this challenge on two indicatives or statements of reality.

First, Paul addresses them as "my beloved brothers." Here, as in 2 Thessalonians 2:13, Paul is reminding the church of their standing in Christ before God the Father. We are loved apart from our performance and moral record. More than that, we are loved and delighted in because of Christ's work and his record. This reality must be recalled again and again if we are going to prosper as Christians, let alone persevere in ministry.

Secondly, he writes, "knowing that in the Lord your labor is not in vain." Our labors have an impact that will literally last forever (cf. 2 Corinthians 4:17)—not because of our gifts or abilities, but because our labor is "in the Lord." If God has called us to ministry, and we are seeking to be faithful in that calling, then God is using us to advance his kingdom. That is an encouraging thought, and it is the only way we will remain *firm and immovable*.

Remember the Resurrection

This challenge from Paul ends his remarkable treatise on the reality and implications of the bodily resurrection of Jesus Christ. All throughout the chapter, the apostle has been making the case that the resurrection is the basis of our faith and our hope as Christians. It is because of the resurrection that we have the ability to go the distance, which is why verse 58 begins with the word *therefore*. One of my mentors in exegesis said that when you see the word *therefore*, you should always look and see what it is *there for*. Most of the time in the New Testament, *therefore* reminds us to look back and consider the context in order to comprehend the verse or passage. The context in this case is the reality that Christ has been raised from the dead. Because Christ has been raised, *therefore* persevere to the end.

How does the resurrection provide persevering stamina? Romans 8:11 is helpful here: "If the Spirit of him who raised Jesus from the dead dwells in you, he who raised Christ Jesus from the dead will also give life to your mortal bodies through his Spirit who dwells in you." This verse certainly has application for overcoming personal sins such as lust, greed, and lying. But it also provides encouragement and staying power to those who are weary in ministry. The very power that raised Christ from the dead is at work in your life and ministry. You have a miraculous power source to tap into that is infinitely beyond yourself. The same Spirit who gave life to Christ dwells within you. "So we do not lose heart. Though our outer self is wasting away, our inner self is being renewed day by day" (2 Corinthians 4:16). Living in the light of the resurrection of Christ means that we can trust God to do miracles in our ministry, that we can have hope even when all seems bleak, and that we can look to a power greater than our own. It compels us to forsake trust in ourselves and put our faith in "him who is able to do far more abundantly than all that we ask or think, according to the power at work within us" (Ephesians 3:20).

Work for Your Heavenly Reward

Earlier in 1 Corinthians 15, the apostle Paul writes, "If the dead are not raised . . . Why are we in danger every hour? I protest, brothers, by my pride in you, which I have in Christ Jesus our Lord, I die every day! What do I gain if, humanly speaking, I fought with beasts at Ephesus? If the dead are not raised, 'Let us eat and drink, for tomorrow we die'" (vv. 29–32). Paul was a realist. If there is no future reward in heaven, he reasons, then forget the whole thing—let's abandon the ministry like everyone else. The startling premise here seems to be that *pastoral ministry is simply not worth it unless you factor in heaven.* Unless heaven is real, let's forget the church and go play video games.

This emphasis on heaven is found throughout Paul's letters. Toward the end of his life, he writes, "I have fought the good fight, I have finished the race, I have kept the faith. Henceforth there is laid up for me the crown of righteousness, which the Lord, the righteous judge, will award to me on that Day, and not only to me but also to all who have loved his appearing" (2 Timothy 4:7–8). Sometimes Christians view it as wrong or selfish to work for a personal heavenly reward. However, John Piper has shown how laboring for our own personal happiness in God and in heaven is not only permissible—it is essential.[6] Finding our deepest pleasure and delight in Christ and in the thought of seeing Christ's face in heaven one day will not minimize our impact or make us selfish—just the opposite. As C. S. Lewis put it, "Aim at Heaven and you will get earth 'thrown in'; aim at earth and you will get neither."[7]

Martin Luther has some brutally honest and very helpful words about how he applied this truth in his own life:

> I often become so angry and impatient with our peasants, townsfolk, and nobility that I think I never want to deliver another sermon; for they carry on so shamefully that a person is inclined to be disgusted with life. Besides this, the devil does not stop plaguing me without and within. Therefore I would almost like to say: Let someone else be preacher in my place. I will let matters take their course, for I am getting nothing but the hatred and envy of the world and all sorts of trouble from the devil. Thus flesh and blood rise in revolt, and human nature becomes dejected and disheartened. In such conditions I must find counsel in the Word of God. . . . "How blest are you, when you suffer insults and persecution and every kind of calumny for my sake. Accept it with gladness and exultation, for you have a rich reward in heaven; in the same way they persecuted the prophets before you" (Matt. 5:11). To these words I cling.[8]

When you are motivated by the gospel in the power of the resurrec-

---

[6]John Piper, *Desiring God: Meditations of a Christian Hedonist* (Sisters, OR: Multnomah, 2003).
[7]C. S. Lewis, *The Complete C. S. Lewis Signature Classics* (San Francisco: HarperSanFrancisco, 2002), 75.
[8]Martin Luther, quoted in Thomas C. Oden, *Classical Pastoral Care: Ministry Through Word and Sacrament*, Vol. 2 (Grand Rapids: Baker, 1987), 13–14.

tion with a view to the future, you are enabled to do some of the things in ministry that tend to make guys quit if left undone.

The Practices of a Determined Man

To speak more practically, I have found several practices essential for cultivating a long-term, sustainable ministry.

Confront Reality

Most pastors live in a fairy-tale world. They refuse to engage the brutal reality that is ministry, opting instead for a safe, plastic world that never involves hard conversations or radical decisions. Dan Allender points out:

> Leaders choose daily, but the real weight on their shoulders lies in the need to decide. And there are no easy decisions. To decide requires a death, a dying to a thousand options, the putting aside of a legion of possibilities in order to choose just one. De-cide. Homo-cide. Sui-cide. The root word for decide means "to cut off." All decisions cut us off; separate us from early infinite options as we select just one single path. And every decision we make earns us the favor of some and the disfavor of others.[9]

Many pastors stay as far away from the front lines as possible and thus live in non-reality, while spending hours a week watching *reality* television. It takes great courage to look the brutal facts right in the face and deal with reality in a God-honoring manner. This means that passive staff members must be motivated. Erring elders and deacons must be confronted. Divisive church members must be rebuked. Nobody enjoys doing such things (if you do, you should be not be a pastor!), but they are necessary in order to have a healthy church over the long haul. If you allow passivity, laziness, and sin to fester, you will soon despise the church you pastor.

Use Your Time Wisely

"Make the best use of the time, because the days are evil" (Ephesians 5:16). "Making the best use of" comes from the Greek word that means

---

[9]Dan Allender, *Leading with a Limp: Turning Your Struggles into Strengths* (Colorado Springs: Waterbrook Press, 2006), 14.

"redeem." Paul is literally saying, "buy back time." How do you buy time? The only way to buy back time is to choose wisely. In a ministry context, this involves a commitment to not waste time. Jonathan Edwards, the great eighteenth-century pastor-theologian, made many personal resolutions before God as an expression of determination in ministry. His fifth resolution had to do with the wise use of time: "Resolved, never to lose one moment of time, but improve it the most profitable way I possibly can."[10]

Determined men take time seriously and are very intentional about how they use it. This does not mean that we never rest—far from it! But it does mean that we should be intentional about when and how we rest. For most of us, for example, redeeming the time probably does *not* mean spending hours each night watching television or surfing YouTube. Such activities may feel relaxing for the moment, but they are often a huge drain on our energy and ability to serve God and people well. For most of us, redeeming the time will mean that we work hard to eliminate unnecessary time suckers in our week, that we design a system for answering e-mails efficiently, that we think through our weekly schedules and priorities beforehand, and so on. You will be amazed at how much this kind of Edwardian discipline and intentionality will give you energy and refresh your ministry over the long stretch.

Take Responsibility for Your Physical Well-being

Edwards's twentieth resolution was, "resolved, to maintain the strictest temperance in eating and drinking."[11] Determined men are physically fit men. I am not advocating that all of us aspire to make the cover of *Men's Fitness*, but I am saying that you should be in shape. Why? Because the more in shape you are physically, the more energy you will have to

---

[10] *A Jonathan Edwards Reader*, ed. John E. Smith, Harry S. Stout, and Kenneth P. Minkema (New Haven, CT: Yale University Press, 1995), 275. Sometimes true determination requires making such commitments, covenants, oaths, vows, and/or resolutions before God. While some Christians view the taking of vows as legalistic, in reality the taking of vows is actually thoroughly biblical. In Scripture, the psalmist takes vows before God (e.g., Psalm 22:25; 56:12; 61:8; 76:11; 116:14), the apostle Paul takes vows (Acts 18:18), God's people take vows (e.g., Genesis 28:20; 50:25; 1 Samuel 1:11), and God himself makes all kinds of various vows, oaths, and covenants (e.g., Genesis 17:7; Psalm 132:11; Jeremiah 31:31). Other Christians may feel that this emphasis puts too much weight on human decision and effort. It is interesting, however, to note that Edwards was a thorough Calvinist with a deep understanding of God's sovereignty. His belief in the sovereignty of God did not make him any less determined in his efforts for God.

[11] Ibid.

do what God has called you to do. God has made us physical creatures, and if we neglect our bodies, it will impact our spiritual and emotional lives. Determined men are careful about what they eat and drink and how they exercise because they know this will make a difference in their ministry and possibly the length of it.

Listen to Wise Counselors

Proverbs 11:14 says, "Where there is no guidance, a people falls, but in an abundance of counselors there is safety." Proverbs 24:6 adds, "By wise guidance you can wage your war, and in abundance of counselors there is victory." Proverbs 12:15 states, "The way of a fool is right in his own eyes, but a wise man listens to advice." Proverbs 15:22 tells us, "Without counsel plans fail, but with many advisers they succeed." To survive the long haul, you must have people around you who do not work for you, do not need your approval, do not idolize you, and are willing to love you by telling you the truth. Most pastors do not have this, but it is a must if you want to stay in the game. Do not be so arrogant as to think you do not need the opinions and counsel of other people.

Take Sabbath Rest

Taking a Sabbath rest is another biblical principle that most pastors ignore. Although it is true that Christians are not bound by the fourth commandment in the same way that Old Testament Israelites were, it is nevertheless, at the very least, a biblical principle from which we have much to learn. Because pastors work on Sunday, many pastors never take a day off. This is a recipe for disaster and burnout. Everyone needs to rest and recuperate now and again.[12] A helpful question we can ask is, would I be comfortable commending my lifestyle to a younger man entering ministry right now? Martin Luther wrote, "Those who take care of souls are worthy of all care."[13] Are you taking care of yourself?

---

[12]For a more in-depth treatment of Sabbath rest, see my sermon "Rest," which was part of a larger series called "Rhythms"; http://www.journeyon.net/sites/default/files/audio/rest-tg-1-11-09.mp3.
[13]Martin Luther, quoted in Oden, *Classical Pastoral Care: Ministry through Word and Sacrament*, 7.

Spend Time with Your Family

Your wife and your children (if you have them) are God's sanctified distractions from ministry idolatry.

I love Pastor Chan Kilgore's story of how God dramatically refocused that undershepherd's attention and affection toward his family.[14]

> During the launch phase of planting Crosspointe, God graced me with a defining moment of repentance for my unhealthy work habits and long hours away from my family.
>
> Just weeks after moving my wife, Stacy—then pregnant with our third child—and two daughters to Orlando to plant the church that only existed in my mind, I was in a crucial meeting with the newly formed core group. On this Sunday evening, I was bringing heat, laying down the core values of the gospel that would define Crosspointe. About thirty minutes into my talk I noticed my wife sitting amongst the core group. I immediately noticed that she wasn't feeling well. She wore the obvious symptoms of some quick-onset illness, and I couldn't look away from her. I'm sure my little gospel lecture started to make less and less sense as my attention was being drawn away from my teaching and toward my wife.
>
> Now what you need to know about Stacy is that she is a very godly woman and she is not a complainer. She's told me plenty of times over the years that one of her ways to help me is to "not get in the way" of what God is doing in and through me. As I looked at her in that meeting, I very clearly heard the Spirit speak to me on her behalf. "Take her home . . . NOW!" he said. It's as if the Spirit was speaking on behalf of my wife who in that moment would not interrupt my gospel proclamation to speak for herself.
>
> I hesitated. Internally, I replied to the Spirit, "But this is important." I'm pretty sure there could be no dumber response to Almighty God than mine in that moment. Immediately came God's reply: "More important than what?"
>
> I resisted for a few seconds. Right in the middle of my lecture I just stopped. God had broken through. I confessed to the group that my wife wasn't feeling well, that I needed to take her home, and that God, in that very moment, was convicting me of my neglect of Stacy in pursuit of the idols of ministry. I took a moment to say to

---

[14]Chan Kilgore is the founding pastor of Crosspointe Church in Orlando, Florida. He is also an Acts 29 board member. Visit Crosspointe's Web site at http://www.xpointe.com.

the group that if I was going to pastor them, I needed to pastor my family well first.

I turned the meeting over to my co-planter, Jay, and took Stacy home. On the way home, she cried tears of thankfulness that God would speak directly to me in defense of her.

The big picture here is that pastors need to be mindful of their spiritual, physical, relational, and emotional needs. Pastors tend not to see themselves holistically. Some pastors focus well on their spiritual lives, but not on their family lives. Others focus well on their family lives, but not on their physical fitness. And so on. What we need is a holistic, practical-oriented, theologically motivated, take-no-prisoners attitude toward the health of our entire being.[15]

Some Questions

We will conclude with some practical questions we all would do well to consider carefully:

1) Am I addressing problems that arise in the church directly and boldly, or am I allowing problems and dysfunctions to fester?

2) Am I making wise use of the time that God has given me? Are there any ungodly hobbies or habits that I need to eliminate from my schedule to further my effectiveness in ministry?

3) Am I being thoughtful about how I am taking care of my body? Am I practicing godly sleeping and eating habits? Am I taking Sabbath rest?

4) Are there any areas of my life that call for me to make a vow before the Lord?

5) Am I surrounding myself with godly influences that will make my ministry sustainable over the long term? Do I have wise counselors and close male friendships to whom I can turn? Am I building a godly marriage and family life?

6) Am I applying the gospel that I preach to others to myself as well? Do I believe that through Christ, God is for me and not against me?

7) Where do I turn when I get discouraged? Is Christ my functional hope and source of refreshment throughout the day?

---

[15]A powerful story of a pastor who has struggled with depression and experienced divine help and break-through is the story of Tommy Nelson, pastor of Denton Bible Church in Texas. You can hear Tommy share his testimony at http://www.dts.edu/media/play/?MediaItemID=6db486780-bfc-4b68-bb025-78cb5f41c70.

8) Am I leaning on the power of the Holy Spirit? Am I trusting God to do what is impossible through my own strength?

All these practices of determination can only be done in conscious dependence upon the Holy Spirit (Ephesians 5:18). A determined man is not a man who is simply driven by his will, but a man who is empowered by the Spirit. As you finish reading this chapter, take a moment to pray and ask the Holy Spirit to encourage and strengthen you in the ministry to which God has called you.

We have spent the first part of this book looking from many angles at what it means to be a man who will honor God with a life devoted to his kingdom and his people. We've acknowledged that the primary qualification for a pastor and church leader is that he acknowledge his need for a rescue and that he depend on the work of Christ to provide it. He must also be the recipient of a special burden and challenge to serve God's church as a vocation. We've looked at the biblical standards for men who aspire to the highest office in the local church, as well as some of the skills that will best serve the church and the man. Finally we've looked at what it means to be a good shepherd of the people placed under a pastor's care and the determination required to live a life that is pleasing to God and reflective of his love for his people. When these elements combine, the result is a man who is fit to carry the message of Jesus into the world. We now turn our attention to that message.

The Message

The great difficulty is to get modern audiences to realize that you are preaching Christianity solely and simply because you happen to think it is *true*; they always suppose you are preaching it because you like it or think it good for society or something of that sort. (C. S. Lewis)[1]

Now there was about this time Jesus, a wise man, if it be lawful to call him a man; for he was a doer of wonderful works, a teacher of such men as receive the truth with pleasure. He drew over to him both many of the Jews and many of the Gentiles. He was [the] Christ. And when Pilate, at the suggestion of the principal men amongst us, had condemned him to the cross, those that loved him at the first did not forsake him; for he appeared to them alive again the third day; as the divine prophets had foretold these and ten thousand other wonderful things concerning him. And the tribe of Christians, so named from him, are not extinct at this day.
(Josephus, a first-century Jewish historian)[2]

[1]Quoted in Michael Horton, *Christless Christianity: The Alternative Gospel of the American Church* (Grand Rapids: Baker, 2008), 97.
[2]Josephus, *Antiquities of the Jews*, 63–64.

8

A Historical Message

The gospel is a true story based on events in history. It tells of a Creator-Redeemer who entered a broken, sinful world in order to rescue his creatures by literally becoming one of them. This Creator-Redeemer entered this world as a screaming, slimy baby in a dirty, smelly manger overwhelmed by the scent of hay and animal dung. In the greatest paradox of all history, God, who is a being of spirit, became a being of flesh. Remaining a being of boundless power, he became weak and hungry and experienced pain. He went from the God of heaven *out there* to being the Lord of earth *right here*. God took the theory of his love for his people and wrapped it in skin and blood and gristle and bone.

The Facts

Jesus, the God-man, grew up and perfectly submitted to his earthly parents. He worked with his dad as a carpenter, no doubt physically laboring in the sun with strong biceps and an even stronger work ethic.[3] Finally, around the age of thirty, after his public baptism when God the Father affirmed his sonship and the Holy Spirit empowered him for the great mission of God, Jesus began his public ministry. He healed the sick, exorcised demons, preached good news, rebuked hypocrites, and started a revolution. Scripture tell us that Jesus was fully human, and thus subject to all the trials and temptations we experience as human beings (Hebrews 2:17–18). This means that he experienced temptation, loneliness, frustration, anguish, and pain, as any man in first-century Palestine would have. But throughout his life, amidst the pain and temptation, he *never* sinned. He did his ministry as he lived his life—*perfectly*.

But despite his moral perfection and miraculous deeds, he was not well received by the religious and political leaders of his day. And that's

---

[3]I love the scene in Mel Gibson's *The Passion of the Christ* that shows Jesus' joy in making tables and chairs.

putting it mildly. He was falsely accused by the Jewish leaders, arrested by Roman soldiers, betrayed by one of his best friends, abandoned by all of his disciples, mocked by Herod, and condemned by Pontius Pilate to die on a Roman cross (Matthew 26:47–27:56; Mark 15:1–41; Luke 23:1–56). John Stott offers a description of what Jesus' crucifixion was like:

> If we had to rely exclusively on the Gospels, we would not have known what happened. But other contemporary documents tell us what a crucifixion was like. The prisoner would first be publicly humiliated by being stripped naked. He was then laid on his back on the ground, while his hands were either nailed or roped to the horizontal wooden beam (the *patibulum*), and his feet to the vertical pole. The cross was then hoisted to an upright position and dropped into a socket which had been dug for it in the ground. Usually a peg or rudimentary seat was provided to take some of the weight of the victim's body and prevent it from being torn loose. But there he would hang, helplessly exposed to intense physical pain, public ridicule, daytime heat and night-time cold. The torture would last several days.[4]

This terrible event was the result of both the predetermined plan of God and the wicked actions of human beings. It took place in history, but it was also the unfolding of God's eternal counsel. Peter brought these two emphases together in his sermon on the Day of Pentecost when he declared to his Jewish listeners, "Men of Israel, hear these words: Jesus of Nazareth, a man attested to you by God with mighty works and wonders and signs that God did through him in your midst, as you your-selves know—this Jesus, delivered up according to the definite plan and foreknowledge of God, you crucified and killed by the hands of lawless men" (Acts 2:22–23).[5] Christianity is a *historical* religion. Against all the esotericism and escapism of early and contemporary Christian heresies, the New Testament insists that Jesus lived, died, and rose in a specific historical setting.[6]

I remember having lunch with one of the leaders of the emerging

---

[4]John Stott, *The Cross of Christ* (Downers Grove, IL: InterVarsity Press, 1986), 48.
[5]Stott comments on the paradox of Peter's words: Jesus "did not die; he was killed. Now, however, I have to balance this answer with the opposite. He was not killed, he died, giving himself up voluntarily to do his Father's will." Ibid., 62.
[6]See, for example, Luke 2:1–2, which places events in Jesus' life in relation to broader events in the Roman Empire, such as a decree by Caesar Augustus and a registration under Quirinius, governor of Syria.

church, Spencer Burke. A former pastor of a megachurch in California, Spencer began to question not only the structure of the church but the theology of the church. He founded *TheOoze*, an online e-zine that helped connect and empower the early adopters of the emerging church. I was delighted to meet the man who had helped me process many of my questions regarding the church and culture as I was preparing to plant The Journey. For the record, Spencer Burke is one of the most pleasant people I have ever met, and I consider him a friend.

Spencer had just written his book *A Heretic's Guide to Eternity,* and because I had not read it, I asked him to give me the lunch version of the book.[7] He began to talk, and I suddenly lost my appetite. Without going into everything that was said, these words came out of Spencer's mouth in front of two other pastors: "It doesn't really matter if Jesus came in the flesh—what matters is the *idea* of Jesus." Many emotions, thoughts, verses, and even a few MMA choke holds came to mind. I pressed Spencer on this, hoping that he had misspoken or that I had misunderstood his Southern California surfer vernacular. However, the more I pressed him to clarify the necessity of a historical Jesus, the more it became clear that Spencer was well on his way toward embodying the title of his recent book, as defined by the New Testament.[8] I hope that Spencer and others like him will realize the danger of this position and turn back toward the historic and orthodox Christian belief that "Jesus Christ has come in the flesh" (1 John 4:2).

The New Testament insists that the eternal God entered into history and acted. God has acted in history: eternity has entered time; the Infinite has become finite. The One through whom the universe was made, and in whom all things hold together, took on a body and was born on earth.[9] These historical events serve as the foundation for the story of the gospel. Graeme Goldsworthy is not speaking in hyperbole when he states, "The gospel of Jesus Christ is the defining revelation to mankind of God's mind, and the defining fact of human history. The

---

[7]For a good critique of Spencer's theology, consult Scott McKnight's review of *A Heretic's Guide to Eternity* at http://blog.beliefnet.com/jesuscreed/2006/07/heretics-guide-to-eternity-1.html.

[8]"Beloved, do not believe every spirit, but test the spirits to see whether they are from God, for many false prophets have gone out into the world. By this you know the Spirit of God: every spirit that confesses that Jesus Christ has come in the flesh is from God, and every spirit that does not confess Jesus is not from God. This is the spirit of the antichrist, which you heard was coming and now is in the world already" (1 John 4:1–3).

[9]John 1:1, 14; Colossians 1:15–20.

person and work of Jesus provide us with a single focal point for understanding reality."[10]

In 1 Corinthians 15:3–6 Paul roots the events of the cross in history, saying that Jesus died according to the Scripture and was buried.[11] Paul continues by stating that Jesus was "raised on the third day," which shows us that Paul wasn't talking about a mere spiritual resurrection but a physical one. Paul goes on to mention that five hundred persons saw the resurrected Christ. Because 1 Corinthians was a public document in a world where the *Pax Romana*[12] enabled people to actually meet these eyewitnesses, Paul was daring skeptics in the first century to corroborate the resurrection, since it happened in history and was viewed by people who were still alive. In other words, if anyone wanted to deny the validity of the resurrection, they would have to get past the fact that five hundred people literally laid eyes on a man who rose from the dead.

The Announcement

The message of the gospel was grounded in history, but what is the nature of the message? The word *evangelion* ("the gospel") or *evangelizdomai* ("to declare the gospel") occurs so often in the New Testament that "clearly the term gospel is a kind of code word for many New Testament writers that summarizes something very basic regarding what the early Christians thought Christian faith was all about."[13] The Greek term *evangelion* distinguished the Christian message from the myriad of other religious ideas that were present in the first century. An "angel" was a heavenly "evangel," herald, or messenger who brought news of a real event that had occurred in history, an event with specific, direct, and dramatic implications for the hearers of that message.

The most common examples in Greek literature are "evangels" who reported the enthronement of a new king or a dramatic victory in a crucial battle. When Christians chose *evangelion* to express the essence of their faith, they passed over words that Hellenistic religions used

---

[10]Graeme Goldsworthy, *Gospel-Centered Hermeneutics* (Downers Grove, IL: InterVarsity Press, 2006), 21.
[11]See, e.g., Isaiah 53:4–6.
[12]The *Pax Romana* was a long period of relative peace and stability throughout the Roman Empire, approximately during the first two centuries A.D.
[13]James V. Brownson, *Speaking the Truth in Love: New Testament Resources for a Missional Hermeneutic*, Christian Mission and Modern Culture Series (Harrisburg, PA: Trinity Press, 1998), 31.

such as "illumination" (*photismos*) and "knowledge" (*gnosis*) and words from Judaism such as "instruction" or "teaching" (*horot*) or "wisdom" (*hokmah*).[14] Of course, all of these words are used to communicate aspects of the Christian message as well, but *evangelion* is the dominant term used in the New Testament. It seems that the Holy Spirit inspired the writers of the New Testament to use a word that signified more than a private ecstatic experience that would quarantine the gospel to the person having the experience. *Evangelion* is the announcement of what God has done objectively in history, not just the subjective experience of one person. The gospel, then, is fundamentally *an announcement*: it is not just about who God is or what he *might* do, but about what God *has done in history*. The gospel is not good advice on how to reach up to God; rather, it is a declaration about what God has *already* done to reach down to us. It is good news about a historical event that changes everything!

This declaration calls for a response. Because Jesus came into history, the gospel has a universal application—Christ is the way, the truth, and the life, the only means for humans to be forgiven and redeemed.[15] It is literally good news for all peoples in all places and at all times. The gospel "identifies Christian faith as news that has significance for all people, indeed for the whole world, not merely as esoteric understanding or insight."[16] As Tim Keller writes, "So the gospel is news about what God has done in history to save us, rather than advice about what we must do to reach God. The gospel is news that Jesus' life, death and resurrection in history have achieved our salvation. We do not achieve it, only accept it. Jesus does not just bring good news; he is the good news."[17]

What is the appropriate response to such a message? It is not to speculate or debate or have a conversation. Because the gospel is revelation about what God has done in history, we must respond with faith, not uncertainty or conjecture. When we realize that the gospel is not a private but rather a public declaration of what God has done in history to draw near to us, we are enabled to respond in faith, believing that

---

[14]Ibid., 46.
[15]John 14:6; Acts 4:12.
[16]Brownson, *Speaking the Truth in Love*, 46.
[17]Tim Keller, "Keller on Preaching to a Post-modern City II: Preaching to Create Spiritually Inclusive Worship"; http://www.redeemer2.com/themovement/issues/2004/august/postmoderncity_2_p3.html.

Jesus is Savior and Lord.[18] The gospel is a different kind of message and therefore calls for a different kind of response. It is more of an address rather than just a simple communication. God is addressing us through the gospel and requires us to respond.

History on Fire

The gospel is the most beautiful story in the history of the world. In fact, the reason that other stories are beautiful—the reason we love movies, novels, and biographies that are saturated with redemption themes—is that they are an echo of *the* story. All good stories follow the same basic plotline of the gospel: the struggle between good and evil before an eventual triumph of good over evil. Tension, then harmony. Redemption. Sacrifice. Betrayal. Love. Suffering. Victory. Screenwriters have co-opted the gospel story to literally make billions of dollars. Pause for a moment and think about how many story lines from how many movies rip off the gospel story. There is a reason for this. The story of redemption captures the human heart, inviting and challenging us to be a part of something bigger than ourselves. This story is movie-ready and myth-like. C. S. Lewis was converted out of atheism as he was enraptured by the beautiful story of the gospel, calling it a "true myth."[19]

It is interesting to note that the English word *gospel* derives from the Old English word *godspell*, which was a combination of *good* and *spell*. Apparently in the old days you knew you'd heard a good story because it put you into a spell that had been cast upon you by the storyteller. The gospel story certainly does that to its hearers because the ultimate storyteller and spell-caster is God. In this way the gospel is not just cold, dry historical facts—it is God's perennial speech to man.[20] The gospel is history on fire. Though grounded solidly in historical events, the gospel story, like the whole of Scripture, is living and active, penetrating down into our very bones.[21]

---

[18]Romans 10:8–10: "But what does it say? 'The word is near you, in your mouth and in your heart' (that is, the word of faith that we proclaim); because, if you confess with your mouth that Jesus is Lord and believe in your heart that God raised him from the dead, you will be saved. For with the heart one believes and is justified, and with the mouth one confesses and is saved."

[19]A helpful account of Lewis's conversion can be found in Alan Jacobs, *The Narnian: The Life and Imagination of C. S. Lewis* (New York: HarperCollins, 2005).

[20]See Louis Berkhof, *Systematic Theology* (Grand Rapids: Eerdmans, 1996), 142.

[21]Cf. Hebrews 4:12; Jeremiah 20:9.

Many people have not been able to navigate the paradox of the gospel as history on fire. The gospel is both objective and subjective, historical and experiential. It happened in history past, but it continues to impact the world every day because the resurrection happened and therefore Jesus is still alive. Because Christianity is objective, it refuses to be lumped into the ecstatic, subjective, and exclusively personal religions. Esoteric religions confine religious experience to the subjective, which then undermines any universal application of any religious message, making everything purely personal and thus relative. But the gospel also refuses to be merely objective, detached, historical events that have no present impact. Though the gospel message is objective and stands outside our experience, it is also subjective because God has revealed himself in such a way that we can know him personally by experiencing the reality of the gospel.[22]

Many thinkers have been ambivalent about the historical aspect of Christianity. Enlightenment thinkers, for example, drove a wedge between the world of history and the world of faith. The German philosopher Immanuel Kant distinguished between the world as we observe it (the *phenomena*) and the world as it is in itself (the *noumena*), setting up a chasm that many subsequent thinkers were unable to bridge. The philosopher and writer Gotthold Lessing spoke of a great, ugly ditch between history and science, declaring that accidental truths of history can never become the proof of necessary truths of reason.[23]

Even before the Enlightenment, early Christian heresies denied the physicality and full humanity of Jesus. Docetism was based upon a worldview that claimed that matter was evil: God, therefore, who was completely holy, could never have taken on a real body, subject to change and being affected by the world. As a result, the Docetists claimed that Christ only *appeared* to have a human body; in fact, he was a spirit. Appollinarianism claimed that Christ did not have a completely human nature. While he had a human body, he did not have a human soul or a

---

[22]It is helpful here to make a distinction between *exhaustive* truth and *sufficient* truth. Cf. D. A. Carson, *The Gagging of God: Christianity Confronts Pluralism* (Grand Rapids: Zondervan, 1996), 103ff. While our earthly knowledge will always be limited and partial, we can truly know about God and the world because God has graciously condescended to us and revealed truth in a way we can understand.

[23]Cf. Lesslie Newbigin, *Proper Confidence: Faith, Doubt, and Certainty in Christian Discipleship* (Grand Rapids: Eerdmans, 1995), 71.

human will. Thus his experience was not fully and completely human, as his divine nature took over many aspects of his being. These heresies (which were condemned by early church councils[24]) and other various forms of Gnosticism all suffered from an unbiblical view that matter is evil, and thus they emasculated the gospel of its historicity.

But the historicity of Christianity and the physicality of Jesus must be defended, because a Christianity not grounded in history is no Christianity at all. If God has truly acted in history, this changes everything. If the eternal God—who is reason, who is truth, who is everything good—has truly entered our world, then we have to reconsider everything in light of this event. As Leonlie Newbigin put it, "If, so to say, the Idea of the Good has actually entered the room and spoken, we have to stop our former discussion and listen."[25]

Moving forward, we need to "listen" to how the gospel displays the accomplishment of our salvation through the perfect life and sacrificial death of Jesus.

---

[24]The early church councils were gatherings of bishops from the whole church to discuss and define Christian doctrine. The error of Appollinarianism, for example, was condemned by the church in the First Council of Constantinople, which took place in 381.
[25]Newbigin, *Proper Confidence*, 11.

The gospel is that Jesus lived the life you should have lived and died the death you should have died, in your place, so God can receive you not for your record and sake but for his record and sake. (Tim Keller)[1]

For the essence of sin is man substituting himself for God, while the essence of salvation is God substituting himself for man. Man asserts himself against God and puts himself where only God deserves to be; God sacrifices himself for man and puts himself where only man deserves to be. (John Stott)[2]

Nothing superficially seems simpler than forgiveness, whereas nothing if we look deeply is more mysterious or more difficult. (B. F. Westcott)[3]

[1]Tim Keller, "Keller on Preaching to a Post-modern City II: Preaching to Create Spiritually Inclusive Worship"; http://www.redeemer2.com/themovement/issues/2004/august/postmoderncity_2_p3.html.
[2]John Stott, *The Cross of Christ* (Downers Grove, IL: InterVarsity Press, 1986), 160.
[3]Quoted in ibid., 110.

9

Salvation-Accomplishing

The gospel is not merely inspiring or insightful or interesting (though it is certainly all these things). The message of the gospel is an active message in which God actually accomplishes salvation. The gospel actually *saves*, because in the gospel the God of the universe *acts*. This work of salvation was promised by God and was awaited by God's people for a long time. It began with the *prolegomenon* (the first preaching of the gospel), in which God, speaking to the Serpent after the fall of humankind, declared, "I will put enmity between you and the woman, and between your offspring and her offspring; he shall bruise your head, and you shall bruise his heel."[4] Human history should have ended when Adam and Eve sinned against God. We can assume that God's perfect justice would have been fully on display if he'd chosen to end humanity in the garden.

Instead, however, God graciously allowed our race to continue and to populate the planet. He even providentially worked to preserve our race from destruction[5] and to set apart a people through whom he promised to one day bring blessing to the whole world.[6] Then, at just the right moment in human history,[7] Christ came to accomplish the predetermined plan of the Father on behalf of his people.[8] God himself invaded our space in order to save us. The remedy for our sickness was acted upon by another. Throughout the Old Testament, God had promised to do something about the two non-personal enemies

---

[4]Genesis 3:15. According to the New Testament, God's plan of salvation goes back even further than Genesis 3; it is the eternal counsel of God. Paul, for example, claims that God saved us "because of his own purpose and grace, which he gave us in Christ Jesus *before the ages began*" (2 Timothy 1:9).
[5]Romans 6–9.
[6]Genesis 12:1–3.
[7]Galatians 4:4: "But when the fullness of time had come, God sent forth his Son, born of woman, born under the law."
[8]Acts 2:22–24: "Men of Israel, hear these words: Jesus of Nazareth, a man attested to you by God with mighty works and wonders and signs that God did through him in your midst, as you yourselves know—this Jesus, delivered up according to the definite plan and foreknowledge of God, you crucified and killed by the hands of lawless men. God raised him up, loosing the pangs of death, because it was not possible for him to be held by it."

of humanity—sin and death.[9] In his death and resurrection, Christ defeated our enemies and accomplished *salvation* from sin and death for his people. As Graeme Goldsworthy says, "The gospel is the event (or the proclamation of that event) of Jesus Christ that begins with his incarnation and earthly life, and concludes with his death, resurrection and ascension to the right hand of the Father. This historical event is interpreted by God as his preordained programme for the salvation of the world."[10]

What kind of salvation did Christ accomplish? That is the question I am addressing in this chapter. The essence of Christ's work of salvation is that he died on a cross for our sins so that we might be reconciled to God. But how does dying on a cross impact our relationship with God? The answer is found in the biblical concept of *atonement*. "The atonement is the work of God in Christ on the cross whereby he cancelled the debt of our sin, appeased his holy wrath against us, and won for us all the benefits of salvation."[11] Atonement is necessary to preserve the justice of God as well as to extend salvation to sinners.

For Whom Did Jesus Die?

Ephesians 5:2 underscores that Jesus' death had both vertical and horizontal aspects. Paul writes, "Christ loved us and gave himself *up for us*, a fragrant offering and sacrifice *to God*." Vertically, Jesus died to satisfy God's justice and wrath. But Christ also died to save those with whom he shared human nature. Jesus was a sacrifice for us and a sacrifice to God. Christ died for God but also for sinners. This is in keeping with Jesus' incarnation as the God-man. In fact, only as the God-man could Jesus serve as the sacrificial "lamb without blemish or spot"[12] and the one who "laid down his life for us."[13]

It is also important to clarify that as God incarnate, the Father, Son, and Holy Spirit were completely united in the effort to uphold the perfection of God's justice and mercy. Stating that Jesus died as a sacrifice

---

[9]We do have a *personal* enemy as well—Satan himself, through whom sin and death entered the world (John 10:10; 1 Peter 5:8; Revelation 12:10).

[10]Graeme Goldsworthy, *Gospel-Centered Hermeneutics* (Downers Grove, IL: InterVarsity Press, 2006), 58.

[11]John Piper, "For Whom Did Christ Die? & What Did Christ Actually Achieve on the Cross for Those for Whom He Died?"; http://www.monergism.com/thethreshold/articles/piper/piper_atonement.html.

[12]Exodus 12:5; 1 Peter 1:19.

[13]1 John 3:16.

to God does not mean that the Father and the Son were at odds with one another. Jesus did not die to simply placate an angry Father. We see in John's Gospel that the Father and the Son are unified. Jesus himself states, "The Father loves the Son and shows him all that he himself is doing" (5:20). A few chapters later, Jesus further denounces any hint of disunity within the Trinity: "For this reason the Father loves me, because I lay down my life that I may take it up again" (John 10:17). While the righteousness of the Godhead must be satisfied, this is accomplished without any implication of a wedge between Father and Son.

To answer the question of for whom Christ died, let's look in turn at Jesus as a sacrifice to God and as a rescuer for sinners.

Jesus Died for God

As shocking as it reads, the second person of the Trinity became a man and died to satisfy the first person of the Trinity. This satisfaction had to do with God's righteous requirements, which were revealed in the Old Testament law. The crux of the law is that we as creatures are to love our gracious Creator with our whole heart, soul, and strength—that is, with everything in our being at all times.[14] The problem is that human beings not only fail to love God as he requires, but that we love to create other substitute gods to worship in the place of God.[15] This is the essence of what we need to be saved from—sin. So the essence of sin is idolatry, whereby we remove God from the altar of our hearts and replace him with functional gods of our own choosing. What does it mean to be saved? It means that Jesus came to satisfy the righteous requirements of the law so that sinners and idolaters could be reconciled to fellowship with God.

Many people in our culture are uncomfortable with the idea of Jesus dying to satisfy God's righteousness. Often the root of this problem is a failure to understand the severity of sin. Sin is not a minor offense that

---

[14]Cf. Israel's *shema*, called by Jesus the greatest commandment, found in Deuteronomy 6:5: "You shall love the LORD your God with all your heart and with all your soul and with all your might."

[15]Cf. Jeremiah 2:12–13: "Be appalled, O heavens, at this; be shocked, be utterly desolate, declares the LORD, for my people have committed two evils: they have forsaken me, the fountain of living waters, and hewed out cisterns for themselves, broken cisterns that can hold no water." I love this metaphor because it speaks to both the nature and the result of idolatry—we create a god and give our heart, soul, and strength to it, which in the end leaves us not only disobedient to the law and dishonoring to God, but also disappointed in the idol and empty, since God is the only true cistern.

can be easily brushed aside like a pesky mosquito on a hot summer day. Sin is the most serious of offenses because it is committed against the most serious, the most glorious of beings.

The Hebrew word for "glory" is *kavod*. *Kavod* comes from the word for "heavy," which is *kaved*. This word was first used to describe things that were actually heavy in a literal, physical sense. So, for example, the Bible describes Eli as "heavy,"[16] which is a polite way of saying that he was, as my grandma used to put it, portly. *Kaved* was also used more figuratively to describe things that were of great importance. So the Bible says that Abram was "heavy," not because he needed to up his cardio, but because he was rich. "Abram had become very 'heavy' in livestock and in silver and gold."[17]

So it's not a stretch for us to see why the Hebrew word for "heavy" eventually came to be used to describe anyone who deserved honor or recognition—generals, kings, judges, and other people of influence and power. In mob and gangster movies, the enforcers, the hitmen, are called "heavies" because the physical and psychological weight they carry demands respect. In Hebrew they were said to be *kavod;* that is to say, they were to be given the utmost respect.

The New Testament word for "glory" has a similar meaning. It is the Greek word *doxa*, and it originally referred to "having an opinion." It eventually came to mean having a high opinion of some great person, like a king. To give someone glory was to give him the honor that his reputation demanded.

So we see why the Bible took these words—the Hebrew word for "heavy" and the Greek word for "honor"—and applied them to God. God has the highest position, the most power, and the weightiest reputation in the whole universe. God is the heavy. He is a heavyweight. He is THE heavyweight.

Therefore, to offend God is to pick a fight with Muhammad Ali, a young Mike Tyson, and Fedor Emalianeko all rolled into one and multiplied infinitely. In other words, offending God is the greatest crime in the universe and deserves eternal punishment.

As John Piper brilliantly articulates, "Sin is not small, because it is

---

[16]1 Samuel 4:18.
[17]Comments on Genesis 13:14 in *Matthew Henry's Concise Commentary* (Nashville: Thomas Nelson, 2000).

not against a small Sovereign. The seriousness of an insult rises with the dignity of the one insulted. The Creator of the Universe is infinitely worthy of respect and admiration and loyalty. Therefore, failure to love him is not trivial."[18] If we fail to understand the depths of our plight as sinners, Christ's death seems unnecessary and superfluous to us. But if we come to terms with our predicament as sinners before a holy God, Christ's death becomes beautiful and precious to us.

The clearest text in the Bible regarding the atonement and its relationship to the justice and righteousness of God is Romans 3:25–26. Here Paul states that God put Christ "forward as a propitiation by his blood, to be received by faith. This was to show God's righteousness, because in his divine forbearance he had passed over former sins. It was to show his righteousness at the present time, so that he might be just and the justifier of the one who has faith in Jesus." Paul is describing the vindication of God's character because of the death of Christ. It would have been unjust, according to Paul, for God to sanction our redemption by simply passing over sin. He would cease to be the righteous moral governor of the universe apart from the brutal death of his Son. The curse of sin must be borne, and the debt of sin must be paid.

A typical question regarding atonement is, why did Jesus have to *die* in order to save us? Why couldn't God simply forgive us? After all, doesn't God command us to forgive one another without demanding payment? But think about a time you or someone you loved was seriously wronged. Were you or the person close to you able to just shrug off the offense or dismiss the wrong without suffering? Of course not! When truly offended, there are two choices. You can either exact revenge and make the one who has wronged you pay, or you can forgive him or her by absorbing the pain of the hurt yourself. On the one hand, you can cause pain to set yourself free; on the other, you can receive the pain of forgiveness and set the other free. If you think forgiveness is not painful, you have never forgiven someone who hurt you deeply. Whether through revenge or forgiveness, *someone* always pays for injustice.

I remember "loaning" money to a drug-user in our church. Let's call him Bob. Bob was not going to be able to provide food for his wife

---

[18]John Piper, *The Passion of Jesus Christ: Fifty Reasons Why He Came to Die* (Wheaton: Crossway, 2004), 21.

and kids if he didn't have my three hundred bucks, or so his story went. So out of the goodness of my pastoral heart I loaned him the money, and he never paid me back. Now I could have exacted revenge and retribution (vandalized his car or laid hands on him in an unbiblical way—both of which I thought about, by the way, out of the wickedness of my pastoral heart), or I could wrestle through the process of forgiving Bob and absorbing that three-hundred-dollar deficit. However, I could not just forgive Bob and erase the three-hundred-dollar debt— I had to *absorb* the loss. In order to forgive Bob, I would have to erase the three-hundred-dollar debt against him. In a real sense, I had to be willing to pay the debt myself.

If this is the case in our interactions with fellow flawed human beings and sinners, how much more must God, our Creator and Judge, not shrug at sin and look the other way! Ultimately the objection that God should simply give a wink and a smile toward our sin overlooks the fundamental difference between us as created beings and God as Creator and moral governor. John Stott offers some helpful words:

> For us to argue "we forgive each other unconditionally, let God do the same to us" betrays not sophistication but shallowness, since it overlooks the elementary fact that we are not God. We are private individuals, and other people's misdemeanors are personal injuries. God is not a private individual, however, nor is sin just a personal injury. On the contrary, God is himself the maker of the laws we break, and sin is rebellion against him.[19]

If you are still having trouble with this idea, think of it like this: the Bible teaches that God is utterly holy and righteous and therefore cannot tolerate *any* evil. Since God is our Creator, and since moral laws are based upon his good nature, our sins have incurred God's righteous judgment. Just as Bob owed me three hundred dollars and an apology, we owe God—except our debt is infinitely greater than Bob's, and a simple apology will not do. We are literally *unable* to repay all that is owed to God. But God, in his great mercy, sent Christ to absorb our debt and pay the penalty of our sin. This is what God has done for us in Christ. He could not simply forgive—he had to absorb our debt by substituting

---

[19]Stott, *The Cross of Christ*, 88.

himself in our place; the Creditor became the debtor. "And you, who were dead in your trespasses . . . God made alive together with him, having forgiven us all our trespasses, by canceling the record of debt that stood against us with its legal demands. This he set aside, nailing it to the cross" (Colossians 2:13–14).

This understanding of the atonement is often called the doctrine of penal substitution—*penal* because Jesus was legally punished for our sins, *substitution* because he did so in our place. Many other perspectives on the atonement have been advocated throughout church history. Many early Christians held that Christ's death was a payment to Satan. Other Christians have understood Christ's death as an example for believers to follow. Others see it as God's way of influencing the world for good by demonstrating his love and kindness in order to move people to repent. For others Christ's death is God's way of restoring harmony to a universe that was disrupted by sin. For still others, Christ's death on the cross is his way of disarming and defeating Satan.[20]

There are glimpses of truth in some of these views, while others are clearly unbiblical. For example, Scripture does teach that Christ conquered Satan and his minions through his death and resurrection.[21] And certainly Christ's death is exemplary for believers.[22] However, the central thrust of the Bible's teaching on the work of Christ is penal substitution.[23] For example, in Colossians 2:15 Christ's conquering of Satan seems to stem from his penal death in Colossians 2:13–14.[24] Lovelace summarizes well: "The substitutionary atonement is the heart of the gospel, and it is so because it gives the answer to the problem of guilt, bondage and alienation from God."[25]

---

[20]If you are interested in learning more about different theories about the atonement, I recommend a brief but helpful resource by Leon Morris titled "Theories of the Atonement"; http://www.monergism.com/thethreshold/articles/onsite/atonementmorris2.html.
[21]Colossians 2:15.
[22]1 Peter 2:21.
[23]Isaiah 53:5, 12; Romans 4:25; 5:8; Galatians 3:13; 1 Peter 3:18.
[24]For a lengthy and helpful defense of the doctrine of penal substitution, see Steve Jeffery, Mike Ovey, and Andrew Sach, *Pierced for Our Transgressions: Rediscovering the Glory of Penal Substitution* (Wheaton: Crossway, 2007). A helpful statement of the practical importance of penal substitution is found, for example, on 153: "A penal substitutionary understanding of the cross helps us to understand God's love and to appreciate its intensity and beauty. Scripture magnifies God's love by its refusal to diminish our plight as sinners deserving of God's wrath, and by its uncompromising portrayal of the cross as the place where Christ bore that punishment in the place of his people. If we blunt the sharp edges of the cross, we dull the glittering diamond of God's love."
[25]Richard F. Lovelace, *Dynamics of Spiritual Life: An Evangelical Theology of Renewal* (Downers Grove, IL: InterVarsity Press, 1979), 97.

Jesus Died for Sinners

One of the metaphors the Bible uses to depict Christ's love for those for whom he died is the relationship between a husband and his bride. In his death Christ demonstrated how he loves his bride, the church.[26] This husband-bride relationship highlights that Jesus died not only out of love for his church but also as a passionate protection of his beloved. Jesus, the Bridegroom, is a passionate lover and defender of his bride. For the men reading this, you may be uncomfortable with this overtly feminine description of the church as a bride. Don't get so distracted by your lack of comfort that you miss the power of the message: Jesus died for you! He didn't die begrudgingly. He didn't die dispassionately.[27] No, Jesus died a tremendously painful death in order to fiercely protect you and show his extraordinary love for you by forgiving you.

Another metaphor used to describe Jesus' relationship to his people is that of a shepherd. Jesus referred to himself as "the good shepherd" and to his people as "sheep," claiming, "The thief comes only to steal and kill and destroy. I came that they may have life and have it abundantly. I am the good shepherd. The good shepherd lays down his life for the sheep" (John 10:10–11). In his death, Christ worked to achieve salvation for the church, his bride, his flock, by rescuing them from destruction and death and giving them abundant life.

The blessings that Christ has procured for us through his death and resurrection are immeasurable. Through his cross-work Christ has provided reconciliation to God,[28] forgiveness of sins,[29] propitiation,[30] the ability to live for God,[31] eternal life,[32] justification,[33] inheritance in heaven,[34] righteousness,[35] healing,[36] bodily resurrection,[37] inter-

---

[26]Ephesians 5:25.
[27]Hebrews 12:2.
[28]2 Corinthians 5:19.
[29]Colossians 2:13.
[30]Romans 3:25.
[31]2 Corinthians 5:15.
[32]John 3:16.
[33]Romans 4:25.
[34]Ephesians 1:11.
[35]Philippians 3:9–10.
[36]1 Peter 2:24.
[37]1 Corinthians 15:22.

cession for the weak,[38] peace,[39] freedom,[40] unity among believers,[41] an example,[42] redemption,[43] advocacy,[44] deliverance from fear of death,[45] hope,[46] wisdom,[47] regeneration,[48] access to God's presence,[49] and all things.[50] In short, Christ's death has given us God. It is literally the difference between eternal anguish and destruction apart from God, and eternal life and happiness with God. The work of Christ is therefore something to be cherished, valued, honored, studied, and proclaimed. Especially in our day, in which there is much confusion about Christ's work, we must not shy away from this aspect of the gospel message. To do so is to deprive sinners of the blessings they might otherwise receive through this message and to obscure the beauty of the gospel for them.

What Does the Death of Christ Mean?

We've seen the dual motivations for Jesus' death. Jesus died for God— meaning that his death appeased God's wrath—and for sinners—meaning that we are the beneficiaries of Christ's perfect sacrifice. What we need now is to understand the implications of this sacrifice.

He Took Our Sin

There is a double imputation in the cross: we receive Christ's righteousness, and Christ receives our sin. "For our sake he made him to be sin who knew no sin, so that in him we might become the righteousness of God" (2 Corinthians 5:21). Martin Luther called this "the great exchange." He prayed, "Lord Jesus, you are my righteousness, I am your sin. You took on you what was mine; you set on me what was yours. You became what you were not, that I might become what I was not."[51]

---

[38]Hebrews 7:25.
[39]Isaiah 53:5.
[40]Galatians 5:1.
[41]Ephesians 2:11–22.
[42]1 Peter 2:21.
[43]Romans 3:24.
[44]1 John 2:1.
[45]Hebrews 2:14–15.
[46]Romans 5:1–11.
[47]1 Corinthians 1:30.
[48]1 Peter 1:3.
[49]Hebrews 10:19.
[50]Romans 8:32.
[51]Quoted in Stott, *The Cross of Christ*, 200.

It must have been a terrible thing for Christ to absorb our sin. The physical agony of the cross was horrific and unimaginable (as we talked about in the last chapter), but it was nothing in comparison to the spiritual agony of becoming sin and enduring the wrath of God. In the Gospel accounts we read that while Jesus was hanging on the cross, darkness came over the land (Matthew 27:45). During this darkness Jesus cried out, "My God, my God, why have you forsaken me?" (Matthew 27:46). This quotation from Psalm 22:1 expressed something of the agony of what Jesus endured; in a very real sense, God literally forsook Jesus on the cross. Though they had eternally loved one another, God the Father turned his back on God the Son. On the cross Jesus looked to heaven and saw only darkness. Jesus cried out to the Father and received only silence in response. Worse, the Father poured out all of his wrath for sin on Jesus. He punished Jesus with the vengeance of a holy and righteous God against all the evil committed by all believers. God's wrath was not mitigated or softened in the least degree. It was poured out on Jesus, who *became* our sin and was punished in our place. "By sending his own Son in the likeness of sinful flesh and for sin, [God] condemned sin in the flesh" (Romans 8:3).

All this happened, though Jesus had never sinned. In his life he had obeyed God perfectly, and from eternity past he had enjoyed a loving relationship with the Father. All this happened, though Jesus was the *eternal God*. He was worthy of infinite praise, but he received infinite wrath. He should have worn a crown of glittering jewels, but instead he wore a crown of jagged thorns. He should have been lauded as king, but he was executed as a shameful criminal. The one worshipped by hosts of angels became the most despised one ever to have existed in the universe.

While we cannot fathom exactly what Jesus experienced on the cross, it is sobering to consider Luther's comment: "Since [Jesus Christ] became a substitute for us all, and took upon himself our sins, that he might bear God's terrible wrath against sin and expiate our guilt, he necessarily felt the sin of the whole world, together with the entire wrath of God, and afterwards the agony of death on account of this sin."[52] Mark Driscoll sums up the practical import of all of this very well: "From

---

[52]Quoted in Mark Driscoll, *Death by Love: Letters from the Cross* (Wheaton: Crossway, 2008), 119.

the beginning of sacred Scripture (Gen. 2:17) to the end (Rev. 21:8), the penalty for sin is death. Therefore, if we sin, we should die. But it is Jesus, the sinless one, who dies in our place 'for our sins.' The good news of the gospel is that Jesus died to take to himself the penalty of our sin."[53]

He Gave Us His Righteousness

"The great exchange" that takes place between Christ and believers on the cross is as good for us as it is bad for Christ. He received our sin, while we receive his righteousness. His loss was our gain, his suffering our joy. "Though he was rich, yet for your sake he became poor, so that you by his poverty might become rich" (2 Corinthians 8:9). Just as our sin was imputed to Christ on the cross, so his righteousness was imputed to us.[54] This means that God literally sees believers as having all of Christ's righteousness, and thus all of Christ's standing and rights, in their lives before God. Quoting Timothy George, Mark Devine once told me, "The reality of imputed righteousness means that our standing before God is as if we possessed the same standing as Christ, which allows the Father to say of us as he did of Christ, 'This is my beloved in whom I am very pleased.'"[55]

In Christ's death we have received propitiation (payment of the penalty of our sin) and expiation (cleansing from the stain of that sin).[56] But the gospel message proclaims even more. Not only has our negative record with God been completely taken away, but a positive status before him has been established. In his death we are clothed with the very righteousness of Christ. This means that our status in God's sight is as secure and beloved as his very Son. Christ becomes for us "wisdom from God, righteousness and sanctification and redemption" (1 Corinthians 1:30). Jesus Christ is the man Jeremiah spoke of: "The LORD is our righteousness" (Jeremiah 23:6).

This righteousness that we receive from Christ is *perfect* because it is a righteousness from God. "As God, he satisfied, at the same time that he

---

[53] Ibid., 20.
[54] 2 Corinthians 5:21.
[55] My former professor and now friend Mark Devine made this remark during a conversation he and I had regarding the impact of imputation.
[56] Driscoll, *Death by Love*, 137: "Propitiation deals with our penalty for sin whereas expiation deals with our cleansing from sin."

obeyed and suffered as a man; and being God and man in one person, he wrought out a full, perfect, and sufficient righteousness for all to whom it was to be imputed."[57]

What about the Resurrection?

You may have noticed that throughout this chapter I have tried to refer to the *resurrection* as well as the *death* of Christ. This is because the two cannot be separated. Though the death of Christ is central to God's accomplishment of our salvation in Christ, it would not be complete without the resurrection. "Blessed be the God and Father of our Lord Jesus Christ! According to his great mercy, he has caused us to be born again to a living hope through the resurrection of Jesus Christ from the dead."[58]

The resurrection is proof that the debt of sin has been paid and that our salvation has been secured. Jesus is not only a Savior who died for sin; he is a King who triumphed over sin. He is not merely a man who experienced death; he is a God in the flesh defeating death. Jesus is not just a servant of God who was bruised by Satan, but the Lord who destroyed Satan's power over the human race. The resurrection is the vindication of all of Jesus' claims and the salvation that is offered by him. It completes our Lord's work and shows beyond all doubt and argument that the salvation he offers is real.

The Journey recently did an apologetics series called "Doubting Your Doubts." I preached a sermon on the resurrection of Christ in which I brought out the implications of Romans 8:11 for the people in our church struggling with doubts. In this verse Paul makes the claim that the same Spirit who raised Christ from the dead is at work in the lives and struggles of believers, to bring strength to us in our frailty, purpose in our confusion. Even the most hostile critics of Christianity confess that if the resurrection of Jesus is real, it is an event of unmatched power and significance with implications that reach deeply into all spheres of our lives. There is life-altering power in the resurrection, and Paul says that the same power that raised Jesus from the dead is available to those who follow Jesus. This is part of the salvation that God offers. All that Christ's

---

[57]George Whitefield, quoted in Jeffery, Ovey, and Sach, *Pierced for Our Transgressions*, 193.
[58]1 Peter 1:3. Cf. also Acts 13:30; Romans 4:25; 2 Timothy 2:8.

death provided is efficaciously *applied* to our lives through the power of Christ's resurrection.

Certainly the resurrection has implications for the renewal of this material world, as we will see in the next section, but Jesus' coming back from death is final proof that Christ's death accomplished our salvation. It brings an end to doubts and evasions and arguments. No one can argue with someone who came back from the dead. If Jesus is alive, he wins the argument.

Summary

The gospel literally means "good news." The gospel is *good* news because Christ actually saves sinners. God's wrath toward sin is no longer aimed at those who trust Jesus as Lord. Instead all that was required for our salvation from sin has been accomplished by Jesus Christ.

The writers of the New Testament refer to the obedient life, sacrificial and atoning death, and powerful resurrection of Jesus as *news* because they are reporting actual events that occurred in history and that both objectively and subjectively free us from the death grip of our sin. Jesus objectively sets us free because he died in our place. In the words of Paul in 2 Corinthians 5:21, God "made him to be sin who knew no sin, so that in him we might become the righteousness of God." Because of Jesus' saving work, we have a clean record, a right standing before a holy God.

Jesus subjectively frees us from sin by revealing the incomplete and inadequate nature of the things upon which we form our identity apart from our sonship in Christ. We no longer have to chase after an identity, a righteousness; it has been brought to us. We are free from guilt and shame and bitterness and disappointment because we believe that our identity and destiny rest securely in the finished work of Jesus on the cross.

In a real sense, then, when we speak of the gospel we speak of Jesus. The gospel rises and falls on the person and work of Christ. Without Christ there is no news concerning a change in our status before God. Without Christ there is no "good" to speak of, because there is no rescue from the slavery of our sin. Without Christ there is no gospel, because the gospel is not just *about* Jesus. Jesus *is* the gospel.

Preach Christ, always and everywhere. He is the whole gospel. His person, offices, and work must be our one great, all-comprehending theme. (Charles Spurgeon)[1]

Apart from Christ, the Bible is a closed book. Read with him at the center, it is the greatest story ever told. (Michael Horton)[2]

In its context every passage possesses one or more of four redemptive foci. The text may be predictive of the work of Christ, preparatory for the work of Christ, reflective of the work of Christ, and/or resultant of the work of Christ. (Bryan Chapell)[3]

[1]Charles Spurgeon, quoted in Sydney Greidanus, *Preaching Christ from the Old Testament: A Contemporary Hermeneutical Method* (Grand Rapids: Eerdmans, 1999), 2.
[2]Michael Horton, *Christless Christianity: The Alternative Gospel of the American Church* (Grand Rapids: Baker, 2008), 142.
[3]Bryan Chapell, *Christ–Centered Preaching: Redeeming the Expository Sermon* (Grand Rapids: Baker, 2005), 282.

10
Christ-Centered

The message of the gospel is centered upon the person and work of Jesus Christ.[4] In the first chapter of this section, we saw how the message of the gospel concerns what God has accomplished in history through Christ. In the last chapter we saw how in the gospel God actually accomplishes salvation through Christ. In this chapter we are going to briefly consider how the gospel is, from Genesis to Revelation, rooted in the promise, person, and work of Jesus Christ. Christ is the center of the Bible, history, the church, and the Christian life and should be proclaimed as such.

Christ Is the Center of the Bible
Christ-centered History

Human history started off so well. The triune God, in perfect fellowship with himself from eternity past, decided in an eternal counsel to create human beings who would share his image and likeness. These human beings were created to know and enjoy God. Adam and Eve enjoyed perfect fellowship with God and with one another. We know this because neither Adam nor Eve wore clothes. This is the Bible's way of saying that they had nothing to hide. There were no barriers between the two of them, and there were no barriers between them and their God. The lack of clothing was the result of the lack of sin. In other words, things were very good.

Unfortunately, things only went downhill from there. Human history went haywire when Adam and Eve decided to be their own gods by ceasing to trust their Father, setting their own rules, and exercising their own authority by eating of the fruit that God had forbidden. Instead of

---

[4] I am greatly indebted to Graeme Goldsworthy for informing this chapter, and I highly recommend his excellent book *Preaching the Whole Bible as Christian Scripture: The Application of Biblical Theology to Expository Preaching* (Grand Rapids: Eerdmans, 2000).

enjoying God and basking in his encouragement to eat freely, our first parents focused on God's prohibition and rebelled, which has been the practice of the human race ever since.[5] God confronted Adam, which is what Adam, as the head of his household, should have done to the Serpent, and essentially asked him why there was separation in his relationship with him and with Eve.[6] Adam, being a typical husband, promptly blamed Eve for the sin, even though he had stood passively by as his wife talked to Satan and partook of the forbidden fruit.[7] Eve then followed her cowardly husband's lead and blamed the Serpent for tempting her.[8] God, who always sees through human rationalization, rejected our first parents' excuses for sin and pronounced judgments on them. He told Adam that his work would be hard, that the ground would rebel against him like he rebelled against God. To Eve he said that her children would cause her pain, just as she caused God pain in turning from him. God also pronounced a curse on the Serpent, and it is here that we have the *proto-evangelium*, the first preaching of the gospel, in which God promised that one of the woman's offspring would crush the Serpent's head.

That offspring was Christ. He was born in history at just the right time.[9] Jesus *enfleshed* among us, meaning that he became one of us.[10] And being human does not mean that he forsook being God.[11] Becoming human did not require the laying down of divinity. "Remaining what he was, Jesus became what he was not."[12] In his life Jesus, the second Adam, did what Adam was supposed to do. He lived his life in perfect submission to his Father, enjoying the Father's presence fully as we all were created to do. Though he did not exercise all his divine attributes as an earthbound human, Jesus modeled what a

---

[5]Adam and Eve, as the church fathers noted, had the ability not to sin. No one since them has had that privilege, except for Jesus, whom the New Testament calls the second Adam.

[6]Genesis 3:9: "But the LORD God called to the man and said to him, 'Where are you?'"

[7]Genesis 3:12: "The man said, 'The woman whom you gave to be with me, she gave me fruit of the tree, and I ate.'"

[8]Genesis 3:13: "Then the LORD God said to the woman, 'What is this that you have done?' The woman said, 'The serpent deceived me, and I ate.'"

[9]Galatians 4:4 notes that God sent his Son "when the fullness of time had come."

[10]John 1:14: "And the Word became flesh and dwelt among us, and we have seen his glory, glory as of the only Son from the Father, full of grace and truth."

[11]Philippians 2:7 teaches that Christ gave up his rights as God, freely volunteering to not exercise all divine attributes. He did not, however, cease to be God.

[12]The church fathers called this paradox the *hypostatic union*—one person, two natures.

human should do, which is to holistically surrender to God and be fully controlled by the Holy Spirit.

Because Jesus became incarnate, he was able to understand the human condition without sinning.[13] As the God-man, he is qualified to be the mediator between us and the Father, the only one who could and would take away our sin.[14] As mediator, Jesus hung on the cross and faced the Father's wrath so we could be received by the Father. He endured the darkness of Good Friday so we could walk in the light of Easter. He died a brutal, sin-bearing, wrath-absorbing death. Three days later Jesus rose from the grave, conquering sin, death, and Satan. This event is the center of human history.

Christ-centered Scripture

When Christ appeared to his disciples on the Emmaus Road, he opened their minds to the true nature and purpose of Scripture and showed them how all of the Bible was related to him.[15] Thus, according to Christ's interpretation, the entire Old Testament is centered upon the promise of his life, death, and resurrection. Ultimately we cannot make sense of Scripture unless we read it through the lens of Christ incarnate, Christ crucified, and Christ resurrected.[16] As Anthony Thiselton states, "The New Testament writers see Christ as an interpretive key for the interpretation and understanding of the Old Testament [and] the Old Testament as a frame of reference for understanding Christ."[17] Sidney Greidanus writes, "Christ is the sum and truth in Scripture."[18]

Another text that teaches the Christ-centered nature of Scripture is 1 Corinthians 2:2. Here Paul reminded the Corinthians that when he was with them, he resolved to know nothing but Christ and him crucified. Paul wasn't saying that all he did was present the "plan of salvation" to the Corinthians, emphasizing simply the way to be saved. What he was saying is that this message—Christ's death for our sin—was the cen-

---

[13]Hebrews 2:17; 4:15.
[14]1 Timothy 2:5–6; 1 John 3:5.
[15]Luke 24:13–35.
[16]"We affirm that the Person and work of Jesus Christ are the central focus of the entire Bible," Article III, Chicago Statement on Biblical Hermeneutics; http://www.churchcouncil.org/ICCP_org/Documents_ICCP/English/02_Biblical_Hermeneutics_A&D.pdf.
[17]Anthony C. Thiselton, *New Horizons in Hermeneutics: The Theory and Practice of Transforming Biblical Reading* (Grand Rapids: Zondervan, 1992), 150.
[18]Sidney Greidanus, *Preaching Christ from the Old Testament* (Grand Rapids: Eerdmans, 1999), 120.

ter of everything he preached. Paul saw the work of Christ on the cross as the foundation for everything—both for salvation and sanctification, for entrance into the Christian life and for growth in the Christian life.[19]

Throughout his letters, Paul constantly connects his practical concerns to Christ and his saving work. For example, when Paul deals with the issue of giving and financial generosity in 2 Corinthians 8, he appeals to Christ's saving work as an example.[20] When he challenges husbands to love their wives in Ephesians 5:25–33, he immediately discusses Christ's relationship to the church. Likewise, when Paul has to confront the Corinthians for making an idol of knowledge and power, he points them to Christ as the power and wisdom of God.[21] So, for Paul money, love, and power—three of the main physical, spiritual, and emotional motivators of the human heart—all find their truest expression in Christ. In Christ alone are true wealth, true intimacy, and true power. Paul responds to the practical concerns of churches filled with flawed and hurting sinners by connecting them back to Christ.

Christ-centered = Gospel-centered

The Bible is not Christ-centered because it is *generally* about Jesus. It is Christ-centered because the Bible's *primary* purpose, from beginning to end, is to point us toward the life, death, and resurrection of Jesus for the salvation and sanctification of sinners. Jesus read the whole Bible in terms of his life, death and resurrection. It's the central truth, the primary thread, the "Big E" on the eye chart when it comes to understanding the Scripture.

Sometimes a focus on being Christ-centered can devolve into looking at Christ primarily as an example to follow for moral improvement. This is not only a shortsighted, flawed hermeneutical practice and a shortchanging of the full impact of Christ in the world, it is actually very dangerous. Those who view Christ primarily as a moral example neglect to see him as the one who would save them from their sin. It is

---

[19]Wayne Grudem defines sanctification this way: "Sanctification is a progressive work of God and man that makes us more and more free from sin and more like Christ in our actual lives." Wayne Grudem, *Systematic Theology* (Grand Rapids: Zondervan, 1994), 746.

[20]2 Corinthians 8:9: "For you know the grace of our Lord Jesus Christ, that though he was rich, yet for your sake he became poor, so that you by his poverty might become rich."

[21]1 Corinthians 1:30: "And because of him you are in Christ Jesus, who became to us wisdom from God, righteousness and sanctification and redemption."

worth noting that Jesus traced his suffering throughout the Bible for the disciples on the road to Emmaus. It seems that Jesus was trying to help them (and us) understand that he is first and foremost a Savior. He was not trying to get them to suffer like he did; he was trying to get them to understand that they *couldn't* suffer like he did and that their fundamental inability to atone for their sin was why Jesus had to suffer. Jesus said to them, "O foolish ones . . . Was it not *necessary* that the Christ should suffer these things?"[22] His suffering was necessary, Jesus was saying, because you and I cannot provide our own salvation from sin. Jesus isn't saying, "Let me show you how to live," so much as he is saying, "Let me show you why I died." Greidanus writes:

> Before you take Christ as your example, you recognize and accept Him as God's gift to you; so that when you see or hear Him in any of His work or suffering, you do not doubt but believe that He, Christ Himself, with such work or suffering of His, is most truly your very own, whereon you may rely as confidently as if you had done that work.[23]

Jesus is first a Savior, and then he is our example. Practically this means that we must recognize our need to be saved from our sin before we can follow his example. Likewise, the key to following his example daily is to daily remind ourselves that he alone is our Savior, that he took our sin and gave us his righteousness.[24] This is in direct contrast to what is preached in the contemporary church. We are told by many in the church today to just focus on following Jesus in practical ways. So it is no surprise that much contemporary preaching is basically an attempt to get hearers to ask the question, "What is God doing in me?"

My point is that the power for responding to what God is doing in me in the present is understanding what God has done for me in the past. This is what the Bible teaches. Graeme Goldsworthy says it succinctly: "It is clear from the New Testament that the ethical example of Christ is secondary to and dependant upon the primary and unique work of Christ for us."[25] The heart of this saving work is not the ethical teach-

---

[22]Luke 24:25–26.
[23]Greidanus, *Preaching Christ from the Old Testament*, 119.
[24]2 Corinthians 5:21.
[25]Goldsworthy, *Preaching the Whole Bible as Christian Scripture*, 4.

ings of Jesus, but his obedient life and death, his glorious resurrection and ascension to the right hand of God on high.[26]

Back in the 1990s, some Jesus junk marketed to the Christian subculture went mainstream. WWJD bracelets exploded onto the fashion scene, with the likes of Justin Timberlake (he of wardrobe malfunction infamy) and Allen Iverson ("We talking about practice, man?"[27]) donning these popular wrist accoutrements. Normally I despise almost everything that emerges from the Christian subculture marketing machine,[28] but I thought WWJD was cool—kind of.

As a youth pastor it was very helpful to use the WWJD thing to engage kids about their relationship with Christ. To get them to consider what Jesus would actually do if he were in their place caused my students and countless others to think more about Christ. Heck, I even wore one (not three like Iverson!) and found it a great reminder to live as he lived.[29] However, WWJD causes us to focus on Jesus as an example but fails to point us to why he did what he did. Perhaps there should have been a WWJM bracelet. Understanding WWJM (What Was Jesus' Motivation) brings us into gospel awareness of what actually empowers us to do what Jesus did if he were in our place. What was Christ's motivation? At his baptism Jesus heard the Father's voice: "This is my beloved Son, with whom I am well pleased" (Matthew 3:17). Before he lifted a finger to touch a wounded body or spoke a word to transform a wounded spirit, before he accomplished any ministry whatsoever, Jesus knew in the depth of his being that he had his Father's approval. His motivation for his life and ministry was the gratitude that he had because of the Father's approval apart from his performance.

Most people think that Christianity is spelled DO: they look at the Bible or the life of Christ, and they simply try hard to live like Jesus. Christianity is really spelled DONE: it is what Christ has done that enables us to live a life of obedience.[30]

Our problem is that we confuse the order of the indicative (what is

---

[26]Ibid., 6.
[27]If you don't understand this reference, please view the following link: www.youtube.com/watch?v=FUYjD7A75HQ
[28]For example, New TestaMints and "God is my copilot" bumper stickers.
[29]1 John 2:6 reminds us that to love God is to live as Jesus did.
[30]I heard this DO/DONE distinction in a talk that Bill Hybels gave years ago.

true) and the imperative (what to do). As Bryan Chapell often says, "We put our 'do's' before our 'who's.'"[31] The indicative is what is true about us in Christ. We are loved and accepted because of what Christ has done on our behalf. The imperative is what we do in obedience out of love for Christ. The key to the Christian life is to live out of the reality of who we are so that we can do what God has revealed in Scripture.[32]

Christ-centered Preaching

This consistently reminding ourselves of our gospel identity is the key to preaching the true gospel of grace and avoiding gospel preaching counterfeits. Greidanus writes, "We can define 'preaching Christ' as preaching sermons which automatically integrate the message of the text with the climax of God's revelation in the person, work, and/or teaching of Jesus Christ as revealed in the New Testament."[33] Without this focus and grid, the preacher is left with a Bible that is fragmented and a sermon that is based on nothing more than his own ideas and preferences.[34]

To drive this point home, let's take a look at several popular counterfeits to Christ-centered preaching: moralism, relativism, self-helpism, and activism.[35]

Moralism

Moralism can be defined as an attempt to appease God's wrath toward sin with our good deeds. It is an enemy of the gospel because, at best, it says that salvation = Jesus + my moral effort. At worst it ignores Jesus' atoning work altogether. In moralism we give God our moral record and demand that he bless us because of our compliance with God's law. Moralistic preaching, then, tends to place the wrath and holiness of God above the love and grace of God.[36]

---

[31]I have heard Dr. Chapell use this phrase in numerous lectures and conversations. I have not found it in his writings.

[32]As Richard Lovelace wrote, "Few know enough to start each day with a thoroughgoing stand upon Luther's platform: you are accepted, looking outward in faith and claiming the wholly alien righteousness of Christ as the only ground for acceptance, relaxing in that quality of trust which will produce increasing sanctification as faith is active in love and gratitude." *Dynamics of Spiritual Life: An Evangelical Theology of Renewal* (Downers Grove, IL: InterVarsity Press, 1979), 101.

[33]Greidanus, *Preaching Christ from the Old Testament*, 10.

[34]Goldsworthy, *Preaching the Whole Bible as Christian Scripture*, 99.

[35]I realize there are many other counterfeits that could be elaborated on here. I am focusing on the ones that I see as major temptations to young pastors.

[36]This is true, but in another way moralism and legalism weaken God's law to our own level of obedience.

Moralistic preaching puts pressure on a person's will to comply with God's law. This kind of preaching produces hyper-rigid and über-critical people. Richard Lovelace writes:

> Christians who are no longer sure that God loves and accepts them in Jesus, apart from their present spiritual achievements, are subconsciously radically insecure persons—much less secure than non-Christians, because they have too much light to rest easily under the constant bulletins they receive from their Christian environment about the holiness of God and the righteousness they are supposed to have. Their insecurity shows itself in pride, a fierce defensive assertion of their own righteousness and defensive criticism of others. They come naturally to hate other cultural styles and other races in order to bolster their own security and discharge their suppressed anger. They cling desperately to legal, pharisaical righteousness, but envy, jealousy and other branches on the tree of sin grow out of their fundamental insecurity.[37]

Christ-centered preaching doesn't discount God's holiness. It honors that holiness more than moralistic preaching because Christ-centered preaching asserts that we can't be holy enough—only Christ was. It asserts that we are only practically holy when we understand and live in the reality of our positional holiness in Christ.[38] It causes us to ponder and bask in the free grace of God in Christ, which motivates us toward practical holiness.

Relativism

Though relativism is considered the opposite of moralism, they are really two sides of the same counterfeit coin. Where moralism teaches us that God is primarily a stern judge and we are to approach him with our best self-effort, relativism teaches that truth is self-determined and that we are to approach God (if there is one) with what seems best to us. In relativism we create our own God and obey our own law. Relativistic preaching, therefore, elevates the love and grace of God above the wrath and holiness of God. This kind of preaching appeals to the emotions, encouraging people to follow their own hearts. Relativistic preaching

---

[37]Lovelace, *Dynamics of Spiritual Life*, 212.
[38]See Ephesians 2:6; Colossians 3:1–3; 2 Corinthians 5:17.

produces mushy, milquetoast people. One postmodern pastor whom I spoke with told me that his main goal in preaching is not to declare the truth of the Bible but to dialogue with his community, so that his hearers can evolve into the true way of Jesus. Curiously this pastor was certain that truth could not even be known.

Christ-centered preaching doesn't belittle the love and grace of God; it magnifies it because such preaching asserts that God's love and grace cost Jesus his life. It moves us outside our own subjective "law" by motivating us to obey God's revealed law out of love for Christ, who perfectly kept the law.

Self-helpism

Self-help appeals to the will of people by challenging them to apply biblical principles without necessarily applying the gospel to their hearts. In self-helpism Christ as example is placed above Christ as Savior. Self-help preaching, then, focuses on Christ as example, forgetting Christ as Savior. Self-help preaching does not take the pervasiveness of sin seriously because it assumes that people want to obey and can obey, they just need to be told how to do it.[39] Such preaching is not biblical because it completely discounts the reality of human resistance to obeying God.[40]

Self-help preaching many times makes the Bible character "like us." We are David, and our problems are like Goliath and so forth. A straight line is drawn directly from the character's struggle or victory to us without connecting any of it to the person and work of Christ.[41]

Thus, it produces consumeristic, shallow people because it does not bring them face-to-face with God. As Edmund Clowney notes: "Preaching which . . . again and again equates Abraham and us, Moses' struggle and ours, Peter's denial and our unfaithfulness; which proceeds only illustratively, does not bring the Word of God and does not permit the church to see the glory of the work of God; it only preaches man, the

---

[39]This is the opposite of what Romans 1:18 says about human beings, who "by their unrighteousness suppress the truth."
[40]Cf. Romans 1:18.
[41]Goldsworthy laments, "Texts are taken out of context; and applications are made without due concern for what the biblical author, which is ultimately the Holy Spirit, is seeking to convey by the text. Problem-centered and topical preaching becomes the norm, and character studies treat the heroes and heroines of the Bible as isolated examples of how to live." Goldsworthy, *Preaching the Whole Bible as Christian Scripture*, 16.

sinful, the sought, the redeemed, the pious man, but not Jesus Christ."[42] In our attempt to be relevant, we might become irrelevant: "The complexity of the interrelationships of biblical themes and doctrines can often elude us when we allow our preaching to become focused on the practical situations and problems in the hope of being known as a relevant preacher."[43]

Christ-centered preaching refuses to run too quickly to application without grounding its hearers in gospel reality: we are completely sinful, but fully accepted in Christ. It shows us that we can't help ourselves because we are full of sin. It shows us that we are, in ourselves, helpless. But it also gives us hope because Christ's work and the power of his Spirit are at work in our lives.[44] Christ-centered preaching goes much further than merely providing suggestions for how to live; it points us to the very source of life and wisdom and explains how and why we have access to him. Felt needs are set into the context of the gospel, so that the Christian message is not reduced to making us feel better about ourselves.[45] In this vein, Christ-centered preaching keeps us from imposing our sermon upon the text and allows us to simply expose the text, allowing Christ to speak from it. John Stott notes, "Whether [the text] is long or short, our responsibility as expositors is to open it up in such a way that it speaks its message clearly, plainly, accurately, relevantly, without addition, subtraction or falsification."[46]

Activism

Activism is the other counterfeit. This is the old-school social gospel message of Protestant liberalism, which has been rekindled today as many urban churches are being forced to deal with poverty and injustice. Activist preaching focuses on the corporate renewal of Christ at the expense of the personal saving work of Christ by overemphasizing the corporate work of the kingdom of God and underemphasizing the personal work of the King. Activist preaching produces cause-oriented

---

[42]Quoted in ibid., 3.

[43]Ibid., 73.

[44]Galatians 2:20: "I have been crucified with Christ. It is no longer I who live, but Christ who lives in me. And the life I now live in the flesh I live by faith in the Son of God, who loved me and gave himself for me."

[45]It is important to preach the text as it is written, that is, to consider the genre (prophecy, narrative, psalm, epistle, etc.) as a guide to how to preach it.

[46]John Stott, *Preaching Between Two Worlds: The Challenge of Preaching Today* (Grand Rapids: Eerdmans, 1994), 126.

people whose lives are not centered on Christ. Ultimately this approach undercuts the ability to effect true societal change because genuine societal change begins with a changed heart. Care for the poor, for example, is very important,[47] but it should not be divorced from Jesus Christ and the message of personal salvation that is connected with his life, death, and resurrection. We should work for the good of our cities, serve the poor, and fight injustice and oppression as a sign of the kingdom to come and as a sign that we know the King. But Christ-centered preaching doesn't forsake the *personal nature* of the gospel in order to simply focus on the *corporate aspects* of the gospel. Instead it provides the ultimate grounds and larger context for gospel-motivated mercy for the poor and oppressed.[48]

An Overview

All of these counterfeits have their appeal. Moralism and self-helpism appeal to the will, relativism to the heart, and activism to the hands. But ultimately only Christ-centered preaching can motivate people holistically (head, heart, and hands) to love Christ, his people, and his world.

The secret of gospel preaching is also the key to gospel living. The gospel must be central in the heart of the preacher if it is to remain central in the pulpit. Gospel power comes when the gospel is central. If you settle for moralism or self-helpism, you might assist people in reforming their behavior, but this will only breed self-righteousness (I'm better than that guy!) and radical insecurity before God (Am I being faithful enough?). Such preaching will produce outward modification, but it will not bring inner transformation. Liberal, relativistic preaching will boost people's self-esteem, but it will not challenge them to die to themselves so that they might truly live. Similarly, activist preaching can improve the cultural and social fabric of your city, but it will leave people unregenerate and thus bound for eternity without Christ.

Many people don't realize it, but Jesus had a Bible. It is what we call the Old Testament. And Jesus read his Bible from a gospel-centered perspective. According to Luke 24:45–46 (among other places), Jesus said that the entire Old Testament, rightly understood, is about him.

---

[47]See James 1:27; 1 John 3:17.
[48]At my church, The Journey, we have started a social justice ministry for our city called Mission St. Louis. Check it out at http://missionstl.org.

And since we know that both Testaments are God-breathed, we can safely say that the whole Bible is about Jesus and his life, his death, and his resurrection.[49] Through his perfectly obedient life, brutal death, and powerful resurrection, Jesus is the hero of the entire Bible. The Bible is not mainly about us; it is about Jesus. The gospel is an announcement of what God has done for us in Christ.

> The gospel is saying that, what man cannot do in order to be accepted with God, this God himself has done for us in the person of Jesus Christ. To be acceptable to God we must present to God a life of perfect and unceasing obedience to his will. The gospel declares that Jesus has done this for us. For God to be righteous he must deal with our sin. This also he has done for us in Jesus. The holy law of God was lived out perfectly for us by Christ, and its penalty was paid perfectly for us by Christ. The living and dying of Christ for us, and this alone is the basis of our acceptance with God.[50]

We will close this chapter with a lengthy quote from Tim Keller about how we should read the Bible and think about Christ even in the Old Testament:

> Jesus is the true and better Adam who passed the test in the garden and whose obedience is imputed to us.
> Jesus is the true and better Abel who, though innocently slain, has blood now that cries out, not for our condemnation, but for acquittal.
> Jesus is the true and better Abraham who answered the call of God to leave all the comfortable and familiar and go out into the void not knowing whither he went to create a new people of God.
> Jesus is the true and better Isaac who was not just offered up by his father on the mount but was truly sacrificed for us. And when God said to Abraham, "Now I know you love me because you did not withhold your son, your only son whom you love from me," now we can look at God taking his Son up the mountain and sacrificing him and say, "Now we know that you love us because you did not withhold your Son, your only Son, whom you love from us."
> Jesus is the true and better Jacob who wrestled and took the blow of justice we deserved, so we, like Jacob, only receive the wounds of grace to wake us up and discipline us.

---

[49]2 Timothy 3:16.
[50]Graeme Goldsworthy, *Gospel and Kingdom* (Carlisle, UK: Paternoster Press, 1994), 86.

Jesus is the true and better Joseph who, at the right hand of the king, forgives those who betrayed and sold him and uses his new power to save them.

Jesus is the true and better Moses who stands in the gap between the people and the Lord and who mediates a new covenant.

Jesus is the true and better Rock of Moses who, struck with the rod of God's justice, now gives us water in the desert.

Jesus is the true and better Job, the truly innocent sufferer, who then intercedes for and saves his stupid friends.

Jesus is the true and better David whose victory becomes his people's victory, though they never lifted a stone to accomplish it themselves.

Jesus is the true and better Esther who didn't just risk leaving an earthly palace but lost the ultimate and heavenly one, who didn't just risk his life, but gave his life to save his people.

Jesus is the true and better Jonah who was cast out into the storm so that we could be brought in.

Jesus is the real Rock of Moses, the real Passover Lamb, innocent, perfect, helpless, slain so the angel of death will pass over us. He's the true temple, the true prophet, the true priest, the true king, the true sacrifice, the true lamb, the true light, the true bread.

The Bible's really not about you—it's about him.[51]

---

[51] This is from a talk Tim Keller delivered at the 2006 Resurgence Conference.

Unable to preach Christ and him crucified, we preach humanity and it improved. (Will Willimon)[1]

The clergyman cannot minimize sin and maintain his proper role in our culture. (Dr. Karl Menninger)[2]

The cross . . . signifies as nothing else could possibly do the awful seriousness of our sin, and therefore the depth and quality of the penitence that is required of us and that only the remembrance of it and the appropriation of its meaning can create in us. (John Knox)[3]

On one occasion I had tea with Martyn Lloyd-Jones in Ealing, London, and decided to ask him a question that concerned me. "Dr. Lloyd-Jones," I said, "how can I tell whether I am preaching in the energy of the flesh or in the power of the Spirit?" "That is very easy," Lloyd-Jones replied, as I shriveled. "If you are preaching in the energy of the flesh, you will feel exalted and lifted up. If you are preaching in the power of the Spirit, you will feel awe and humility." (Edmund Clowney)[4]

[1]Quoted in Sidney Greidanus, *Preaching Christ from the Old Testament* (Grand Rapids: Eerdmans, 1999), 34.
[2]Quoted in John Stott, *The Cross of Christ* (Downers Grove, IL: InterVarsity Press, 1986), 91.
[3]Quoted in Greidanus, *Preaching Christ from the Old Testament*, 5.
[4]Edmund Clowney, *Preaching Christ in All of Scripture* (Wheaton: Crossway, 2003), 55.

11
Sin-Exposing

One of the things that both drew me and repelled me from the Christian faith was its doctrine of sin. As I began to study Scripture, I realized that one of the main components of the Christian message was to show in vivid detail the ugliness of sin and how it destroys people made in God's image. As a young, rebellious man, I realized that if Christianity was true, this meant that God had a big problem with me because of my sin against him. And if God had a big problem, I had a big problem too, namely, God's wrath.

What Is Wrath?

In the first chapter of his letter to the Roman church, Paul goes into specific detail about where sin came from and what God's attitude toward human sin is. He describes God's reaction to human unrighteousness, unbelief, and sin as *wrath*. Paul says in Romans 1 that when God gives human beings what they want—freedom to pursue the lusts and desires that eventually destroy them—he is executing his wrath.[5] But wrath is not simply the passive consequences of our sin;[6] it also refers to God's active judgment of sin. Wrath is God's "steady, unrelenting, unremitting, uncompromising antagonism to evil in all its forms and manifestations."[7] God feels wrath toward human sin and rebellion because he is utterly holy, and his holiness compels him to recoil against and oppose all evil. The Bible teaches that whoever has not received God's mercy is an object of God's wrath.[8]

---

[5]Cf. especially Romans 1:24–32.

[6]Some would argue that wrath is often used impersonally, that is, apart from God. Stott, *The Cross of Christ*, 105 makes some helpful reflections on this point: "To be sure, sometimes the word is used without explicit reference to God, and with or without the definite article, but the full phrase 'the wrath of God' is used as well, apparently without embarrassment, by both Paul and John. . . . Perhaps the reason for Paul's adoption of impersonal expressions is not to affirm that God is never angry, but to emphasize that his anger is void of any tinge of personal malice. . . . And just as *charis* stands for the gracious personal activity of God himself, so *orgē* stands for his equally personal hostility to evil."

[7]Ibid, 173.

[8]"Whoever believes in the Son has eternal life; whoever does not obey the Son shall not see life, but the wrath of God remains on him" (John 3:36).

Wrath should not be compared to some story of poetic justice or revenge that you would see on the Lifetime network. Nor is wrath some vindictive temper tantrum that occasionally comes upon God. As Stott explains, "God is entirely free from personal animosity or vindictiveness; indeed, he is sustained simultaneously with undiminished love for the offender. . . . God's holiness exposes sin; his wrath opposes it."[9] Wrath exists because evil and sin exist. Sin is what separated the creation from the Creator, and sin is what necessitated and eventually caused Christ's death. Sin is a serious issue to God, which is why God has a wrathful disposition toward it.[10] As Jack Miller states, "Man's total existence is inglorious. As an image of God he was made to reflect in an accurate way the splendor of God. But now he lives only to the praise and honor of himself and the idolatrous creations of his mind and hands. No one is excluded from this condemnation."[11]

What Is Sin?

There are a multitude of reasons why the gospel message is wildly unpopular. At the apex is the painful reality that Scripture repeatedly defines what is good and bad, much like an umpire calls balls and strikes. For instance, in Proverbs the writers spend much time calling out people who commit specific sins, using politically incorrect names like "prostitute," "sluggard," and "fool."[12] Scripture is full of examples about what behavior is in bounds and out of bounds with regard to sexuality, money, power, and other spheres of human life. Though it is clear throughout God's Word that God loves his people passionately, this same passionate love does not permit him to ignore our sin.

But all of this begs the question, what exactly is sin? It doesn't take a degree from Harvard to realize that there is something dreadfully wrong in this world. Numerous culprits are blamed for the condition

---

[9]Stott, *The Cross of Christ*, 106.

[10]Many people today have a difficult time understanding how God can be completely good and yet still feel wrath toward evil. Goodness and wrath, however, are not inconsistent. Parents who feel wrath when they discover their child has been abused do not feel wrath despite being good persons but because they are good persons. In their goodness they recoil against the evil that has been committed against their child. In the same way, God feels wrath because he is utterly holy, righteous, and good. If he did not feel wrath, he would not be God.

[11]C. John Miller, *Repentance and the 20th Century Man* (Ft. Washington, PA: Christian Literature Crusade, 1998), 73.

[12]For example, cf. Proverbs 6:6–9; 6:26; 19:24; 10:10; 12:16; etc.

of our world—the erosion of the family, lack of education, war, poor governmental leadership. Systemic problems in these areas contribute to the myriad ways our world is "jacked up." But what is the root of our problems here on the third rock from the sun? It is sin.

The New Testament has a word that describes the nature of sin in the individual: *flesh*. Flesh does not merely refer to our physical bodies; rather, it is that part of us not yet submitted to God's law.[13] The New Testament also describes the corporate nature of sin: *world*. The world is perhaps best described in 1 John 2:16: "All that is in the world—the desires of the flesh and the desires of the eyes and pride in possessions— is not from the Father but is from the world." The world is the product of many individuals living in their flesh, not submitting to God. In the "flesh" and in the "world," we see the impact and result of sin. So we know that sin is individual (private) and corporate (public), but it is still necessary to nail down what it means to sin against God.

Sin Is Living Independently of God

Many have speculated about what exactly caused Adam and Eve to go from perfection to imperfection, from being friends of God to being enemies of God. Most agree that the manifestation of their rebellion was in their act of disobedience by eating the forbidden fruit, but there is disagreement over the ultimate underlying motivation for this act. One way of looking at their action is considering their desire for *independence*. Their choice to eat the fruit and disobey God was preceded by a choice to live independently of God. From that point forward, this has been our ultimate problem as human beings—desiring and attempting to live independently of God. As Stott puts it, "We have rejected the position of dependence which our createdness inevitably involves, and made a bid for independence."[14] In a real sense, every human being has said, "God, thanks for creating me and for giving me commands so that I can enjoy you and my life, but no thanks. I am going to take over now. I will set my own standards, obey my own rules, and be my own god." At the heart

---

[13]Cf. Romans 8:7: "For the mind that is set on the flesh is hostile to God, for it does not submit to God's law; indeed, it cannot."
[14]Stott, *The Cross of Christ*, 90.

of sin is the feeling that God's commands are a burden to rebel against rather than a blessing to be obeyed.[15]

Another way to talk about living independently of God is pride. We see the origin of pride in the garden of Eden. Adam and Eve considered God and his Word to be insufficient. They chose instead to listen to the Serpent, trusting their own instincts and desires to define good and evil and to be the final arbiters of truth. Pride is self-sufficiency, which is the consistent refusal to acknowledge and submit to God.[16]

When Adam and Eve sinned, they lost their innocence, which is demonstrated by the fact that they immediately clothed themselves with fig leaves. Instead of going to God to repent of their sin and seek God's forgiveness and help, they tried to cover their sin and atone for it through their own effort with fig-leaf Fruit of the Looms. They ran from God with the expectation that they could save themselves from their sin. This is self-righteousness, the pursuit and presumption of righteousness apart from God. Pride frequently expresses itself in self-righteousness.[17]

Sin Is Self-protection

The fig leaves not only helped Adam and Eve hide from God, but also from one another. The fig leaves formed a barrier that wasn't supposed to be there. They covered themselves up so as not to have to own up to sin, but the covering also caused them to separate from each other. Sin is self-protection. Self-protection is the consequence of sin upon human community. Instead of freely sharing all of who we are—our desires, hurts, and concerns—we hold back because we fear rejection, judgment, and/or misunderstanding. This is sin because it violates God's intent for authentic human community, which is expressed in the New Testament command to allow others to bear our burdens.[18]

When God confronted Adam about his sin, Adam blamed his wife

---

[15]The idea that God's commandments are a burden and are too difficult is, of course, a lie. First John 5:3 says, "For this is the love of God, that we keep his commandments. And his commandments are not burdensome." James 1:25 promises that we will be "blessed in [our] doing" of God's Word. There is no more fulfilling and happy way to live than by following God's commandments (Psalm 1:1–2).

[16]The psalmist describes the self-sufficient person: "In the pride of his face the wicked does not seek him; all his thoughts are, 'There is no God'" (Psalm 10:4).

[17]"All who rely on works of the law are under a curse; for it is written, 'Cursed be everyone who does not abide by all things written in the Book of the Law, and do them.' Now it is evident that no one is justified before God by the law, for 'The righteous shall live by faith'" (Galatians 3:10–11).

[18]Galatians 6:2.

for tempting him and his God for bringing Eve into his life in the first place.[19] This is interesting because Adam had just composed the first love song in human history, praising Eve and thanking God for his great gift of a wife.[20] Eve, when confronted by God about her sin, blamed Satan.[21] From the very beginning, we see that sin is self-deceiving, causing us to view ourselves as victims and to blame anyone and everyone else for our own wrongdoing.

Sin Is Breaking God's Law

At the heart of sin is the choice to deliberately break the revealed command of God. Robert Peterson writes, "In spite of the modern aversion to the use of legal categories in religion, the Bible depicts God as Judge, sin as violation of his law."[22] "Sin is any want of conformity unto, or transgression of, the law of God."[23] Sin is rebellion against God through willful disregard of his law. It is interesting that even *Webster's Dictionary* defines sin as "any voluntary transgression of the divine law, or violation of a divine command; a wicked act; iniquity."

The New Testament uses several terms to describe the reality of sin. One term is *hamartia*, which means "missing the mark." James uses this term to describe sin when he writes, "So whoever knows the right thing to do and fails to do it, for him it is sin" (James 4:17).[24] Another common term is *adikia*, which means "unrighteousness." The apostle Paul uses this term in Romans 1:18 when he writes, "For the wrath of God is revealed from heaven against all ungodliness and unrighteousness of men, who by their unrighteousness suppress the truth."[25] Yet another term is *paraptoma*, which means "to trespass, crossing a known boundary." The apostle Paul uses this term to describe Adam's sin when he writes that "many died through one man's trespass" (Romans 5:15).[26] A final term is *anomia*, which means "lawlessness, violation of a known law." Paul uses this term when he asks, "What partnership has righteousness with

---

[19]Genesis 3:12.
[20]Genesis 2:23.
[21]Genesis 3:13.
[22]Robert Peterson, *Hell on Trial: The Case for Eternal Punishment* (Phillipsburg, NJ: P&R Publishing, 1995), 47.
[23]Westminster Shorter Catechism, question 14.
[24]Cf. also Matthew 12:31; John 8:11; Romans 5:12; 1 John 3:4.
[25]Cf. also John 7:18; 2 Thessalonians 2:12.
[26]Cf. also Romans 5:20; 11:12.

lawlessness?" (2 Corinthians 6:14).[27] Quite simply, to sin is to break the righteous, revealed law of God.

Sin Is Misdirected Passion

On one occasion Jesus was being challenged about the nature of God's law, which is explicated in the Ten Commandments. He summed up the first four commandments by telling the hyper-fundamentalists of his day to love God with all their heart, soul, and mind. He then summed up the last six commandments by telling them to love their neighbor as much as they love themselves. In this summation Jesus is telling us something important about the nature of sin. Sin is when we love something or someone more than we love God and others. Sin is when we fail to love God with everything we are. Sin is when we are more passionate about anything more than God. Sin is when we fail to love God as he demands to be loved and when we fail to love people as they deserve to be loved as people made in God's image.

The result of our misdirected passion is not that we merely fail to love God, but also that we begin to love other things in the place of God. This is the case that Sören Kierkegaard makes in his very difficult to read book *The Sickness unto Death*. Though we will get into this idea in more detail in the next chapter, it is important to mention here that sin is when we look to something or someone other than Jesus Christ to gain our primary significance and baseline security. Our human tendency is to look to a person, a product, a lifestyle, or a hobby to make us feel personally significant, emotionally connected, and socially satisfied. We begin to experience a *disordering* of our loves, as Saint Augustine noted. Our passion takes us away from God, but it leads us to something or someone who must function as God in order for us to be at rest.[28] Again, we will consider this idea more fully in the next chapter, but what we need to know for now is that the church's proclamation of the gospel must orient people back to their primary love. Not only does this kind of preaching require significant exposure of God's grace and mercy, but

---

[27]Cf. also Romans 6:19; 1 John 3:4.
[28]When I say at rest, I don't mean a restful rest but an idolatrous rest. Augustine was spot-on when he said, "Our hearts are restless until they find their rest in Thee."

also significant exposure of our failure and inability to keep the greatest commandments.

Preaching a Sin-exposing Message

Scripture is exceedingly clear about what God loves and what God hates. This is why Scripture is extremely offensive to people. Jesus warns us that this offense will often be so strong that it will cause people to persecute us when they hear our message.[29] While in most countries of the world you will not be harmed or killed by the government for preaching the gospel, the reality is that you will be persecuted in one way or another. In Western culture, almost any talk about sin will incur mocking, ridicule, and slander. In fact, the only "sin" upheld and exposed by our culture is to call something a sin.

Yet it is clear that we are to preach Scripture, thereby exposing both the sin of the church and the sin of the culture. If there is no challenging of the sinful heart, there is no gospel preaching. If there is no astonishment at the forgiveness of sins, there is no gospel preaching. If there is no joy in Christ's victory over indwelling sin, there is no gospel preaching. Contemporary preaching tends to soften the offense of the gospel so that its message will be more palatable to modern sensibilities.[30] We minimize sin in order to minimize offense. But in so doing, we subvert God's Word with human words, commit the sin of idolatry, and rob people of the joy of forgiveness found in the gospel.

In saying that we must preach God's laws, I am not saying we must preach legalistically. The law of God[31] has many functions. That law protected the nation of Israel by helping them separate morally from the pagan nations and thus have a witness to them.[32] The law discouraged evildoers from sinning and restrained evil in Israelite society. The law

---

[29]Matthew 5:11–12: "Blessed are you when others revile you and persecute you and utter all kinds of evil against you falsely on my account. Rejoice and be glad, for your reward is great in heaven, for so they persecuted the prophets who were before you."

[30]This is a lot like the situation Paul envisioned in 2 Timothy 4:3: "For the time is coming when people will not endure sound teaching, but having itching ears they will accumulate for themselves teachers to suit their own passions." Don't make your church the fulfillment of this prophecy.

[31]In the Reformed tradition, the Old Testament law has been subdivided into three categories—the civil, ceremonial, and moral. This is one way to understand the continuing relevance of the law to modern Christian believers. In terms of the uses of the law, the Reformed tradition has generally focused upon three: (1) the law exposes sin; (2) the law restrains evil; and (3) the law is a guide for believers.

[32]Deuteronomy 4:6–8.

also names our sin[33] by stirring up our deep rebellion and exposing the deep depravity of our hearts,[34] not unlike my toddler son who clearly heard "my law" about not playing in the toilet one minute, yet was playing with the Tidy Bowl Man not three minutes later. The law also reveals to us the heart of God and the norm for a believer's life. Finally, the law drives us to Jesus.[35]

Ultimately the law beats us up and leaves us hopeless because it shows us our inability to live up to God's standard.[36] While the law teaches us about God's heart and about how to live wisely and righteously in a corrupt world, the truth is that we are never able to completely follow the law because of our sin. This reality is evidenced in the fact that the same God who gave the law also gave the sacrificial system to deal with our lack of obedience to the law. Therefore, preaching from the law will inevitably provoke our need for a Savior.[37]

If you don't know how dirty you are, you won't see the need for a bath. If you do not know how sinful you are, you feel no need of salvation. "Only he who knows the greatness of wrath will be mastered by the greatness of mercy."[38] Sin-exposing preaching helps people come face-to-face with their sin and their great need for a Savior.

Sin-exposing preaching works with the Holy Spirit in the life of the hearer to bring about conviction and repentance of sin. It is important to note the three internal dynamics that occur when an individual is confronted with law. Some simply feel guilty—that is, they feel bad but not broken. Others feel condemned, which means they feel broken but

---

[33]Romans 7:7.
[34]Romans 7:8.
[35]Galatians 3:23–24.
[36]Romans 3:23.
[37]This perspective must factor into the way that we choose biblical texts from which to preach. Since the entire Bible is God's Word, we must not shy away from hard texts but rather allow ourselves to be corrected by them. William H. Willimon, *Pastor: The Theology and Practice of Ordained Ministry* (Nashville: Abingdon Press, 2002), 126 offers some helpful words: "We must read the Bible in a way that is more careful and respectful than simply going to the Bible, rummaging about, picking and choosing on the basis of what we consider to be possible and permissible within our present context. To do so is not to align our lives with the witness of the saints, but rather to, in Barth's word, 'adorn ourselves with their feathers.' The temptation is to discard that which makes us uncomfortable or that which does not easily fit into our present conceptual scheme of things. Therefore, an appropriate hermeneutical question is not simply, What does this text mean? but rather, How is this text asking me to change?"
[38]The complete quote goes like this: "It is partly because sin does not provoke our own wrath, that we do not believe that sin provokes the wrath of God.' . . . 'where the idea of the wrath of God is ignored, there also will there be no understanding of the central conception of the Gospel: the uniqueness of the revelation in the Mediator.' Similarly, 'only he who knows the greatness of wrath will be mastered by the greatness of mercy'" (Stott, *The Cross of Christ*, 109).

not hopeful. Conviction, on the other hand, brings true contrition of heart but woos the heart with the joy of embracing Christ and forsaking sin.[39]

The message of the gospel exposes our sin, but it does not end there. Kierkegaard once complained that the preaching he heard in his day was like someone reading a cookbook to a starving person.[40] If all we do is preach to expose sin, then we fall under Kierkegaard's critique. We must also point people to Christ and the forgiveness and healing that he brings. If we expose sin without magnifying Christ, we have failed. "A guilty conscience is a great blessing, but only if it drives us to come home."[41] The goal of sin-exposing preaching is to help people turn from their sin to the joy and forgiveness found solely in the gospel.

---

[39]Ibid., 101: "To recover the concepts of human sin, responsibility, guilt and restitution, without simultaneously recovering confidence in the divine work of atonement, is tragically lopsided. It is diagnosis without prescription, the futility of self-salvation in place of the salvation of God, and the rousing of hope to dash it to the ground again."

[40]Willimon, *Pastor*, 148.

[41]Stott, *The Cross of Christ*, 98.

The opposite of the gospel is idolatry. (Mark Driscoll)[1]

When we try to fit God into our life movie, the plot is all wrong—and not just wrong but trivial. When we are pulled out of our own drama and cast as characters in his unfolding plot, we become part of the greatest story ever told. (Michael Horton)[2]

The human heart is an idol factory. (John Calvin)[3]

[1]Mark Driscoll, *Death by Love: Letters from the Cross* (Wheaton: Crossway, 2008), 92.
[2]Michael Horton, *Christless Christianity: The Alternative Gospel of the American Church* (Grand Rapids: Baker, 2008), 94.
[3]John Calvin, *The Institutes of the Christian Religion*, 1.11.

12
Idol-Shattering

As we discussed in the last chapter, the Bible is very clear in its definition and denunciation of sin. But we can press this a little further—what kind of sin or sins in particular does the Bible denounce? One might expect that sexual sin or injustice or murder would be most decried in the Bible. While these sins are often confronted and challenged, the sin that receives the most frequent and forceful denunciation in Scripture is the sin of idolatry.[4]

Throughout Scripture we are warned about both the dangers of and our propensity toward the creation of idols. Here are but a few examples:

- *Leviticus 19:4:* Do not turn to idols or make for yourselves any gods of cast metal: I am the LORD your God.
- *Isaiah 42:8*: I am the LORD; that is my name; my glory I give to no other, nor my praise to carved idols.
- *Jonah 2:8*: Those who pay regard to vain idols forsake their hope of steadfast love.
- *Habakkuk 2:18*: What profit is an idol when its maker has shaped it, a metal image, a teacher of lies? For its maker trusts in his own creation when he makes speechless idols!
- *1 Corinthians 10:14*: Therefore, my beloved, flee from idolatry.

The roots of idolatry trace all the way back to the beginning. Adam and Eve were created to worship and serve God alone. They were not created because God was lonely or because God needed them; they were created to love and enjoy God. Their lives were not

---

[4]"In the Bible there is no more serious charge than that of idolatry. Idolatry called for the strictest punishment, elicited the most disdainful polemic, prompted the most extreme measure of avoidance, and was regarded as the chief identifying characteristic of those who were the very antithesis of the people of God." Brian S. Rosner, "Idolatry," in *New Dictionary of Biblical Theology: Exploring the Unity and Diversity of Scripture*, ed. T. Desmond Alexander, Brian S. Rosner, D. A. Carson, and Graeme Goldsworthy (Downers Grove, IL: InterVarsity, 2000), 570.

just to be lived in vertical worship to God. They were to worship God horizontally by ruling over God's creation under God's authority.[5]

One day, as Adam and Eve were loving and enjoying God, Satan, the deceiver, approached our first parents and essentially said to them, "You can't really trust God. He's so restrictive. He's so bossy. He is so absorbed with his own agenda. You need to trust me and take your life into your own hands so you can ensure your own happiness."[6] Tragically, our first parents decided that their well-being and happiness could not be entrusted to God, so they took control of their own lives, trusting "the father of lies"[7] over "the Father of lights."[8]

Theologians typically describe this original rebellion as "the fall."[9] Though I don't object to this terminology, it can be a bit simplistic in understanding the nature of sin. Adam and Eve didn't just fall into sin like someone falls into a ditch, nor did they catch sin like you catch the swine flu. They made a fundamental choice that led to the break in their relationship with God. That choice was the first act of idolatry, when Adam and Eve willfully placed their trust, significance, identity, security, and future in something other than God. When Paul describes the root of human rebellion, he talks about sin as not just a breaking of the law but rather as an exchange of worship: "[They] exchanged the glory of the immortal God for images."[10]

Idolatry Is Exchanging and Replacing the Proper Object of Worship

The clearest expression of God's desire and direction for his people can be found in the Ten Commandments. These rules regarding human morality are God's laws, the conduct that nourishes our covenant relationship with God. Interestingly, three of the Ten Commandments deal with the sin of idolatry. The first commandment says that God

---

[5]Genesis 1:26, 28.
[6]Genesis 3:1–5.
[7]John 8:44.
[8]James 1:17.
[9]Historically, Christians have been referring to our first parents' disobedience since the time of the church fathers. Louis Berkhof, *Systematic Theology* (Grand Rapids: Eerdmans, 1932, 1996 reprint), 219 notes that "the idea that [the origin of evil] originated in the voluntary transgression and fall of Adam in paradise is already found in the writings of Irenaeus."
[10]Romans 1:23.

demands exclusive worship because he is Lord of the Earth, which was in opposition to the prevailing wisdom in the ancient Near East that deities only served particular nations or regions. "Don't worship other gods because I am the God of gods," says Yahweh.[11] The second commandment is a warning against creating and worshipping a god as we would want him to be, instead of worshipping the true God as he is.[12] The last command says in effect, don't covet—don't desire your neighbor's house, your neighbor's stuff, your neighbor's wife, your neighbor's anything, more than you desire God.[13] The New Testament clearly links coveting with the greater sin of idolatry.[14] All three of these commands, therefore, speak to the temptation to take "god imposters" (false gods—people and stuff) and put them in the place of worship that is reserved for God alone.

What we put in the place of God captures our imagination and heart, and then we become servants of our object of worship. The word *worship* actually comes from the Old English phrase "worth shape," which implies that the object of our worship will necessarily shape us (our worth) in a comprehensive way. Our object of worship will always be the primary influencer of our thoughts, our emotions, our actions, and, of course, our lives. This is why we cannot be both servants of God and also of idols. Ultimately we worship God or we worship idols. As the psalmist declares, "Who shall ascend the hill of the LORD? And who shall stand in his holy place? He who has clean hands and a pure heart, who does not lift up his soul to what is false"[15]—that is, to an idol.

Many times the psalmists connect worship with glory.[16] To worship is to glorify something. We talked earlier about the Hebrew word *kabod* (glory), which has the idea of weightiness, substance, or supreme

---

[11]Exodus 20:3: "You shall have no other gods before me."

[12]Exodus 20:4–5: "You shall not make for yourself a carved image, or any likeness of anything that is in heaven above, or that is in the earth beneath, or that is in the water under the earth. You shall not bow down to them or serve them, for I the LORD your God am a jealous God, visiting the iniquity of the fathers on the children to the third and the fourth generation of those who hate me."

[13]Exodus 20:17: "You shall not covet your neighbor's house; you shall not covet your neighbor's wife, or his male servant, or his female servant, or his ox, or his donkey, or anything that is your neighbor's."

[14]Colossians 3:5: "Put to death therefore what is earthly in you: sexual immorality, impurity, passion, evil desire, and covetousness, which is idolatry." Cf. also Ephesians 5:5: "You may be sure of this, that everyone who is sexually immoral or impure, or who is covetous (that is, an idolater), has no inheritance in the kingdom of Christ and God."

[15]Psalm 24:3–4.

[16]See, e.g., Psalm 8:1; 24:7; 26:8; 29:1; 57:11; 66:2; 71:8; 145:11.

importance. Idols are objects or persons to which we give inordinate attention. Idols are things that we glorify other than God. An idol is anything that gets more glory, more weight, more importance in our eyes than God does. The heart of sin is when we sacrifice our love for (and from) God in order to pursue and embrace false lovers.[17]

Idols are pictured in many verses as seductresses that seduce us and draw us into complete intoxication, enslavement, and dependence.[18] They steal the love that should be directed toward God alone. But this does not relieve us of responsibility for our tragic choices. In idolatry we willfully exchange what our hearts should love for a cheap prostitute. Because our object of worship is what captures our heart and imagination, we will necessarily become lovers of our object of worship. If God captures our heart and imagination, then we worship and love him. If something else captures our heart and imagination, then we will worship and love it.

Idolatry Is Worshipping Created Things in the Place of God

In Romans 1 Paul says that in idolatry we worship created things instead of our Creator.[19] In our idolatry we "inflate something to function as a substitute for God."[20] In this way, idolatry is a reversal of God's intention in creation. Instead of worshipping God and ruling over creation, we worship creation and are ruled by it. Where we should be faithful stewards, we become unjust managers. Where we should be masters, we become slaves, because we are necessarily ruled by that which we worship. Whatever we place as at the center of our hearts becomes the shaper of our values and the primary director of our lives.[21]

---

[17]"Therefore say to the house of Israel, Thus says the LORD God: Repent and turn away from your idols, and turn away your faces from all your abominations" (Ezekiel 14:4–6, especially v. 6). "With their idols they have committed adultery" (Ezekiel 23:37). "Thus says the Lord God, Because your lust was poured out and your nakedness uncovered in your whorings with your lovers, and with all your abominable idols . . ." (Ezekiel 16:36).

[18]E.g., Psalm 106:36: "They served their idols, which became a snare to them."

[19]Romans 1:25: "They exchanged the truth about God for a lie and worshiped and served the creature rather than the Creator, who is blessed forever! Amen."

[20]Os Guinness and John Seel, eds., *No God but God: Breaking with the Idols of Our Age,* (Chicago: Moody, 1992), 32.

[21]Many thanks to Tim Keller for all of his insights through the years in both his teachings and in personal conversations, including one regarding idolatry. He, more than anyone else, has shaped my understanding of this grievous sin.

According to Paul's chain of reasoning in Romans 1, worship is unavoidable for human beings. When we stop worshipping God, we don't stop worshipping altogether. Rather, we worship some kind of substitute instead of God. This means that everyone is a worshipper at heart. We were simply made to put something outside of ourselves at the center of ourselves. As Mark Driscoll writes, "Everyone is a worshiper for the simple reason that we were made by God to worship and cannot help ourselves."[22] The fact of our worship doesn't change; only the gods we worship do.

This is a radical reality: every single human being on the planet is a worshipper. Humans make knowledge, power, fame, music, money, sex, sports, hobbies, work, and toys their object of worship, ultimate focus, and central identity. Which is to say, they are always worshipping something—either God or something or someone in the place of God. Martin Lloyd-Jones defines an idol as "anything in my life that occupies the place that should be occupied by God alone. An idol is anything that holds such a controlling position in my life that it moves and rouses and attracts me so easily that I give my time, my attention, my energy and my money to it effortlessly."[23]

Because the human heart was made to worship someone outside itself, it continually seeks a place to *rest*. It seeks an object on which to set its hope. We simply must go to someone or something to feel at peace. Scripture teaches that human beings will ultimately look either to God or to something else, be it achievement, relationships, family, status, popularity, or even a hobby to make us feel socially connected, personally significant, and emotionally secure.

And whatever we look to, whatever we pursue, whatever we are faithful to then drives everything in our lives. This is why the Bible doesn't treat idolatry as a sin like gluttony, lust, or lying. It treats it as *the only alternative to worshipping and loving the one true God*. Sin happens because we treasure our idols more than we love our God. When we don't actively love God, we actively love something else. When God is not the center of our lives, something else is.

---

[22]Driscoll, *Death by Love*, 92.
[23]Martin Lloyd-Jones, *Life in Christ: Studies in I John* (Wheaton: Crossway, 1994), 729.

Idolatry is the Sin underneath Most Sins

I remember hearing this "sin underneath the sin" concept while listening to one of the hundreds of Tim Keller sermons I have heard over the years.[24] The early church father Tertullian was so bold as to say that every sin comes from idolatry, which was echoed by Martin Luther's insight into the Ten Commandments.[25] Luther's reasoning is that since there are only ten commandments, and the first two of them both deal with idolatry—have no other gods, make no graven images—then God is saying something. It seems that the other commandments are all related to idolatry. If we break commandments 3–10—if we steal, if we dishonor our parents, if we engage in sex outside of the marriage covenant, and so on—it is because we have broken commandments 1–2. The real issue is idolatry. All sin flows from valuing something more highly than we value God.

David Powlison, in his wonderfully enlightening article "Idols of the Heart in Vanity Fair," first alerted me to the reality that John ends his first epistle (verse 105 of 105) with the challenge to "keep yourselves from idols."[26] Interestingly, there has been no mention of idols in the previous 104 verses! In other words, John has not talked about idolatry (at least directly) throughout his whole letter. The two possibilities for this unique insertion in the very last verse of the letter are: (1) John is changing his subject matter at the very end of the letter, or (2) John is summarizing the subject matter of the entire letter. It would seem more than a bit odd that he would change the subject. John, like any thoughtful writer, is helping his listeners understand what he has been talking about throughout his Spirit-inspired letter.

What has John been talking about?

1 John 1:5–7: After establishing the case that God's light symbolizes his knowledge and purity John urges followers of Jesus to "walk in

---

[24] I like to say that Tim Keller is to pastors much like Johnny Cash is to musicians—everybody rips him off, but few give him credit.

[25] See Tim Keller's "Talking about Idolatry in a Postmodern Age"; http://www.monergism.com/post modernidols.html.

Keller writes, "Luther saw how the Old Testament law against idols and the New Testament emphasis on justification by faith alone are essentially the same. He said that the Ten Commandments begin with two commandments against idolatry. It is because the fundamental problem in law–breaking is always idolatry. In other words, we never break the other commandments without first breaking the law against idolatry. Luther understood that the first commandment is really all about justification by faith, and to fail to believe in justification by faith is idolatry, which is the root of all that displeases God."

[26] "Idols of the Heart in Vanity Fair," *The Journal of Biblical Counseling*, Vol. 13, No. 2 (Winter 1995), 35.

the light."[27] To walk in the light means to pursue knowledge of God through relationship with him and to pursue holy living in relationship with other believers.

1 John 2:3–6: John now explains that holy living is actually a natural by-product of knowing God. To claim to know God and yet disobey his commands is to speak lies.

1 John 3:16–18: John summarizes the Christian life by comparing it directly to the life, specifically the death, of Christ. To live like Christ, John says, is to sacrifice as Christ did—by laying down his life so others would know that God's love and power are real.

If we understand the last verse in the epistle as the summary of the letter, then John's command to walk in the light, to keep God's commandments, and to love others is ultimately an admonition to keep ourselves free from idols. Freedom from idolatry seems to power obedience. Therefore, when you have a "walking in the light" problem or a "laying your life down for your brother" problem, that means you have an "idol" problem. The great burden of John's letter is simple: love God and love people in accordance with Christ's summarization of the Ten Commandments,[28] which is the core of Christianity. What John seems to be saying is that idols are the source-obstacle that keeps Christians from loving God and loving people. Idols are the fertile soil that grows sin, which hinders us from obeying God. They are the root and fuel of what grows and powers sinful behavior.

Questions That Expose Idols

The following questions can help expose our idols by demonstrating where our ultimate source of trust is.[29]

- What do I worry about most?
- What, if I failed or lost it, would cause me to feel that I did not even want to live?
- What do I use to comfort myself when things go bad or get difficult?
- What do I do to cope? What are my release valves? What do I do to feel better?

---

[27]"Introduction to 1 John," *ESV Study Bible* (Wheaton: Crossway, 2008).
[28]Matthew 22:37–39.
[29]These questions are adapted from chapter 7 of David Powlison's *Seeing with New Eyes* (Phillipsburg, NJ: P & R, 2003). Powlison calls these "X-ray questions."

- What preoccupies me? What do I daydream about?
- What makes me feel the most self-worth? Of what am I the proudest? For what do I want to be known?
- What do I lead with in conversations?
- Early on what do I want to make sure that people know about me?
- What prayer, unanswered, would make me seriously think about turning away from God?
- What do I really want and expect out of life? What would really make me happy?
- What is my hope for the future?

The answers to these questions reveal what a person is truly trusting in, no matter whom he or she professes to worship. The answers to these questions describe what a person has elevated to the place of God in his or her life—that person's functional lord.

Definitions That Expose Idols

Many writers have sought to classify idols according to different classes.[30] Several years ago I listened to a lecture from Dick Kaufman at one of our Acts 29 conferences. Kaufman described two categories of idols: far and near, which he confessed that he had borrowed from Dick Keyes. Over the years I have read Keyes and others, and I have found the categories too confusing for my pea brain. So, in an effort to understand these definitions given by Kaufman, I have renamed these categories "source idols" and "surface idols."

Surface Idols

Of the two idol categories, surface idols[31] are easier to spot because they are closer to the surface. Thus many people recognize them as the cause of many of the problems they have in their relationships with both God and people. Jack Miller calls these kinds of idolatry "branch-sins" because they are simply shoots off the less observable root sins.[32] These surface idols include:

---

[30]For example, Dick Keyes in *No God but God* and David Powlison in "Idols of the Heart in Vanity Fair."
[31]Kaufman (again following Keyes) calls these *near idols*.
[32]C. John Miller, *Repentance and the 20th Century Man* (Ft. Washington, PA: Christian Literature Crusade, 1998), 38.

Image idolatry: "Life only has meaning/I only have worth if I have a particular kind of look or body image."

Helping idolatry: "Life only has meaning/I only have worth if people are dependent on me and need me."

Dependence idolatry: "Life only has meaning/I only have worth if someone is there to protect me and keep me safe."

Independence idolatry: "Life only has meaning/I only have worth if I am completely free from obligations or responsibilities to take care of someone."

Work idolatry: "Life only has meaning/I only have worth if I am highly productive and getting a lot done."

Achievement idolatry: "Life only has meaning/I only have worth if I am being recognized for my accomplishments, if I am excelling in my career."

Materialism idolatry: "Life only has meaning/I only have worth if I have a certain level of wealth, financial freedom, and very nice possessions."

Religion idolatry: "Life only has meaning/I only have worth if I am adhering to my religion's moral codes and am accomplished in its activities."

Individual person idolatry: "Life only has meaning/I only have worth if this one person is in my life and happy there and/or happy with me."

Irreligion idolatry: "Life only has meaning/I only have worth if I feel I am totally independent of organized religion and have a self-made morality."

Racial/cultural idolatry: "Life only has meaning/I only have worth if my race and culture is ascendant and recognized as superior."

Inner ring idolatry: "Life only has meaning/I only have worth if I am allowed to be part of a particular social grouping or professional grouping or other group."

Family idolatry: "Life only has meaning/I only have worth if my children and/or my parents are happy and happy with me."

Relationship idolatry: "Life only has meaning/I only have worth if Mr. or Ms. Right is in love with me."

Suffering idolatry: "Life only has meaning/I only have worth if I am hurting and in a problem; only then do I feel noble or worthy of love or am able to deal with guilt."

Ideology idolatry: "Life only has meaning/I only have worth if my political or social cause or party is making progress and ascending in influence or power."

Source Idols

Whereas surface idols are more readily understood and even recognizable to many people, source idols, by nature, are more subversive. According to Kaufman, source idols include comfort, approval, control, and power.[33] These are the idols that drive all other idolatries in our lives. These idols match up both with the teachings of Jesus[34] and with the personality theory work of Alfred Addler.[35]

Kaufman's chart describes: (1) what we seek (the source idol); (2) the price we are willing to pay to get that idol; (3) our greatest nightmare and how others feel when we are operating through the idol; and (4) our problem emotion that reveals our idol. The language "life only has meaning/I only have worth if . . ." is a little hyperbolic, but it accomplishes its goal by causing readers to examine their hearts.

To put flesh on these source idols, I'd like to examine each one through the lens of a consistent metaphor that is familiar to all of us—money. With each source idol listed below, we will look at what is ultimately sought through the idol, the price we are willing to pay to continue in our worship of it, the greatest fears that feed it, the impact it has on those closest to us, the problem emotions associated with it, and what role it plays in the context of our money metaphor.

Comfort idolatry: "Life only has meaning/I only have worth if I have this kind of pleasure experience, a particular quality of life."

What we seek: comfort (privacy, lack of stress, freedom).

Price we are willing to pay: reduced productivity.

Greatest nightmare: stress, demands.

---

[33]Kaufman, following Keyes, calls these *far idols*.
[34]Each of these motifs, for example, figures prominently in Jesus' Sermon on the Mount (Matthew 5–7). Much of Jesus' teaching bears upon the fundamental human needs of approval (5:3–10; 6:2–4, 14–15), power (6:19–24), control (6:25–34), and comfort (7:7–11).
[35]One of the derivatives of Addler's work is the DISC personality profile; http://www.discprofile.com/whatisdisc.htm.

Others often feel: hurt.

Problem emotion: boredom.

In regard to money: People with comfort idolatry earn and spend money in an attempt to insulate themselves from the needs of others and from the demands of daily life. They avoid boredom at all costs; so they are continually purchasing new gadgets and toys and investing deeply in their hobbies and other distractions from day-to-day life. Worshippers of comfort see other people, even those closest to them, as potential obstacles to their comfort. Not surprisingly, authentic relationships do not come easily and as a result are only invested in if they provide an adequate layer of insulation from hassle.

Approval idolatry: "Life only has meaning/I only have worth if I am loved and respected by _____."

What we seek: approval (affirmation, love, relationship).

Price we are willing to pay: less independence.

Greatest nightmare: rejection.

Others often feel: smothered.

Problem emotion: cowardice.

In regard to money: We were all created with a desire to be loved. This desire is healthy and natural. The problem for persons with an approval idol, however, is that they are not ultimately satisfied with God's love for them and seek love and affirmation from those they deem important. So people who worship approval will do just about anything to make a loved one happy, including excessive spending in an attempt to literally buy the acceptance of others. They may also use their earning potential as a way to make someone important to them proud of their accomplishments. Approval worshippers often overcommit, over-promise, and overstate in order to gain affirmation from others. They are radically insecure in their identity in Christ and fear rejection of people above a biblical fear of God's hatred of sin. This leads to a worry about what others think of them. Often those closest to someone with an approval idol feel smothered by the neediness of the idolater, whose desire to be loved cannot realistically be met by a mere human being.

Control idolatry: "Life only has meaning/I only have worth if I am able to get mastery over my life in the area of _____."

What we seek: control (self-discipline, certainty, standards).

Price we are willing to pay: loneliness, spontaneity.

Greatest nightmare: uncertainty.

Others often feel: condemned.

Problem emotion: worry.

In regard to money: Lightheartedness aside, those who worship control are often obsessed with making things go exactly as they planned and often pay for it through deep-seated anxiety and worry. The mantra of a true control worshipper is, "If I want it done right, I have to do it myself," though he or she may also frequently say, "It's my way or the highway." We see this in such persons' view of money. People with a control idol know where every penny goes, and they often self-righteously look down their nose at those who appear less in control of their finances. Wealthy or poor, the control idol brings about worry. "Will I make enough?" or "Am I saving enough?" are common questions. The marks of control idolatry most obviously surface when change or unexpected events, like economic recessions, threaten to ruin the plans of the idolater.

Power idolatry: "Life only has meaning/I only have worth if I have power and influence over others."

What we seek: power (success, winning, influence).

Price we are willing to pay: being burdened, responsibility.

Greatest nightmare: humiliation.

Others often feel: used.

Problem emotion: anger.

In regard to money: Someone with a power idol gains identity in competition—the fiercer the challenge the better. There is nothing wrong with competition; it can be very helpful, especially, I think, in the lives of men. But remember that all idol worship is taking something good that God has given as a gift and making it an ultimate source of identity. In this case, that good thing is challenge or competition; more accurately it is victory. However, another way to describe power worshippers is to say that their primary motivation in life is not so much to win as it is to avoid losing. In regard to money, the person with a power idol is driven to earn more and is determined to spend more than anyone else. Such persons may develop an addiction to gambling, enjoying the built-in challenge of the game of choice. All is well with power worshippers as long as they are winning. But losing exposes their deep insecurity. Losing brings anger, often accompanied with verbal or even physical abuse. Losing can bring hatred of self and disdain for those who "cost" them the victory. Those close to a person with a power idol very often feel used, undervalued, and exhausted from the up-and-down cycle of winning and losing.

At any given moment, one may be operating from several of these source idols; ultimately, however, I believe there is one that is central, one that drives most other sins and idolatries in one's life. Source idols are the root, and surface idols are the fruit.

Repenting of Idols

When Jesus came and began to declare the kingdom of God, he proclaimed to all who would hear him in Galilee, "Repent and believe in the gospel."[36] This is the essence of what it means to be a follower of Christ: *to repent and believe the gospel.* This is the key to removing idols from your life and installing Christ in the center of your being. I think a visual model is helpful at this point to understand how we dethrone idolatry and exalt Christ in our lives.[37]

Figure 12-1

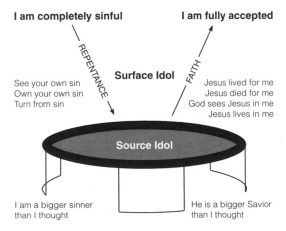

At the top of this trampoline model, we see the two pillars of the gospel: we are completely sinful and unable to remedy our condition, but we are completely accepted by God because of Christ's work.[38] The two slopes represent how we can appropriate the gospel in our lives—repenting from sin and placing our faith in Christ.

In repentance we must do three things in relation to sin: see it, own it, and turn from it. To see our sin specifically is to understand that it is grievous to God and hostile to his law.[39] To own our specific sin, we must not just see the sin as wrong in general, but that we have sinned specifically and definitely. It is to take responsibility not just for the law-breaking, but to acknowledge that we are lawbreakers. Finally, we turn from our sin; that is, we forsake it.[40] Idolatry occurs when we turn our backs on God and turn our whole selves to sin. Repentance occurs when we turn our backs on our idols and turn our whole selves to God.[41]

In accordance with the trampoline image, repentance is a lot like trying to double jump someone who is on the trampoline with you. When you want to propel your buddy skyward, or to the emergency room, you must bounce deep. Likewise with repentance, we must bounce deep in order to turn from not just our surface sins and idols but also from our source idols, the things that drive much of the other sin and idolatries in our lives. One milestone of repentance is that we begin to see we are bigger sinners than we thought. The bad news is actually worse than we thought.

However, the good news is better than we thought. Though in repentance we see that we are bigger sinners than we thought, through faith in the gospel we see that Jesus is a bigger Savior than we thought. "Repentance can only be genuine and lasting when the evildoer sees that God's mercy is available to him."[42]

As we begin to embrace our acceptance in Christ, we see that we

---

[38]Luther referred to this reality as *simul justus et peccator*—righteous and sinner at the same time. This refers to the reality that when we are in Christ, we have indwelling sin in our lives, but we are clothed with Christ's righteousness at the same time.

[39]Romans 8:7: "The mind that is set on the flesh is hostile to God, for it does not submit to God's law; indeed, it cannot."

[40]The Greek word for repentance, *metanoia*, literally means "to change one's mind."

[41]I love Jack Miller's words regarding repentance: "God has not called us to be attorneys acting in our own defense, but beggars humbled before the throne of grace, refusing to leave until bread is forthcoming." *Repentance and the 20th Century Man*, 35.

[42]Ibid., 77.

don't have to be perfect in this life because Christ was perfect in his life for us. We don't have to put up with condemnation from Satan or think that God is punishing us for our sin because Christ died and took all of God's wrath and punishment for us. So because we are *in Christ*,[43] Christ's perfect life and atoning death constantly substitute for our imperfect life and our deserved punishment. Because of this reality, when God looks upon us he sees his Son, because our life is "hidden with Christ in God,"[44] and our continued life with God is lived by faith as Christ's life is lived through us.[45]

The way to deal with sin and idolatry is to repent of them and believe the gospel.[46] Satan's main temptation is to convince us that we are half the sinner we actually are and that we have half of Christ's acceptance as we actually do.[47] In Paul's first letter to the church at Thessalonica, Paul praises the church for how they "turned to God from idols to serve the living and true God."[48] May this be said of us and of our churches as we repent and believe the gospel.[49] We'll close this chapter and section with the words of the late Jack Miller: "The more that you know that you are stained to the bone with selfish impulses, the more that you see how you hold out against the will of the Lord, the more you go to Christ as a thirsty sinner who finds deeper cleansing, more life and greater joy through the Spirit."[50]

---

[43]"In Christ" is Paul's frequent designation (for example, Romans 8:1; 1 Corinthians 15:58; 2 Corinthians 5:17; Galatians 3:26) for union with Christ.

[44]Colossians 3:3.

[45]Galatians 2:20.

[46]"The standing temptation is for the believer to allow his life to fill up with sins and to slip back into the old habit of self-assertion and self-trust. When this happens, his 'repentings' often lose their power because self-trust has led him to legalistic grounds as a basis for his acceptance with God. Without faith in Christ, repentance because soul-chilling remorse." Miller, *Repentance and the 20th Century Man*, 93.

[47]Ibid., 103.

[48]1 Thessalonians 1:9.

[49]At The Journey we did a series on idolatry in the fall of 2007. I encourage you to listen to the sermons from this time for further reflection on this topic. You can find them at http://journeyon.net/media/transformation.

[50]Miller, *Repentance and the 20th Century Man*, 55.

The Mission

We are able to see the "upside of messy" only because Jesus went into the mess first in order to heal it. He left heaven for a womb, a stable, a wilderness, and a cross, so that the world would be saved through him. We are able to love and pursue the healing of messy people because Jesus did it first—befriending tax collectors, sinners, pimps and prostitutes, and then making many of them his apostles! (Scott Sauls)[1]

---

[1] Scott Sauls, *Gospel* (Unpublished).

13
The Heart of Mission: Compassion

I will never forget hearing the pastor in the first church I joined preach a message on the need to reach out to those who were far from God. He asked an interesting question: "What is the one act of obedience that you can do on earth that you can't do in heaven?" He then answered his own question: "We can worship in heaven, and we can talk to God in heaven, and we can read our Bibles in heaven, but we can't share the gospel with our lost friends in heaven." I remember being shaken to the core by this reality. It caused me to remember that I had been one of the lost just a few months earlier but had been found by Jesus through the relationship of two friends.

Though our Acts 29 Network is thoroughly Reformed in its understanding of the nature of salvation, we are desperate in our desire to share the gospel with all peoples so that they may be saved.[2]

Men who are qualified, called, and armed with the gospel message are on a mission with Jesus, who came to seek and save the lost.[3] It is important to call attention to the mission that Jesus is on, but it is also important to speak to the motive of the mission. See if you can discern the motive behind the mission in the following verses.

Matthew 9:20–22: "And behold, a woman who had suffered from a discharge of blood for twelve years came up behind him and touched the fringe of his garment, for she said to herself, 'If I only touch his garment, I will be made well.' Jesus turned, and seeing her he said, 'Take heart, daughter; your faith has made you well.' And instantly the woman was made well."

Matthew 9:35–36: "And Jesus went throughout all the cities and villages, teaching in their synagogues and proclaiming the gospel of the kingdom and healing every disease and every affliction. When he saw

---

[2]Romans 10:14–17.
[3]Luke 19:10; cf. 5:31–32.

the crowds, he had compassion for them, because they were harassed and helpless, like sheep without a shepherd."

Matthew 14:14: "When he went ashore he saw a great crowd, and he had compassion on them and healed their sick."

Matthew 15:30: "And great crowds came to him, bringing with them the lame, the blind, the crippled, the mute, and many others, and they put them at his feet, and he healed them."

Matthew 15:32: "Then Jesus called his disciples to him and said, 'I have compassion on the crowd because they have been with me now three days and have nothing to eat. And I am unwilling to send them away hungry, lest they faint on the way.'"

Mark 1:40–41: "And a leper came to him, imploring him, and kneeling said to him, 'If you will, you can make me clean.' Moved with pity, he stretched out his hand and touched him and said to him, 'I will; be clean.'"

Mark 10:20–21: "And he said to him, 'Teacher, all these I have kept from my youth.' And Jesus, looking at him, loved him, and said to him, 'You lack one thing: go, sell all that you have and give to the poor, and you will have treasure in heaven; and come, follow me.'"

From these passages it is clear that compassion motivated Jesus' ministry. In his book *Love Walked Among Us*, Paul Miller notes that compassion is the dominant emotion that the Gospel writers ascribed to Jesus.[4]

Compassion was demonstrated when Jesus raised from the dead the only son of the woman at Nain.[5] Jesus not only raised the young man up but also consoled the woman. The compassionate Jesus wasn't so distracted by the supernatural healing of the son that he missed the hurting heart of the mom.[6] To be on mission is to have a heart full of compassion for people—to see them the way Jesus did.[7]

I glory in the invention of TiVo, which makes total commercial

---

[4] Paul Miller, *Love Walked Among Us* (Colorado Springs: NavPress, 2001).
[5] Luke 7:11–17.
[6] Miller, *Love Walked Among Us*, 28.
[7] There is debate among some theologians about whether or not God "feels" emotions like we do, which directly impacts the way one thinks about a compassionate God. I believe Scripture overwhelmingly supports God's passibility. Wayne Grudem proves helpful here. "The idea that God has no passions or emotions *at all* clearly conflicts with . . . Scripture. . . . Quite the opposite is true, for God, who is the origin of our emotions and who created our emotions, certainly does feel emotions: God rejoices (Isaiah 62:5). He is grieved (Psalm 78:40; Ephesians 4:30). His wrath burns hot against his enemies (Exodus 32:10). He pities his children (Psalm 103:13). He loves with everlasting love (Isaiah 54:8; Psalm 103:17). He is a God whose passions we are to imitate for all eternity as we like our Creator hate sin and delight in righteousness." Wayne Grudem, *Systematic Theology* (Grand Rapids: Zondervan, 1995), 166.

avoidance possible, because I hate most commercials. But have you ever noticed how uncomfortable it is to watch those "feed the children" commercials? It is so uncomfortable—I confess that I rarely watch one in its entirety, and not just because of TiVo. There is a deeper reason why I avoid watching commercials highlighting the hunger of real children with their bloated, malnourished stomachs: I don't want to look at desperate human need when I am desperately trying to escape from human reality. To look on a hungry child would take me out of consumer mode into compassion mode. As a Christian anytime you look at someone who is hurting, you *will* (as in, must) feel compassion, unless you make a choice to turn your head and harden your heart. The Gospel writers describe Jesus compassionately looking at people nearly forty times, indicating that it was a regular practice.[8]

In the parable of the good Samaritan, we see how easy it is for religious folks to avoid looking upon the pain of another. Both the Levite and the priest refused to look because they were drained of compassion. The Samaritan, on the other hand, took pity on the hurting person; he saw the man and didn't look away.

When we look—not glance, but look—we see the person, not the problem. When we look at the person, we see that he or she matters to God and ought to matter to us. When we look, we see a person to be loved, not a problem to be handled. Only when we look can we experience compassion.

Being on mission means having open eyes that are looking for the hurting—the married couple living next door struggling with fertility, the frat boy who disguises his alcoholism with the statement, "Hey, this is what college is all about," the single mother who waits on you at the restaurant even though she has no idea how she and her child will eat tomorrow after her tips buy food tonight.

To open your eyes is to risk losing your life and living with a broken heart for the sake of the lost. As C. S. Lewis reminds us, the alternative to a compassionate heart is a dead heart:

> To love at all is to be vulnerable. Love anything and your heart will
> be wrung and possibly broken. If you want to be sure of keeping it

---

[8]Miller, *Love Walked Among Us*, 31.

intact, you must give your heart to no one, not even to an animal. Wrap it carefully round with hobbies and little luxuries; avoid all entanglements; lock it up safe in the casket or coffin of your self- ishness. But in that casket—safe, dark, motionless, airless—it will change. It will not be broken; it will become unbreakable, impen- etrable, irredeemable.[9]

The motive for mission is compassion. We join Jesus on his mission not because we want to grow our church or because we like to dispense apologetic insights to skeptics or even because we like to hang out with unbelievers. We go on the mission of the Savior because we share the compassionate heart of the one who sees people as sheep without a shepherd.

The Enemies of Compassion

Busyness

When I first went into full-time ministry, I had an overwhelming sensa- tion that I was alive for the first time. I was utterly consumed with teach- ing, shepherding, leading, and counseling, to the point that I neglected other responsibilities in order to do more ministry. I could not imagine not enjoying ministry. Over the years I have realized that the joys of ministering to people are often crowded out by the demanding schedule of ministry. I find that I can get so immersed in the busyness of ministry that I lose the pleasure of ministry.

One of the first signs that busyness is threatening to kill joy is a lack of compassion for those God has placed under a pastor's care. I have seen this in my own ministry. Many times I have sat across a booth or a desk or a dinner table with a person or couple ravaged by the effects of their sin and/or the sin of others against them, and instead of lis- tening with "spiritual ears" and waiting for the direction of the Spirit, I tuned out the person who was speaking and began worrying about the twenty-five tasks that wouldn't get done because of that meeting. Worse still are the times when I am not only anxious about the things I need to get done but am angry at the people I'm meeting with for being sinners! In situations like these, instead of having a heart filled

---

[9]C. S. Lewis, *The Four Loves* (Eugene, OR: Harvest House, 1971), 121.

with compassion I have a heart filled with conceit, contemplating my agenda, my anxieties, my needs, my wants, my comfort level . . . my . . . my . . . my . . . my . . . my.

To be clear, a pastor (or any other spiritual leader for that matter) is not obligated to be "on the hook" for every problem his flock is experiencing. But when the needs of people consistently make you angry, when you avoid people because you're afraid they might need something from you, when you frequently tune out during counseling situations, you need to know that you are no longer caring for people. You and I may offer excuses, but there is no excuse for not offering care to the sheep when we are shepherds of the flock. And one consequence of this busyness is that we regularly miss one of the greatest blessings God gives to pastors, which is the pleasure of knowing that you've been the hands and feet of our Savior to someone in great need.

Hurriedness

There is a difference between simply being busy and being hurried. Being busy is about the things you have to do. Being hurried is the spiritual, mental, and emotional state that you are in when trying to do the things you have to do. You can be busy without being hurried. As a new pastor I could not even understand a journal entry like this:

> I'm tired, Lord. Bone weary from the inside out. I'm tired of a constantly cluttered desk and an overcrowded calendar. I'm tired of problems I can't solve, and hurts I can't heal. I'm tired of deadlines and decisions—duties done without any pleasure. I can't remember the last time I walked barefoot outside or took time to smell the air after the rain. I can't recall the last time I smelled coffee and paused to enjoy it. I want to feel. I want to laugh. I want to cry. I want to live life to the fullest. I want to love, and be loved.[10]

After a few short years in the trenches, I was writing entries just like this. Hurriedness is like a strong wind that blows on the waters of your heart. If the waves are too high, you forget about others and focus on your own survival, making compassion toward others impossible.

---

[10]Richard Exley, *The Rhythm of Life* (Tulsa: Honor Books, 1987), 37.

Self-righteousness

There is a vertical aspect to self-righteousness (I am trying to gain right standing with God with my good work instead of Christ's). But there is also a horizontal aspect to self-righteousness (I am trying to be right before God because I compare my sin with others').

The horizontal form of self-righteousness is one of the main reasons people don't forgive people close to them, much less be compassionate toward people not close to them. As Miroslav Volf, who witnessed his family and friends being murdered and raped in the Balkan wars of the 1990s, astutely says, "Forgiveness flounders because I exclude the enemy from the community of humans and I exclude myself from the community of sinners."[11]

Here I believe that Volf lists the main two pillars that keep people from exercising compassion on others.

1. Believing that others are less than human (they are excluded from the community of humans, in my mind).
2. Believing that I am more than human (I am excluded from the community of sinners, in my mind).

Compassion grows in the human heart and bursts out onto others when we understand that others are humans made in the image of God and that we are sinners before God.

Self-protection

One of the hardest things to overcome in loving hurting people is absorbing their hurt, rejection, and shame without pulling back emotionally. The root of the word *compassion* in English means "to be together [com] with someone's pain [passion]."[12] So to demonstrate compassion toward someone is to agree at that moment to enter into suffering with them, to choose to enter their reality—hopes, dreams, sins, and rebellion. If your heart is clogged up with protecting yourself, you are unable to enter into the loves of other people because all your energies will be

---

[11]Miroslav Volf, *Exclusion and Embrace: A Theological Exploration of Identity, Otherness, and Reconciliation* (Nashville: Abingdon Press, 1996), 124.
[12]Ronald A. Heifetz and Marty Linsky, *Leadership on the Line: Staying Alive Through the Dangers of Leading* (Boston: Harvard Business School Publishing, 2002), 235.

consumed with avoiding their pain. Compassion is the only way not to focus on your own comfort. Compassion is the God-given emotion that enables us to be distracted from our own wants and focused on others' needs.

An interesting word picture is imbedded in the Hebrew word *racham*. In the Old Testament the word *racham* is normally translated "to love" or "to have compassion."[13] Interestingly, it is a derivative of the word *rechem*, normally translated "womb." I believe it is no strange coincidence that the word *compassion* is rooted in a mother's womb. Just like the love a mother feels for her baby is from a place deep within her, so compassion is meant to come from deep within the heart of servants of Jesus. There is a special compassion that a mother has for the child that surpasses even the father's, and there should likewise be a special compassion easily recognized in the life of a Christ-follower.

Compassion, most assuredly, is deep within us as followers of Christ. We know this because the same Spirit who moved Jesus with compassion lives in us, and that same Spirit yearns to move us toward compassion just as he moves preachers to preach and leaders to lead. Just as we need the Spirit's guidance to reveal truth to us in Scripture, so do we need the guidance of the Spirit to birth compassion in us regularly. God, when he revealed himself to Moses, described himself as compassionate.[14] Ultimately, not tapping into this well of compassion is an issue to be taken up with the Lord himself. Consider the words of Saint Theresa of Avila:

> Christ has no body on earth but yours,
> no hands but yours, no feet but yours.
> Yours are the eyes through which
> Christ's compassion for the world is to look out;
> Yours are the feet with which He is to go about doing good;
> And yours are the hands with which He is to bless us now.

---

[13]David Patterson, *Hebrew Language and Jewish Thought* (New York: Routledge, 2005), 21.
[14]Exodus 34:5–7: "The LORD descended in the cloud and stood with him there, and proclaimed the name of the LORD. The LORD passed before him and proclaimed, 'The LORD, the LORD, a God merciful and gracious, slow to anger, and abounding in steadfast love and faithfulness, keeping steadfast love for thousands, forgiving iniquity and transgression and sin, but who will by no means clear the guilty, visiting the iniquity of the fathers on the children and the children's children, to the third and the fourth generation.'"

The church is the church for the sake of the world. (Hans Kung)[1]

The church exists by mission as a fire exists by burning. (Emil Brunner)[2]

We could as meaningfully talk of the missional basis of the Bible as of the biblical basis of mission. (Christopher Wright)[3]

[1]Quoted in Randy Wilson Coffin, *The Collected Sermons of William Sloane Coffin*, Vol. 1 (Louisville: Westminster John Knox Press, 2008).
[2]Quoted in Wilbert R. Shenk, *Write the Vision* (Harrisburg, PA: Trinity Press, 1995), 87.
[3]Christopher J. H. Wright, *The Mission of God* (Downers Grove, IL: InterVarsity Press, 2006), 29.

14
The House of Mission: The Church

Matthew 16:18: "And I tell you, you are Peter, and on this rock I will build my church, and the gates of hell shall not prevail against it."

Ephesians 3:10: ". . . so that through the church the manifold wisdom of God might now be made known to the rulers and authorities in the heavenly places."

I was working as a campus minister in a parachurch college ministry. I spent my days teaching, discipling, and counseling college students. I loved ministry but had given up on the church. I had grown tired of the lack of life, the legalism, and the loss of leadership development that I experienced in the church. When I went to church, I was not inspired or challenged. When I hung out with pastors, I got angry and depressed. Looking back, I was clearly an arrogant, self-righteous young man who should have submitted to and served in a local church. It was around this time that I was introduced to the ministry of Willow Creek Community Church, and I began to be hopeful about the church.

I first read about "The Creek" in *Christianity Today* magazine. Pastor Bill Hybels was featured on the cover with the title, "Selling Out the House of God?"[4]—which I now know was a play on words (Willow Creek was exploding in growth but was also being questioned for possibly compromising the gospel).[5] In that interview Hybels talked about being a church that built up believers and reached unbelievers. My heart was captured. This is what I was called to do: to start churches that equipped God's people to love Jesus and to share that truth with and live among the lost. Ever since, I have had a glorious vision of what the church can and should be: the very vehicle of God's blessing to the whole world. The church is God's Plan A to redeem the world. And God has no Plan B.

---

[4]Interview of Bill Hybels, "Selling Out the House of God?" *Christianity Today*, July 18, 1994.
[5]For more on the self-assessment of Willow Creek, read the *Reveal* Study Series by Greg Hawkins and Cathy Parkinson, published by the Willow Creek Association or for an outside critique read *Willow Creek Seeker Services: Evaluating a New Way of Doing Church* by G. A. Pritchard (Grand Rapids: Baker, 2005).

In college I had ministered to a weird blend of people—athletes (because that is what I was) and artists (because that is what my girlfriend and future, first, and only wife was). I realized that I wanted to plant a church for all kinds of people, not just one narrow demographic. I wanted a church where the "jockiest" of the jocks and the "artsiest" of the artsy could both worship. I began to believe that the church should be a diverse community of people who love Jesus and embrace his mission.

As I came to understand more about how the church was God's primary tool to carry out his mission, I began to study the nature of the church more closely. The technical word for this study is ecclesiology, which simply means the study of the church—what the church is, what the church is supposed to be like, how the church is supposed to function in the world, and how it carries out its mission. Defining the church is a nuanced and confusing task, as there are so many opinions regarding what exactly the church is.[6] Sadly, few church leaders work from a solid definition of the church.[7] It is very important to define and understand what the church is biblically before we attempt to plant, lead, and serve local churches. If we do not understand what it is that we are serving or leading, or what it is that we are starting, not only are we unlikely to be successful, but we will not even know what success *is*.

What Does the Church Look Like?

The Bible uses many images to communicate the nature of the church.[8] She is called the temple of the living God (1 Corinthians 3:16–17).[9] But what does the church actually look like? What distinguishes the church from other groups and institutions?

In their book *Vintage Church*, Mark Driscoll and Gerry Breshears do a

---

[6]Some estimate the number of Protestant denominations to be over thirty thousand. See *World Christian Encyclopedia*, 2nd edition, ed. David Barrett, George Kurian, and Todd Johnson (New York: Oxford University Press, 2001).

[7]This has been my experience as well as Mark Driscoll's. See Mark Driscoll and Gerry Breshears, *Vintage Church* (Wheaton: Crossway, 2008), 35.

[8]I have adapted the following from D. J. Tidball, "Church," in *New Dictionary of Biblical Theology: Exploring the Unity and Diversity of Scripture*, ed. T. Desmond Alexander, Brian S. Grosner, Graeme Goldsworthy, D. A. Carson (Downers Grove, IL: InterVarsity Press, 2000), 410.

[9]The church is also called the new humanity (Ephesians 2:15), a body with many significant parts and members (1 Corinthians 12:12–31), the bride of Jesus Christ (Ephesians 5:25–33), God's field (1 Corinthians 3:9), and a holy nation (1 Peter 2:9). The church began with the nation of Israel as the offspring of Abraham (Genesis 17:7) and the covenant people of God (Exodus 19:5–6) and continues today as the true children of Abraham, those who put their faith in Christ (Galatians 3:7; Philippians 3:3).

thorough job of discussing the definition and nature of a New Testament church:

> The local church is a community of regenerated believers who confess Jesus as Lord. In obedience to Scripture they organize under qualified leadership, gather regularly for preaching and worship, observe the biblical sacraments of baptism and Communion, are unified by the Spirit, are disciplined for holiness, and scatter to fulfill the Great Commandment and the Great Commission as missionaries to the world for God's glory and their joy.[10]

This definition contains eight qualifications that are helpful in understanding what it means to be a local church.

Regenerated Church Membership

This simply means that the church is made up of people who have ceased trying to save themselves and have trusted Christ as Savior and Lord.[11] Obviously there are people who come to worship services and other events who are not Christians, as well as children who will hopefully hear the gospel, trust Christ, and participate in the life of the church. Simply put, regenerated church membership means that those who are members have been regenerated by the Holy Spirit, resulting in both saving faith and persevering faith in the members.

Qualified Church Leadership[12]

The church was built upon the prophets and apostles.[13] The apostles then appointed elders[14] and set in motion the office of deacon.[15]

The two offices of the church are elders and deacons.[16] Elders are the highest office in the church and are responsible to serve the church by leading.[17] Deacons are to lead the church by serving.[18] In addition, lay leaders

---

[10]Driscoll and Breshears, *Vintage Church*, 38–39.
[11]Acts 2:38: "And Peter said to them, 'Repent and be baptized every one of you in the name of Jesus Christ for the forgiveness of your sins, and you will receive the gift of the Holy Spirit.'"
[12]For more on the biblical rationale for elders and deacons, see chapter 3, "A Qualified Man," in this book.
[13]Ephesians 2:20.
[14]Acts 14:23.
[15]Acts 6:1–4.
[16]Philippians 1:1.
[17]1 Timothy 3:1–7.
[18]1 Timothy 3:8–13.

serve the church without holding an office in the church. I personally dislike the term *staff* if it is disconnected from the office of elder or deacon. *Staff* is a term that isn't found in Scripture, and its qualifications tend to be divorced from the clear biblical qualification for elders and deacons in many churches. What I have found in many contemporary churches is that the qualifications for staff do not directly correspond to the qualifications for elder or deacon, which are explicit in the Pastoral Epistles.

Preaching and Worship

The first three thousand people in the new church at Jerusalem became Christians because they heard the gospel preached.[19] This wasn't a one-time experience, as these first converts continued to discipline themselves to listen to God's Word and respond in worship. Early Christian churches continued to gather for worship, instruction, and mutual edification.[20]

Rightly Administered Sacraments

The church is charged with the responsibility of administering baptism and the Lord's Supper.[21] In these sacraments, the presence of Christ is administered to his people.

Spirit Unity

The church of Jesus Christ echoes the prayer of Jesus, who asked God the Father "that they may all be one, just as you, Father, are in me, and I in you, that they also may be in us, so that the world may believe that you have sent me."[22] This does not mean that godly Christians cannot disagree on specific issues of doctrine or method. It does mean that all orthodox Christians share a fundamental unity in their ultimate identity and mission.

Holiness

Because the church has been made positionally holy,[23] it seeks to maintain practical holiness by repenting of sin and believing the promises of

---

[19]Acts 2:41.
[20]1 Corinthians 14:26.
[21]Matthew 28:19–20; 1 Corinthians 11:23–26.
[22]John 17:21.
[23]2 Corinthians 5:17; Ephesians 1:3.

the gospel, as exhibited by obedience to Scripture. The church rebukes those who are caught in sin[24] and disciplines those who are unrepentant in sin.[25] The church should stand out as different from the world because it is holy.[26]

The Great Commandment to Love

Jesus summed up the heart of God's desire for how we treat other human beings in his second greatest commandment: "love your neighbor as yourself."[27] The New Testament epistles put more flesh on this commandment as they command believers to show hospitality to others (Romans 12:13).[28] Where such things occur, there is the church. Where such things are absent, there is no church.

The Great Commission to Evangelize and Disciple the Church

The church is a place where the lost are found by God through the clear proclamation and demonstration of the gospel. The church doesn't just make converts; it makes disciples by teaching the church to do all that Jesus commanded.[29]

From Where Did the Church Come?

To answer this question, you have to go to eternity past. God has always existed as a community of persons comprising one God: Father, Son, Holy Spirit. This divine community was on a mission. Before the beginning of time, this triune God planned the church as a people whom he would adopt through Jesus Christ.[30] At creation, the triune God made Adam and Eve to bear his image and to rule and reign over creation in

---

[24]Galatians 6:1.
[25]Matthew 18:15–17.
[26]Philippians 2:15.
[27]Matthew 22:39.
[28]Believers are also told to bear with one another (Romans 15:1), edify one another (1 Corinthians 14:26), restore one another (Galatians 6:1), forgive one another (Ephesians 4:32), submit to one another (Ephesians 5:21), consider one another more significant than themselves (Philippians 2:3), speak truth to one another (Colossians 3:9), share with one another (Hebrews 13:16), confess sin to one another (James 5:16), and have unity of mind with one another (1 Peter 3:8).
[29]Matthew 28:18–20.
[30]Ephesians 1:4–5.

God's name.[31] In other words, the first family in the history of the world was a community on mission.

After things had gone from bad to worse,[32] God judged the world with a flood,[33] humbled human pride,[34] and then decided to start again with a new family, Abraham and his offspring,[35] who would form another community on mission.[36] Then we get into the New Testament and the first time the church is mentioned (Matthew 16:18). Here Jesus pictured "the called out ones," who are on a mission to storm the gates of hell. The church is part of God's plan from all eternity and is connected to God's mission from creation. As Christopher Wright puts it, "Mission was not made for the church; the church was made for mission—God's mission."[37] God himself has always been a community on mission, and he has always empowered his people to be a community on mission.

What Does the Church Do?

At the same time as I was reading about Willow Creek and noticing the need for churches for artists and athletes, I began reading the book of Acts. Acts 2:41–47, in particular, gripped me:

> So those who received his word were baptized, and there were added that day about three thousand souls. And they devoted themselves to the apostles' teaching and the fellowship, to the breaking of bread and the prayers. And awe came upon every soul, and many wonders and signs were being done through the apostles. And all who believed were together and had all things in common. And they were selling their possessions and belongings and distributing the proceeds to all, as any had need. And day by day, attending the temple together and breaking bread in their homes, they received their food with glad and generous hearts, praising God and having favor with all the people. And the Lord added to their number day by day those who were being saved.

---

[31]Genesis 1:27–28.
[32]Genesis 6:5.
[33]Genesis 7:23.
[34]Genesis 11.
[35]Genesis 12:1–3.
[36]Isaiah 49:6: "I will make you [Israel] as a light for the nations, that my salvation may reach to the end of the earth."
[37]Wright, *The Mission of God*, 62.

It is not an understatement to say that these verses wrecked my life. I began to realize that the parachurch was a reaction to the church not doing its job. I began to see how the local church is God's eternal plan to both edify his people and evangelize the world. In these verses I began to see everything the church should be and could be:

- believers built up by the clear teaching of Scripture (v. 42)
- believers praying fervently together (v. 42)
- believers in awe because of the supernatural power of the Spirit (v. 43)
- believers not allowing class distinctions to divide them (v. 44)
- believers sharing their possessions with those in need (v. 45)
- believers living life together in community (v. 46)
- unbelievers attracted and converted to Christ (v. 47)

Unfortunately, throughout its history the church has focused on one of these functions to the reduction or neglect of the others. In other words, sadly, the church of Jesus Christ often lives well below its divine mandate and rich identity. We will now consider some models of various contemporary churches.

What Are Some Models of the Church?[38]

The Teaching Church (Doctrine-driven)

The teaching church focuses on a commitment to "the apostles' teaching" (Acts 2:42). This is the church where the pastor has an advanced seminary degree and is a good teacher. These churches glory in the proclamation of doctrine and take responsibility for teaching the whole counsel of God's Word. Numerous theological classes are taught, and small groups operate with the primary goal of theological education rather than personal relationships.

The strengths of this model are that the church is taught sound doctrine, and members are encouraged to study the Scripture for themselves and to think about deep truths through consistent theological reflection. The weakness of this model is that it tends to produce Pharisees who are proud of their theological knowledge but fail to exercise compassion

---

[38]This subsection is informed heavily by the teaching of Richard Lovelace. A helpful resource is his *Dynamics of Spiritual Life* (Downers Grove, IL: IVP, 1979).

to outsiders. Likewise, teaching churches tend to get stuck in an era,[39] which causes them to resist adapting their ministry to reach emerging culture. This guarantees that the only growth they have is biological, stemming from transfers from other churches.[40]

The Devotion Church (Worship-driven)

The devotion church is committed to prayer, worship, and the display of the Holy Spirit's power. The pastor is energetic and often leads out in corporate worship and prayer, which is the focus of the church. These churches revel in God's presence, often having services that last upwards of three hours, full of music, prayer, and prophetic words.[41]

Because of its experiential nature, the strength of this model of church is that members are encouraged to go to God for their own sanctification.[42] Another great strength of devotion churches is that they tend to have greater racial diversity than other churches. The weakness of this model is that the church is often led into a mystical relationship with God that is not grounded in sound doctrine, resulting in prophetic words and other supernatural experiences that are often elevated above Scripture.

The Community Church (Community-driven)

The community church devotes itself to fellowship within the body through connected relationships that often transcend socioeconomic barriers. Pastors in community churches are more likely to be adept at empowering ministry than teaching the Word. From the top down, members are implored to "be the church" and not to rely on the paid clergy to do the work of ministry.[43]

The strength of these churches is that ministry and relationships are decentralized in small groups, which results in a vibrant "body life." Likewise, members' needs are quickly known and thoroughly met in the

---

[39]Ed Stetzer often says that many tradition churches are perfectly contextualized for 1954! I heard this in an Acts 29 conference in October 2006.

[40]Larry Osbourne calls this drift from one church to another for deeper teaching "maturity migration."

[41]For a good understanding of this gift, read Wayne Grudem, *The Gift of Prophecy in the New Testament and Today* (Wheaton: Crossway, 2000).

[42]Sanctification is a progressive work of God and man that makes us more and more free from sin and more like Christ in our actual lives. See Wayne Grudem, *Systematic Theology* (Grand Rapids: Zondervan, 1995), 746.

[43]The theological basis for this idea is the priesthood of all believers.

community church. The weakness of these churches is that it is difficult for outsiders, especially unbelievers, to break into the community. With regard to decision-making, it is almost impossible for the pastor to lead in a community church because everyone feels empowered to "weigh in" on almost every decision.

The Seeker Church (Evangelism-driven)

The seeker church devotes itself to sharing the gospel with the lost, both privately and corporately, so that the Lord can add to the church daily those who are being saved. Seeker churches utilize cutting-edge technology in their worship services to help unbelievers understand the basic tenets of the gospel. Pastors in seeker churches are passionate about evangelism, and that passion bleeds into every aspect of the church's programming.

The strength of the seeker church is that it is very accessible to the unchurched and de-churched,[44] and it is willing to innovate to respond to the ever-changing culture. The weakness of this model is that because of the emphasis on practical, topical, "how to" sermons, the church tends to be a mile wide and an inch deep. "Hard truths" are often ignored in order to meet the felt needs of the people.

The Social Justice Church (Social-concern-driven)

The social justice church devotes itself to serving marginalized people. The poor are valued and served, and races are encouraged to reconcile. The social justice church often starts several nonprofit community development organizations. The pastor in this model tends to be more a releaser of ministry than an equipper of the saints.

The strength of this kind of church is that it challenges its members to love "the least of these," forsaking the tendency of the contemporary church to settle for affinity.[45] The social justice church promotes a simple lifestyle among its members so they can identify with the poor and marginalized. Also the social justice church empowers ministry that extends beyond the four walls of the church building.

---

[44]The de-churched are people who were formally part of a church but no longer attend. Unchurched people are people who have never been a part of the church.
[45]Affinity is when we surround ourselves with people just like us.

The weakness of this model is that it tends to focus on the corporate aspects of the gospel to the neglect of the personal.[46]

All of these models have strengths, but none of them is all that the church is meant to be. Acts 2 shows us that the church must not settle for one particular function but must be a teaching, praying, awe-inspired, classless, possession-sharing community on mission.

How Does the Church Reproduce?

The book of Acts reveals a church that was gospel-centered in teaching (it preached Christ as the climax and hero of every text) and missional in practice (it talked and lived out the Christian faith in ways that were comprehensible to unbelievers). Because the New Testament church is centered on the life and work of Christ, it takes the commands of Christ seriously.

Consequently, gospel-centered, missional churches in the twenty-first century will imitate churches in the book of Acts by planting new churches wherever the Holy Spirit leads them. Sadly, along the way the church stopped planting churches. This caused it to become ingrown and stale, losing its missional impact and forsaking its original intention.[47] It got distracted from the mission by focusing on its own structure. This temptation is as serious now as it was in church history. Driscoll writes wisely that "a church needs to be as formally organized as is necessary to get on and stay on mission, and no more."[48] When the church loses its mission, it loses its foundation, its power, and its influence.

In New Testament times churches planted churches, and these churches both repelled and attracted unbelievers.[49] Because such churches focus on Jesus, not on politics, legalism, or simple activism, onlookers are able to, without distraction, respond to Christ. Because members of such churches understand that they are saved by pure grace

---

[46]For a helpful resource for better understanding this weakness, see the paper written by Steve Boyer and the elders of Capitol Hill Baptist Church in Washington, D.C., "Whar Does Scripture Say about the Poor?"; http://sites.silaspartners.com/partner/Article_Display_Page/0,,PTID314526|CHID598014|CIID2376562,00.html#vi.

[47]James Brownson said it best: "The early Christian movement that produced and canonized the New Testament was a movement with a specifically missionary character," in his book *Speaking the Truth in Love: New Testament Resources for a Missional Hermeneutic*, Christian Mission and Modern Culture Series (Harrisburg, PA: Trinity Press, 1998), 14,

[48]Driscoll and Breshears, *Vintage Church*, 145.

[49]Acts 5:13; 9:31.

(they contributed nothing to their salvation), they are able to live out their faith with confidence, knowing that Christ's perfect life substitutes for their life before God on a constant basis. Likewise, members are humble because they are completely aware of their own sin, and they know that it was for their sin that God slaughtered his Son. This humble confidence[50] is very attractive to those outside the Christian community. Those peeking over the fence into Christianity look on these people, who are like them but not like them, who are confident but not judgmental, who are humble but not depressed. Disciples like this are attractive because they don't exude an "I am better than you" persona but just the opposite—an "I am probably worse than you, but God saves bad people like us" persona. This kind of disciple is grown in the soil of the local church. It is then that the local church begins to be populated with non-Christians who come to find out where these people come from and why they have such hope. Once this begins to happen, you have a New Testament church where believers are built up and the lost are evangelized. This kind of church will plant new churches.

---

[50]I first learned of this concept from Tim Keller.

Contextualization is about making the church as culturally accessible as possible without compromising the truth of Christian belief. In this, what is sought is timeless truth and timely methods. In other words, contextualization is not making the gospel relevant, but showing the relevance of the gospel. (Mark Driscoll)[1]

We now recognize that Western culture is not the realm of Christendom that must be brought to the rest of the world as a part of God's mission; rather, the gospel must be addressed in fresh ways to a Western culture that no longer understands or discerns God's gracious activity in the world. (James V. Brownson)[2]

In order for the Christian message to be meaningful to people it must come to them in language and categories that make sense within their particular culture and life situation. (Dean E. Flemming)[3]

[E]very statement of the gospel in words is conditioned by the culture of which those words are a part, and every style of life that claims to embody the truth of the gospel is a culturally conditioned style of life. There can never be a culture-free gospel. (Lesslie Newbigin)[4]

---

[1]Mark Driscoll and Gerry Breshears, *Vintage Church* (Wheaton: Crossway, 2008), 228.
[2]James V. Brownson, *Speaking the Truth in Love: New Testament Resources for a Missional Hermeneutic* (Harrisburg, PA: Trinity Press International, 1998), 4.
[3]Dean E. Flemming, *Contextualization in the New Testament: Patterns for Theology and Mission* (Downers Grove, IL: InterVarsity Press, 2005), 13.
[4]Lesslie Newbigin, *The Gospel in a Pluralist Society* (Grand Rapids: Eerdmans, 1989), 306.

15
The How of Mission: Contextualization

Thus far in the book we have seen that God calls a man who is prepared in character and gifts to live and preach the gospel. However, a called and qualified man who is armed with the gospel is simply not enough. That man must be able to preach his message in a way that his hearers can comprehend. This does not imply that the gospel does not have power in and of itself, as some critics of contextualization maintain;[5] it simply recognizes that all gospel proclamation takes place within a context and that the gospel must be explained in ways that the people in that context can understand.[6]

What Is Contextualization?

Contextualization is a word that was originally used by missionaries to describe the process of taking the gospel to different cultures.[7] Contextualization is the church's gospel-response to culture. It is simply the taking of the unchanging gospel into an oft-changing culture by restating the meaning of the gospel in a way that is comprehendible to those who are hearing the gospel.[8]

Contextualization is not a rejection of the absolute, objective truth of the gospel in favor of the latest fad of relativism. D. A. Carson says it best: "No truth which human beings may articulate can ever be articulated in a culture-transcending way, but that does not mean that the truth

---

[5]For an example of some critics of contextualization, check out http://teampyro.blogspot.com, and especially this article: http://teampyro.blogspot.com/2008/03/context-and-contextualization.html.

[6]Tim Keller, "Contextualization: Wisdom or Compromise?" (Connect Conference, Covenant Seminary, 2004), 3 writes: "Missionary strategy consists of two parts: a) On the one hand, be sure not to remove any of the offensive essentials of the gospel message, such as the teaching on sin, the need for repentance, the lostness of those outside of Christ, and so on. b) On the other hand, be sure to remove any nonessential language or practice that will confuse or offend the sensibilities of the people you are trying to reach. The key to effective mission is to know the difference between essential and un-essential."

[7]See http://www.pcusa.org/calltomission/presented-papers/young.htm.

[8]Graeme Goldsworthy, *Gospel Centered Hermeneutics* (Downers Grove, IL: InterVarsity Press, 2006), 26.

thus articulated does not transcend culture."[9] Carson is pointing out the simple reality that every time we communicate truth, we do so within a context. This means that while there is only one unchanging gospel, there is not only one way to communicate this unchanging gospel. To communicate the gospel in one static form with no regard to a culture's language, customs, politics, and belief systems would result in undermining the gospel by under-contextualizing it.

However, contextualization can be a risky endeavor. In the same way that there is a danger of allowing fear of culture to lead to under-contextualizing the gospel, there is also a danger of over-contextualizing by essentially placing the gospel under the authority of culture. Look again at Carson's quote above. The back half of Carson's quote points to the reality that though the gospel exists within a context, its truth transcends, or goes beyond, that context. He's right. God's truth is *extra-local*, meaning that it is true for all times in all places for all peoples. To believe that the gospel is less than this is over-contextualizing. So both going "over" and "under" with regard to contextualization results in ineffective ministry.

Tim Keller has written brilliantly and extensively in this area. He says: "Contextualization is adapting gospel ministry from one culture into another culture by 1) changing those aspects of ministry that are culturally conditioned, and 2) maintaining those aspects of ministry that are unchanging and Biblically required. Contextualization 'incarnates' the Christian faith in a particular culture. It is the process by which we present the gospel to people of a particular world-view, in forms that the 'receptor-hearers' can understand."[10] Keller's definition demonstrates the delicate balance in contextualization. Faithful gospel ministry consists of both firmness and flexibility. On one hand, we "*contend* for the faith that was once for all delivered to the saints" (Jude 3). We are to stand fast and hold true to even the most unpopular and difficult Christian doctrines. On the other hand, we *contextualize* the gospel, as Paul did: "I have become all things to all people, that by all means I might save some" (1 Corinthians 9:22).[11] Both components are crucial.

[9]D.A. Carson, "Maintaining Scientific and Christian Truths in a Postmodern World," *Science & Christian Belief,* Vol. 14, No. 2 (October 2002), 107–122; www.scienceandchristianbelief.org/articles/carson.pdf.
[10]Keller, "Contextualization: Wisdom or Compromise?," 1.
[11]I heard Ed Stetzer use this language of "contend" and "contextualize" in a training event we did together in Springfield, Missouri in 2005.

Many critics of contextualization label it as compromise—simply changing the gospel to please the culture.[12] This is a misunderstanding of the nature of this vital biblical principle. Contextualization is speaking to people with their terms, not on their terms. As Keller puts it, "Contextualization is not 'giving people what they want' but rather it is giving God's answers (which they may not want!) to questions they are asking and in forms that they can comprehend."[13] In other words, there is an *attracting offensiveness* to contextualization. The attractiveness of contextualizing the gospel is that we actually listen to the questions that people are asking. We are able to listen patiently to the hopes, challenges, and fears that people in a culture express through art, theater, literature, and film and to communicate the gospel in a way that connects with these hopes, challenges, and fears. Many unbelievers in our cultural setting will be attracted to the gospel as they come to understand how it connects to them in the deepest possible ways. The culture begins to see the church as a place of depth and honesty, and many will give the claims of Christ a hearing. People are actually *drawn* to the church rather than repelled by the church.

Contextualization shows the attractiveness of the gospel, but it also reveals the offensiveness of the gospel.[14] We enter the culture to listen, but we don't give *our* answers—we give God's answers, which most of the time, as Keller notes, are not what people want to hear! So, though many are attracted to the character, demeanor, and lifestyle of the people in the church, they are repelled because of the Savior of the church. As the church explodes the categories of liberal or conservative and other reductionist labels, it removes stumbling blocks to the Christian faith. This causes people to come face-to-face with *the* stumbling block, which is Jesus Christ himself.[15]

Dean Flemming gets at the heart of the matter when he writes,

---

[12]You can watch some critiques of contextualization at http://www.youtube.com/lanechaplin.

[13]Keller, "Contextualization: Wisdom or Compromise?," 2.

[14]1 Corinthians 1:18.

[15]1 Peter 2:6–8. Of course, unbelievers will often take offense at believers themselves—their conduct, their words, their lifestyles. Just as people hated Daniel for praying three times a day (Daniel 6), and just as Peter and John were persecuted for healing and for preaching the gospel (Acts 4:1–22), so believers today will earn persecution through righteous living. My point is that when the church strips away unnecessary elements of church culture, unbelievers are able to come to terms more directly with the gospel itself. Instead of seeing "conservative or "liberal" headquarters, they see Jesus Christ himself. In this way, Christ, and not the church, becomes the ultimate ground for offense.

"Contextualization is the dynamic and comprehensive process by which the gospel is incarnated within a concrete historical or cultural situation."[16] This definition demonstrates the kind of flexibility needed to appropriately contextualize. Adapting gospel ministry into a culture requires nimbleness, pliability, and creativity. A good preacher, for example, must be able to exegete not only the text but also the culture of the hearers in order to be a faithful and fruitful missionary. We are to bring the gospel through the church to the world and avoid allowing the world to influence the church and corrupt the gospel.

This definition also hints at the thoroughness required in contextualization. It must be comprehensive. This involves examining every aspect of the text being preached and the truth being explained through the eyes of those who are listening to that truth.[17] This is why a missional pastor should always preach as if there are unbelievers in the crowd. He should never assume that his audience is comprised only of those already convinced of the truth and power of the gospel. We must literally consider everything we do through the lens of the unbeliever, always asking the question, "How does this come across to unbelievers?"[18]

My thoughts on taking the "text" into a "context" were crystallized through a conference that was held at Covenant Theological Seminary in 2004 called "Connect Conference." During this conference Tim Keller presented a paper entitled "Contextualization: Wisdom or Compromise?" This paper not only helped define contextualization, but it also delineated the tensions that arise from trying to take the unchanging gospel into changing cultures.

In that paper Keller states that "there is no universal, de-contextualized form or expression of Christianity."[19] His point is that, much to the dismay of certain fundamentalist Christians in our setting,[20] the church always blends with culture. It is simply impossible for the church

---

[16]Flemming, *Contextualization in the New Testament: Patterns for Theology and Mission*, 19.
[17]A great resource on this tension is John Stott's *Between Two Worlds: The Challenge of Preaching* (Grand Rapids: Eerdmans, 1994).
[18]Cf. Paul's concern in 1 Corinthians 14:24–25.
[19]Keller, "Contextualization: Wisdom or Compromise?" 1. Brownson, *Speaking the Truth in Love*, 64, makes the same point: "There is no noncontextualized telling of the gospel narrative."
[20]By "fundamentalist," I mean people who are anti-culture and who tend to see church vs. culture relations in purely black and white categories and who believe their "type of church" has the perfect balance.

to not allow some aspects of culture to come into its worship or programming.[21] He explains:

> The minute we begin to minister we must "incarnate," even as Jesus did. Actual Christian practices must have both a biblical form or shape as well as a cultural form or shape. For example, the Bible clearly directs us to use music to praise God. But as soon as we choose a music style to use, we enter a culture. As soon as we choose a language, as soon as we choose a vocabulary, as soon as we choose a particular level of emotional expressiveness and intensity, as soon as we choose even an illustration as an example for a sermon, we are moving toward the social context of some people and away from the social context of others. At Pentecost, everyone heard the sermon in his or her own language and dialect. But since Pentecost, we can never be "all things to all people" at the very same time. So adaptation to culture is inevitable.[22]

Contextualization is a two-way process.[23] Because this process involves declaring the unchanging truth of God, a large part of contextualization is to correct the idols of the culture. Likewise, when Christians incarnate in another culture, they see their own idols. As missionaries have pointed out for centuries, the crossing of cultures is a major catalyst in the personal holiness and ministry effectiveness of the missionary. The process of contextualization allows the missionary to discern his own cultural biases that violate the truth of the gospel. Keller points out:

> . . . while the Bible cannot be corrected by non-Christian cultures, Christians can be. (A refusal to allow your own Christianity to be corrected means you assume your Christianity is perfectly Biblical.) A non-Christian philosophy can point out something that is a Biblical

---

[21] Keller cites a practical and cultural example of this: "Korean Christians have a heavy pre-layer of Confucian culture (which makes an idol of human tradition and worships ancestors). So when they read the Bible, they see the emphasis on submission to authority, loyalty, commitment. American Christians have a heavy pre-layer of Western individualism (which makes an idol of individual feelings and needs). So when they read the Bible, they see the emphasis on freedom and personal decision. But Korean Christians will be able to pick up American Christians' phobia about commitment and hatred for authority (i.e., where they 'screen out' Biblical truth), and American Christians will be able to pick up Korean Christians' tendency toward authoritarianism in their institutions and to enshrining human traditions in a Pharisaical way (i.e., where they 'screen out' Biblical truth). The church is simply unable to not be affected, in some aspect, by the culture it finds itself in." Keller, "Contextualization: Wisdom or Compromise?" 2.

[22] Ibid., 1.

[23] Ibid., 2.

insight but which the Christians have missed. Such a process shows us what part of our own framework is really Biblical, and what part was our own cultural or emotional baggage.[24]

Keller continues, "Contextualization is a balance of accepting and rejecting, of entering and challenging."[25] There are parts of culture that we can accept and enter into because of God's sustaining and preserving common grace, given to all people and all cultures. For instance, in our cultural setting the values of community (we should live life together) and social justice (we should serve the poor) are deep-seated values for many people outside the Christian faith. These values are biblical values. The church can accept and enter into the human desire to connect and to help the less fortunate because both community[26] and serving the poor[27] are biblical. This emphasis on community and service is one of the keys to why many Acts 29 churches are growing in the difficult soil of urban contexts. We enter into culture realizing that it is both broken and beautiful because culture comes from the hearts of people, and people are both made in the image of God and are sinners. Therefore, culture has elements within it that can be entered into, such as the desire for community and justice.

The church, realizing that it is a missionary entity,[28] must realize that people in culture have deep-seated beliefs about their lives that must be addressed by the gospel if they are going to give Christianity a hearing. To reach people with the gospel, we have to address a person's view of the nature of truth, history, science, and, at times, politics. Gospel-sharing and preaching that does not address the cognitive aspects of culture may tweak the emotions but may not transform the worldview of the person.

Likewise, gospel-sharing and preaching must engage the values of the person in culture. This involves entering into the heart-values of people. A good missionary will examine the things people orient their

---

[24]Ibid.

[25]Ibid., 3.

[26]E.g., Acts 2:42–47.

[27]E.g., Proverbs 14:31: "Whoever oppresses a poor man insults his Maker, but he who is generous to the needy honors him." Cf. Galatians 2:10.

[28]For a good description of the church being sent to a context, read *The Missional Church in Context: Helping Congregations Develop Contextual Ministry*, ed. Craig Van Gelder (Grand Rapids: Eerdmans, 2007).

lives around—how they are investing their time, money, and energy. They will look into the questions that the culture is asking, what they rally around, and what things transcend normal social barriers. In my context it is baseball. People in St. Louis, Missouri "love them some" St. Louis Cardinals. They are proud citizens of Cardinal Nation. I am continually amazed at how every segment of society comes to The Temple of St. Louis, which is Busch Stadium. Artists, soccer moms, urban hipsters, NASCAR aficionados, and everyone in between are educated and passionate about Cardinal baseball. It is something that people in my city rally around, as demonstrated by the time, money, and energy they devote to it. One way to contextualize in St. Louis, Missouri is to educate yourself about its professional baseball team. The church must be willing to enter into Cardinal Nation armed with a working knowledge of the game, and specifically the team, that shapes the passions of so many.

There are things we must receive about a culture as the gospel advances into it. Of course, there are also things in culture that we must reject and challenge. The Western values of relativism (all truth is subjective and personal) and its close cousin, tolerance (you may not judge another's personal beliefs), are examples of values we should reject and challenge. To appropriately contextualize is to discern the culture's core beliefs and then bring the truth of God to bear on them, confronting and exposing them and challenging people to embrace Christ.

"Contextualization is entering, challenging, and re-telling the culture's basic 'story-lines' and 'cultural narratives.'"[29] Every culture has a story, a plot, and an answer to these questions:

1) How are things supposed to be?
2) What has gone wrong? What is the main problem with things?
3) What is the solution and can it be realized?[30]

The answers to these questions form the worldview of individuals and thus the cultural ethos. A large part of contextualization involves connecting the answers to these foundational questions to the person and work of Christ. This is what the apostle Paul seems to be doing to

---

[29]Keller, "Contextualization: Wisdom or Compromise?" 4.
[30]Ibid.

the most jacked-up church in the New Testament, the church in Corinth: "For Jews demand signs and Greeks seek wisdom, but we preach Christ crucified, a stumbling block to Jews and folly to Gentiles, but to those who are called, both Jews and Greeks, Christ the power of God and the wisdom of God."[31]

The Jews saw power as the answer to many of their cultural questions. But the cross was utter weakness, and offensively so. The Greeks craved wisdom as their cultural plot. But the cross was complete foolishness. Paul challenges the cultural narratives of power and wisdom and then points people to Christ, who embodies true power and wisdom.[32] In true contextualization, there is both a yes and a no, an affirmation and a denial. The questions people ask are heard and addressed, but they are challenged by the answers supplied by the gospel.

Biblical Examples of Contextualization

Pentecost, the Reverse Babel

Quite possibly the apex of human stupidity and rebellion is when we tried to build a tower to heaven. God put a stop to this monument to human potential by creating a multitude of cultures, causing those at Babel to speak different languages.[33] Once united by language, the human race was now scattered because of language. So God chose a man who quite possibly could have been a tower-builder to be the man whom God would bless and use to build a nation that served as a light back to God through those scattered by God at Babel. We often read the Bible as if mission began with the Great Commission of Matthew 28. The reality is that the Bible is missional from the outset. Already in Genesis 12:1–3, God calls Abraham and sends him out to be a missionary. Mission begins in the Old Testament as the nation of Israel was intended to be a missionary agent to the surrounding nations.[34] But ultimately it was the church, the new Israel, that would reverse the events at the tower of Babel.

In Acts 2 God again dealt with languages. God the Holy Spirit filled the disciples and enabled them to speak in languages they had not

---

[31] 1 Corinthians 1:22–24.
[32] K.eller, "Contextualization: Wisdom or Compromise?" 4
[33] Genesis 11:1–9
[34] Cf. Deuteronomy 4:6–8; 1 Kings 8:41–43. For more on Israel as a missionary to the nations, read Walter C. Kaiser Jr., *Mission in the Old Testament: Israel as a Light to the Nations* (Grand Rapids: Baker, 2000).

learned. These languages were not random but were the specific ones of the people who had gathered for the feast of Pentecost, enabling the gathered to hear "the mighty works of God" in their own language (v. 11). This supernatural event caused the crowd to pay attention to the apostle Peter who preached the sermon that drew the three thousand converts who birthed the church.

At Babel God divided people through language. At Pentecost God united people through language. The purpose of the tongues-speaking in Acts was not simply to demonstrate the power of the Holy Spirit (though certainly it did that). The larger significance of Pentecost in redemptive history is that God used the breaking down of cultural and linguistic barriers as a way to launch and set the direction and method of his church. God enabled his people to supernaturally speak cross-culturally. However, this event only happened once in human history. Normally missionaries must work hard to learn the basic grammar of a new language and, much more, the nuances of a cultural use of language. Though Pentecost had unique spiritual power, it did not have a unique missional focus. Because we live in the church age, an era in which God calls us to take the gospel across language and cultural boundaries, we must do the hard work of contextualizing the message so that it can be understood from one culture/language to another.

The Nature of the New Testament

Some argue that instead of contextualizing, all we need to do is "preach the Bible." But such a framework overlooks the fact that the Bible itself is an act of contextualization. The Bible was written in specific languages within specific historical and cultural settings. God is the ultimate con-textualizer. He accommodates himself to our finite thoughts and catego-ries so we can understand him. Every book of the New Testament, for example, was written in order to be intelligible to a specific people who lived in a specific time and situation.[35] Throughout the New Testament we see writers inspired by the Holy Spirit declaring the unchanging gos-pel through various metaphors, narratives, and images that appealed to

---

[35]This is also the case in the Old Testament, which communicates to Israel with specific customs, idioms, and historically specific concepts that were intelligible to those to whom it was written.

the various settings of the audiences. As Flemming puts it, "Each book of the New Testament represents an attempt by the author to present the Christian message in a way that is targeted for a particular audience within a given socio-cultural environment."[36]

Mark Driscoll's table on the next page helps us grasp with even more clarity the way the authors of each Gospel were keenly aware of their audiences and how God inspired each man with the same core content, but with different languages and emphases depending on each man's context.[37]

Flemming writes again, "Paul's writings are less a collection of doctrinal studies than a series of theological conversations between the apostle and his diverse audiences within their life circumstances."[38] We see this in Galatians, where Paul's redemption metaphor directly combats a false gospel that overemphasized circumcision and adherence to the law. We see this in 1 Corinthians, where Paul pushes against a culture that praised rhetorical skill and philosophical wherewithal by stating that the gospel was foolishness to Greeks and a stumbling block to Jews. In Philippians the gospel is proclaimed through political and military language, fitting for Philippi, a Roman colony. In his personal letter to his chief disciple Timothy, Paul employs accounting language about the gospel as a "deposit," which resonated with a young pastor dealing with believers who were wasting or inappropriately leveraging their wealth.[39] Even in similar epistles like Galatians and Romans, Paul argues and emphasizes analogous points differently because of the situation in the church he is addressing. In Galatians his tone is strident, and he focuses especially on where the Galatians have erred, whereas in Romans he proceeds more systematically due to the theological distinctives that existed between Jews and Gentiles in Rome. Paul the theologian is always Paul the apostle/missionary, and his letters can never be divorced from the concrete particulars of his context.

---

[36]Flemming, *Contextualization in the New Testament*, 15.
[37]Mark Driscoll, *The Radical Reformission* (Grand Rapids: Zondervan, 2004), 56–57.
[38]Flemming, *Contextualization in the New Testament*, 105.
[39]William D. Mounce, *Word Biblical Commentary: Pastoral Epistles* (Nashville: Nelson Reference & Electronic, 2000), 371 notes that Paul's term "deposit" (used in, for example, 1 Timothy 6:20) refers to "valuable property entrusted to a person for safe keeping."

Figure 15-1

	Matthew	Mark	Luke	John
Author	Jewish Christian; former despised tax collector	Jewish Christian; cousin of Barnabas	Gentile Christian doctor	Jewish Christian and Jesus' youngest disciple
Primary Audience	Jews	Romans	Gentiles	Greeks
Portrait of Jesus	Jewish Messiah and king	Faithful servant	Perfect man	God
Jesus' Genealogy	Traced to Abraham and David, showing Jesus as the fulfillment of Old Testament prophecy	No genealogy, since Jesus' accomplishments, and not his family, are what is important	Traced to Adam to show that Jesus was fully human	Jesus as the eternal Word of God
Notable Features	Roughly 60% of the book is Jesus' words from his teaching as a rabbi; about fifty Old Testament quotes	Briefest Gospel; few Old Testament quotes; explains Jewish words and customs for non-Jews; 150 present-tense verbs emphasizing Jesus' actions; thirty-five miracles; 40% of the book is Jesus' words	Roughly 50% of the book is Jesus' words; thirteen women mentioned who are omitted from other Gospels; Jewish customs explained; a focus on Jesus' early years and emotional life	Roughly 90% is unique to John; no parables or exorcisms; seven "I am" statements of Jesus prove he is God

It isn't just Paul's writings that were contextualized. James writes to "the twelve tribes in the Dispersion" (1:1) by employing Jewish language and concepts. Peter, writing to those who were being persecuted by Nero, unpacks the gospel particularly in terms of the hope it gives in the middle of first-century persecution. Jude challenges his readers to "contend for the faith that was once for all delivered to the saints" (v.3) so that the church would stand in the face of the nut-job heretics who had infiltrated the church. In the grand perspective, the New Testament letters were divinely inspired and ad hoc, or contextualized, on the ground level. I believe these dual distinctives actually contribute to the *timelessness* and *timeliness* of Scripture.

The Example of Jesus and Paul

The Bible, however, is not the ultimate act of contextualization. God's greatest act of contextualization is the incarnation. "And the Word became flesh and dwelt among us, and we have seen his glory, glory as of the only Son from the Father, full of grace and truth" (John 1:14). When God became a man, he became a first-century, Aramaic-speaking, Jewish man. "Although he offered a radically new teaching he did not coin a new language to express it."[40] Jesus was virtually indistinguishable from other men in his historical context. He wore the same clothes, ate the same food, and used the same language as the average first-century Jewish man. As Mark Driscoll puts it, "Jesus is the greatest missionary who ever lived or ever will live. In fact, Jesus' incarnation was in many ways a mission trip led and empowered by God the Holy Spirit."[41]

Because of this, Jesus' ministry is the model for how we do mission. As Jesus contextualized, lived among people, and spoke their language, so must the church. "So there may be two kinds of churches. One kind says to its community: 'You can come to us, learn our language, our interests, and meet our needs.' The other kind says to its community: 'We will come to you, learn your language, learn your interests, meet your needs.' Which of these approaches imitates the incarnation?"[42] Churches that imitate Jesus are those that are willing to incarnate the gospel by meeting people where they are. At my home church, The Journey, our Midrash ministry (http://midrashstl.com) is dedicated to engaging culture through monthly film nights as well as monthly forums on politics, ethics, and other topics of interest in the broader culture. We also established The Luminary Center for the Arts as a way to reestablish relationship between the church and artists in St. Louis (http://theluminaryarts.com). Many Acts 29 network churches do the same.[43]

---

[40]Flemming, *Contextualization in the New Testament*, 21.
[41]Driscoll and Breshears, *Vintage Church*, 19.
[42]Keller, "Contextualization: Wisdom or Compromise?" 4.
[43]The Acts 29 church Sojourn Community Church in Louisville is reaching artists through The 930 Art Center. The 930 works to bring cultural renewal through the arts, hosting visual art exhibitions and concerts, under the framework of the doctrine of *imago Dei*—everyone is creative because everyone is made in the image of God the Creator. For more information see http://sojournchurch.com/site-management/the-930.

We see the same principle in the ministry of the apostle Paul. Paul was so zealous to win people for Christ that he was willing to adapt his methods and lifestyle in order to be as winsome as possible. He also took great care to adapt his sermon style to more effectively reach different groups of people. Because he was preaching in radically different settings, Paul adapted and communicated the gospel message differently in his different sermons. It is interesting, for example, to compare Paul's different sermons in Acts. In Acts 13 Paul preached the gospel directly and clearly to the Jews at Antioch by using the Old Testament as a pointer to the gospel.[44] In the very next chapter, Paul took the unchanging gospel to the pagan Gentiles at Lystra.[45] In that sermon Paul begged the Lystrans not to worship him and Barnabas, mere human beings, declaring to them that God is not a part of creation but is the Creator. He then appealed to something they all understood. Instead of using the revealed truth of God (the Old Testament), of which they had no knowledge, he appealed to their experience of the grace of God through rain that caused them to be able to grow crops, feed their animals, and eat.

In Acts 17 Paul encountered another unique group of people who needed to hear the gospel in their vernacular. Despite being deeply disturbed by the sin and idolatry at Athens,[46] he entered into their highly spiritual but gospel-less worldview by going to the epicenter of religious debate, the Aeropagus.[47] Paul did not simply reason in the synagogue like he did in Acts 13, nor did he just go to the streets as he did in Acts 14. Instead Paul sought out a new platform[48] at Athens, to a people who "spent their time in nothing except telling or hearing something new."[49] Paul spoke the language of these pluralistic hipsters by quoting from

---

[44]Paul quotes from the Old Testament five times during the sermon.

[45]For a great book on Paul and paganism, read Peter Jones, *Capturing the Pagan Mind: Paul's Blueprint for Thinking and Living in the New Global Culture* (Nashville: Broadman & Holman, 2003).

[46]Acts 17:16: "Now while Paul was waiting for them at Athens, his spirit was provoked within him as he saw that the city was full of idols."

[47]Matthew P. Ristuccia defines the Areopagus as "the first-century Athenian version of the editorial board of *The New York Times*: an incredibly influential set of gatekeepers for what was to be deemed urbane, thoughtful and chic. The Areopagus wore the mantle of Greek greats like Plato and Socrates and Aristotle." Cf. "Mere Christianity in Athens"; http://web.princeton.edu/sites/chapel/Sermon%20Files/2005_sermons/050105athens.htm.

[48]My friend Jonathan McIntosh has helped me with his many insights into Acts 17. He defines platform as "cultural permission."

[49]Acts 17:21.

memory two Greek poets/playwrights/philosophers: "'In him we live and move and have our being'; as even some of your own poets have said, 'For we are indeed his offspring.'"[50]

Paul wasn't just throwing out some random names in order to have "street cred." One of the philosophers he quoted was Epimenides, who hundreds of years earlier was called to help Athens during a severe plague. Supposedly it was his knowledge of the unknown god that led to the restoration of the city.[51] Paul, well versed in biblical exegesis, was also dedicated to cultural exegesis and knew enough of Athenian history to quote from the very man who introduced this unknown God to them.[52] Paul worked very hard to declare that God is Creator (v. 24), self-sufficient (v. 25), and sovereign (v. 26). But he worked equally hard to compassionately help the spiritual, but lost, Athenians to see that God was near to them and could be known by them in Christ.[53]

Paul explains his philosophy of contextualization in this important passage in 1 Corinthians:

> For though I am free from all, I have made myself a servant to all, that I might win more of them. To the Jews I became as a Jew, in order to win Jews. To those under the law I became as one under the law (though not being myself under the law) that I might win those under the law. To those outside the law I became as one outside the law (not being outside the law of God but under the law of Christ) that I might win those outside the law. To the weak I became weak, that I might win the weak. I have become all things to all people, that by all means I might save some. I do it all for the sake of the gospel, that I may share with them in its blessings. (9:19–23)

The gospel is the message of our mission, and contextualization

---

[50]Acts 17:28. These quotations are from Epimenides of Crete and Aratus respectively.

[51]Cf. Don Richardson, *Eternity in Their Hearts: Startling Evidence of Belief in the One True God in Hundreds of Cultures Throughout the World* (Ventura, CA : Regal, 2006), 17.

[52]Cf. Mark Driscoll: "As a missionary, you will need to watch television shows and movies, listen to music, read books, peruse magazines, attend events, join organizations, surf websites, and befriend people that you might not like to better understand people that Jesus loves," *The Radical Reformission*, 103.

[53]Jonathan McIntosh has helped me understand that because culture involves human beings who are glorious because of the image of God in them and yet broken because of sin, it is easy to either completely reject or completely absorb culture. In other words, it is easy to either focus entirely on the glory (image of God) of human beings or entirely on the gory aspect of human beings (depravity). Conservatives tend to focus on depravity, and liberals tend to focus on the *imago Dei*. Effective missionaries are able to maintain the tension that comes from recognizing both the beauty and the brokenness.

is the method of our mission. If, like Paul, we love the gospel (v. 23), we will, like Paul, contextualize it (vv. 19–23). We take the unchanging gospel into the ever-changing culture so that persons in a specific time and a specific culture can comprehend the truth of the gospel and be saved by it.

16
The Hands of Mission: Care

When I moved to St. Louis, I was struck by the beauty of this great city. Being an older city with a rich history, St. Louis had beautiful architecture and old-world character. But like many other Rust Belt cities, St. Louis was sucked into the vortex of urban sprawl that had left the city decimated, deserted, and swimming in racial tension.[1] I realized that planting a church in a city with this kind of history and brokenness would require a commitment to the gospel as Word but also the gospel as deed.

The Great Co-Mission

The Gospel according to Matthew closes with Jesus charging his followers to carry on the work he initiated, instructing them to:

1. Gather disciples from all nations (28:19).
2. Baptize those disciples in the name of the Father, Son, and Holy Spirit (28:19).
3. Teach the disciples to observe all that Jesus commanded (28:20).

Now, who knows whether Jesus was as succinct as Matthew's rendering of this farewell address, but our Lord did have a way of packing a lot of meaning into a few words, so this could very well have been his final speech in its totality. If you ever have a day when you are confused about what Christ wants you and the church to be about, review the last few words of Jesus in the Gospel of Matthew.

Here Jesus sums up the role his followers are to play. We are to make disciples of all peoples through our teaching and our living. Because the truths of the gospel apply to all men, women, and children from all

---

[1]See http://www.urbandictionary.com/define.php?term=rust+belt for a definition of "Rust Belt" and http://en.wikipedia.org/wiki/Urban_sprawl for a definition of "urban sprawl."

nations, and because heaven is the epitome of diversity, the result of our gathering should look, sound, and smell pretty diverse.

Once disciples are gathered, we are to baptize those disciples under the authority of the Father, Son, and Holy Spirit. This means, in a nutshell, that Jesus wants his followers to display outwardly the transformation that has occurred inwardly, which begins with the sacrament of baptism. So far Jesus has commanded nothing terribly controversial or over our heads. This is what every individual follower of Jesus and every church bearing his name is supposed to be doing.

The third point is where some confusion seems to have crept into the church. Jesus' third instruction is to teach disciples all that he commanded. But teach what? Specifically Jesus says to teach disciples to "observe" all that he commanded. A couple of things stand out in this instruction.

First, notice that Jesus is calling the church to point people to the gospel *before* doing anything regarding their behavior. The role of the church is not to create a society of well-intended, morally superior people. The church, according to Jesus, is supposed to champion the gospel and let the Holy Spirit do the work of transforming people from the inside out. For many American churches the focus has been almost exclusively on converting people to a code of Christian conduct with the hope that they will "behave" their way to salvation. This couldn't be further from the intent of the gospel of grace.

Second, Jesus is calling his disciples to learn to *observe* all that he commanded. The word "observe" here means "obey."[2] Jesus does not want his followers to settle for a head full of knowledge about theology; he wants his followers to actually obey (i.e., keep, do, live out) the revealed teaching of God's Word. And what is it that he wants us to obey? What does it mean to observe all that he commanded? Jesus summed it up with two commandments.

In Mark 12:30–31 Jesus sums up the law by explaining the two most important commandments. "'And you shall love the Lord your God with all your heart and with all your soul and with all your mind and with all your strength.' The second is this: 'You shall love your neighbor

---

[2]Study note in *ESV Study Bible* (Wheaton, IL: Crossway Bibles, 2008).

as yourself.' There is no other commandment greater than these." To observe all that Jesus commanded is primarily going to look like loving God and loving people. In other words, Jesus is calling the church to *do* something, to carry out the mission of God as the hands and feet of the resurrected and now ascended Lord of heaven and earth. And not just as a bunch of ministry renegades. Jesus is indicating that he wants the church, the unified body of all believers, to strategically seek, reach, teach, and serve people.

The story that closes this section is about how The Journey is attempting to love the Lord our God and love our neighbors as ourselves. These efforts are led by Journey pastor Josh Wilson who, before he was a pastor, was a Journey intern with a heart to do mercy ministry with the urban poor in St. Louis. Great goal, difficult task. What follows is how Pastor Josh went from being a struggling, naive intern to the founder and executive director of Mission: St. Louis. In the process he became one of the strongest leaders at The Journey. As you read, especially those of you who are attempting to address similar issues in your contexts, please recognize that our efforts are not perfect. We have not solved the problems of poverty; neighborhood stabilization; un- and underemployment; severe racial division; drug, sex, and human trafficking; and high crime rates. Nor have we even come close to solving them. What we have done is build relationships with those most in need of the healing power of the gospel, and in this process we have also grabbed the attention of many of our own Journey folks who have exchanged their nice individual pursuits of God for an opportunity to get into the nitty-gritty of loving their neighbors as themselves.

The Beginning

What does it look like to serve the city? This is the question that drove Pastor Josh's internship when he first arrived at The Journey. After two years of working with kids in the inner city prior to starting his internship, Josh saw firsthand the effects of poverty in St. Louis. With the weight of this experience, he began a mercy ministry in July 2006 at The Journey. He and the team he gathered started trying to "fix it all." Josh says, "We were involved in every kind of typical activity imaginable related to serving the poor in the city—from soup kitchens to women's shelters, to walking the late-night streets downtown in search of homeless people to evangelize, and everything in between."

After a three-month flurry of well-intended but unfocused activity, Josh realized that his team was attempting to do a lot of good things. And they were failing miserably. "We had not built any relationships, shared struggles, carried burdens, or really loved our neighbors the way we should have. We thought we knew what the poor needed without really listening to, identifying with, or knowing any of them," says Josh. He continues, "Despite all our busyness, we were not actually accomplishing anything. We were not empowering economic, social, or developmental change. Our once eager volunteers were burnt out. After trying to fix the city without a vision or a mission, we had actually done more harm than good. We didn't really know those whom we were serving, and we didn't know who Mission: St. Louis was or where we were going."

The Turning Point

Not content to fold his hands, Josh did some deep introspection about his calling and the mission God had set before him. He opened up dialogue with other leaders he trusted and began a process of radical critique of his ministry efforts. Josh prayed for God to show him and his team very clearly the direction he wanted Mission: St. Louis to go. In typical fashion, God's answer came as a surprise to Josh and the team.

The turning point came in the midst of yet another project—a school supply drive for several elementary schools, including Adams Elementary in the Forest Park Southeast neighborhood, located a half mile from The Journey's south city campus. Josh recounts the day he delivered the supplies to Adams.

"The day we delivered supplies, we were met with a gratitude and hospitality that left an impression on us. After dropping off supplies at a few other schools, we felt a very strong feeling that God wanted us to go back to Adams." And so began a relationship between Adams Elementary and Mission: St. Louis. Josh asked the Adams staff about their dreams for the school. The staff was more than happy to share.

Adams Principal Jeanetta Stegall's first response was that they would

love for Mission: St. Louis to help out with school supplies again the following year. Josh pushed for more, asking, "If you could have anything you
wanted, what would it be?" The reply came immediately. She dreamed of
a school where children (her "babies," she called them) were able to read
and had the family support at home to help them succeed. She dreamed
of having male role models in the neighborhood to teach boys how to be
men and girls how they should be treated as women. She dreamed of a
school where families weren't being forced to move because of rising rent
and gentrification. Ultimately her dreams were like those of any other
school administrator—that Adams Elementary would be a place where
every child had a more than decent shot at reaching his or her potential.

Principal Stegall continued to reveal not only serious concerns
about literacy rates in the neighborhood, but she also acknowledged the
increase of family displacement as gentrification of the neighborhood
was reaching its peak. By the close of 2006, Forest Park Southeast saw
rehabbed homes being flipped at a rate of two per day, forcing families
who had spent their whole lives in the neighborhood to move to Section
8 housing in completely different parts of the Metro area. Stegall also
pointed to the lack of men in the neighborhood, commenting that "the
only male role models my kids see are the dealers on the corners and the
hip-hoppers on TV."

As he listened, Josh began to see that there was much more to
this relationship than he had first realized. It turned out that Adams
Elementary was the hub of the Forest Park Southeast neighborhood.
If there was a neighborhood event, it was promoted by and housed
in Adams. If you wanted to know the real problems of the families in
Forest Park Southeast, you asked the teachers and administration at
Adams. In other words, if you wanted to make an impact in that neigh-
borhood, you had to begin by making an impact at Adams Elementary.

Armed with new direction and enthusiasm, Josh and Mission: St.
Louis decided to put all their eggs in one basket. Instead of scattering
their influence all over the city, they decided to put all their financial
and people resources into Adams Elementary and Forest Park Southeast
in the hopes that they would help transform that neighborhood, then
transform the neighborhood next to that, and so on.

"We'd found a school that was inviting, and a neighborhood that was facing tough issues like poverty and gentrification," says Josh. "We began to study and learn how to serve in a way that dealt with the root of these issues. We stopped haphazardly working all over the city and began to narrow our focus and put all our resources into one specific community. We needed a place where we had a relationship that could be built on, where we could really get to know people and their needs, and where we could work toward true community development. For us, that became Forest Park Southeast."

Forest Park Southeast (FPSE)

The first major obstacle for Mission: St. Louis was the fact that they knew very little about their newfound ministry context. They knew the physical location and boundaries that defined the neighborhood, and they were developing what looked like a very fruitful relationship with Adams Elementary. But that was it, and it was not enough to do effective gospel-driven ministry. The team began to do their homework. They hit the streets to converse with the experts of the neighborhood—those who lived there. More specifically, they sought out people who had lived in FPSE for a long time. They gathered anecdotal and observational information, as well as consulting census data and survey results from state and city officials. The results gave Josh and his team a revealing look into the neighborhood where God had called them to serve.

"A hundred years ago, St. Louis was a booming city, population 575,000—one of the largest in the nation," says Josh. He's right. During the 1950s population in St. Louis proper peaked at 857,000. However, the white flight of most American population centers was no different in St. Louis. Middle- and upper-income families moved out of the urban center in order to develop the suburbs commercially and residentially, leaving behind many lower-income city dwellers. Poverty increased, and crime levels rose. Population numbers in 2000 reached new lows at 348,000. Today this trend has begun to shift, with city population rising 0.7 percent between 2000–2007, a significant fact given the previous fifty years of rapid decline. Still, St. Louis faces higher poverty and crime rates than the state as a whole, and in 2006

CBS News reported that St. Louis was ranked "Most Dangerous City" in the United States.[3]

In so many ways FPSE is a microcosm of the plight of St. Louis. According to the census data from 2000, 70 percent of residents of FPSE are African-American. The average age of residents in the FPSE neighborhood in the year 2000 was twenty-two, which is fourteen years younger than the state average (thirty-six) and ten years younger than the city as a whole (thirty-two). The same census showed that the majority of the housing stock in the Forest Park Southeast neighborhood was renter-occupied (66 percent). This rental occupancy rate is higher than both the city and state rental rates of 53 percent and 30 percent respectively. Such statistics, while not necessarily compelling by themselves, give a basic sketch of the neighborhood. Other statistics go deeper.

One of the most shocking statistics that Josh and Mission: St. Louis uncovered gave a stunning look into the economic deterioration of FPSE. The poverty rate in FPSE is 36 percent, which is higher than the St. Louis city rate of 25 percent and the state rate of 12 percent. "In 2007, FPSE had a population of 3,670 individuals, 36% of whom are below poverty level. Our target population is the 1,321 people living below the poverty line, though we understand that real community-level change will involve engaging the other 2,349 residents as well. In the last year, we served over 585 people, which is 44% of the target population," says Pastor Josh.

Making the poverty stats even more troubling is the fact that 35 percent of the FPSE residents over the age of twenty-five have not completed high school, a rate double that of the state rate. The needs for economic stability and increased education became clear immediately. Further still, a survey conducted during the fall semester of 2003 by the Missouri Department of Elementary and Secondary Education asked parents a variety of questions about themselves, their home lives, and their children's school performance. The survey at Adams Elementary School, located in the heart of FPSE, was completed by 189 parents: 82 percent of the survey participants were the mothers, 6 percent were the fathers, 3 percent were the grandmothers, and 8 percent were other rela-

---

[3]Study compiled by Mario Quinto Press and reported by CBS News; http://www.cbsnews.com/stories/2006/10/30/national/main2135998.shtml.

tives. These statistics seemed to confirm the anecdotal evidence gathered by Josh and his team, indicating that the fathers of FPSE were nowhere to be found. Here is more data indicating that the families of FPSE are severely in need:

- 57 percent of households have only one wage earner, 16 percent have no wage earners;
- 25 percent of parents say their child watches more than four hours of TV daily;
- 62 percent of households are single-parent homes;
- 61 percent of families do not have a computer at home;
- 68 percent of families do not have access to the Internet at home;
- 90 percent of students qualify for free or reduced lunch programs.

Not surprisingly, the academic needs of the students are great. Adams Elementary is part of the St. Louis Public School system. School officials self-report that the school has not made Adequate Yearly Progress (AYP) for three consecutive years. Test scores from the school represent the degree to which the students are not achieving their potential. The sixth graders scored a 15 percent on the math portion of the Missouri Assessment Program (MAP) test in 2007, while the state average was 49 percent. Further, sixth graders scored only 5 percent on the communication arts portion, while the state average was 44 percent. The academic needs of the students at Adams Elementary go unmet, putting them at risk for underachievement and, later, dropping out. "At-risk youth,"[4] as defined by the National Association for Gifted Children, describes "students whose economic, physical, emotional, or academic needs go unmet or serve as barriers to talent recognition or development, thus putting them in danger of underachieving or dropping out." The students of Adams Elementary School meet this definition.

With a very clear understanding of some of the most pressing needs in FPSE, Mission: St. Louis began developing strategies to meet them.

Meeting the Needs

The sum of the evidence brought to the fore three specific areas that needed attention in FPSE. Mission: St. Louis began developing strategies

---

[4]See http://www.nagc.org, http://txgifted.org/gifted–glossary.

and programs to confront under-education, gospel-centered empowerment, and economic instability. The result now is that Mission: St. Louis operates programs grounded in measurable success indicators and best practices, thus ensuring a greater likelihood of achieving the best possible results. Below is a glance at how Mission: St. Louis is addressing some of the most pressing needs in FPSE.[5]

Education

Morning Reading Program

The Morning Reading Program (MRP) was designed by a graduate-level reading specialist and Journey member, Brandy Greiner, in consultation with literacy coaches in the St. Louis Public Schools. The program utilizes the six pillars of literacy: phonemic awareness, phonics, fluency, vocabulary, flow, and reading comprehension. Volunteers spend the majority of the twenty-five to thirty minutes reading with the children, and once per month they give each student a book to take home. During the remaining time with the students, volunteers focus on teaching phonemic awareness and higher-level comprehension skills that students may not receive at home or as often in the classroom.

Adopt-a-Classroom

This program is a direct result of a plea from teachers and administrators at Adams Elementary for help in the classrooms. Since research resoundingly shows that smaller class sizes yield better learning, Adopt-a-Classroom provides teachers with a volunteer dedicated to a particular classroom for at least one hour per week. [6]

Empowerment

An Affordable Christmas

The hallmark empowerment event for Mission: St. Louis is An Affordable Christmas. In previous years The Journey participated in holiday programs that were entirely charity-based. Volunteers bought

[5]For more detailed information on these and other Mission: St. Louis ministries, please visit http://www.missionstl.org.
[6]F. Mosteller, "The Tennessee Study of Class Size in the Early School Grades," *The Future of Children: Critical Issues for Children and Youths*, Vol. 5, No. 2 (1995), 113–127.

gifts and delivered them to the families. Pastor Josh noticed something that wasn't quite right on one such delivery run. "I noticed that the kids, moms, grandmas were ecstatic—smiling, laughing, crying, the whole nine yards. But the dads, if they were even there, did their best to sneak out the back door," he says. What Josh picked up on was shame. While charity was helpful in providing a decent Christmas for lots of kids, it was terrible at building up and empowering people in general and men in particular.

Inspired by a program developed by Bob Lupton,[7] Josh set out to change things. Working with the Department of Family Services to identify low-income households in FPSE and surrounding neighborhoods, and using thousands of gifts donated by Journey members and regular attenders, Affordable Christmas focuses on empowerment rather than on charity. It provides low-income parents an opportunity to shop and purchase gifts for their children at a low cost. Christmas is transformed for these families from a holiday filled with dread, worry, and disappointment to one of hope, joy, and pride. And all the money collected from toy sales goes right back into the FPSE neighborhood. In 2008 the third annual Affordable Christmas served eighty families and three hundred children, with help from over six hundred and fifty volunteers.

Cross the Street

Two days a week, volunteers walk around the neighborhood meeting people through a program called Cross the Street (CTS). The six to eight volunteers meet at a home in the neighborhood, and for approximately ninety minutes they actively engage community members in real, meaningful conversation.

Community Bible Study

After walking through the neighborhood during Cross the Street, volunteers meet for a Community Bible Study (CBS). CBS takes place in the homes of FPSE families and is led by indigenous community leaders

---

[7]Robert D. Lupton, *Compassion, Justice and the Christian Life: Rethinking Ministry to the Poor* (Ventura, CA: Regal Books, 2007), previously published as *And You Call Yourself a Christian*.

whenever possible. These weekly studies teach through books of the Bible, with assistance from volunteer leaders from The Journey.

Economic Development

As Josh brought the needs of FPSE to our attention, we sought "out-of-the-box" approaches to meeting them. One of the ideas that came out of that thinking was to get our community groups on mission in FPSE. We launched a new service in a recently renovated space on our campus in South City and invited fifteen of our groups to commit to this service. The purpose was for them to worship together three weekends a month and serve in FPSE on the other weekend. We wanted to be able to say once a month, "The church has left the building."

The very first Community Work Day was a roaring success. After consulting with a local day care with a huge list of necessary physical improvements, the agenda was set. More than a hundred and fifty volunteers worked all day that Sunday replacing windows, painting rooms, laying carpet, landscaping, and constructing a playground for the day care. In all, more than $30,000 worth of labor and materials was donated that day. Not only did the improvements bring a sense of satisfaction for volunteers and folks in FPSE, but many who had no prior connection to FPSE saw firsthand the needs of this hurting community. The workday also sent a message that FPSE is a community of people who are fighting to revive and care for their community.

The future includes more workdays to help homeowners maintain their homes and improve their neighborhood through beautification projects. At the time of this writing, plans are underway to establish a doughnut and coffee shop in the neighborhood in order to provide jobs and a safe haven for authentic community-oriented relationships to grow. The ultimate goal is to empower neighborhoods to be economically healthy, sustainable communities.

Loving God and Neighbor

Mission: St. Louis is not perfect. It took years of failed attempts at doing every imaginable mercy ministry before we realized that something more specific was needed, not just for FPSE but for The Journey as well. "We needed focus, we needed direction," says Josh. "We had all the heart in the world and no eyes to see what was in our own backyard. Once God switched on the light for us, and we were able to see that our resources are best used in long-term relationships, we've been able to at least draw attention to the struggles of living in FPSE, and we've been able to serve some families out of a gospel motivation."

It's tempting for churches to focus on *either* social justice *or* evangelism. After all, Christians naturally lean toward one or the other as a primary expression of the gospel. But the gospel promotes both; it is evangelism *and* social justice. It is loving God and loving neighbor. That's a hard line to walk. Mission: St. Louis has remained firmly in the tension by hiring staff that represent both ends of the spectrum. Some staff are evangelism-driven, while others are social-justice-driven. The results have been promising. As we close this section on the mission of God, I want you to encounter a longtime resident of FPSE. Mr. Ben Jefferson (name changed by request) is a man not unlike the apostle Paul in many ways. He is a man whose life was marked by hostility toward the gospel and toward those who championed it. He was a rebel who answered to no one and did what he wanted when he wanted to do it.

Then he met Jesus. This is his story.

The story actually begins not with Ben Jefferson but with a Mission: St. Louis volunteer named James Allen. James joined Mission: St. Louis because he liked the idea of entering into the brokenness of the city, and he had hopes of participating in its restoration. He entered FPSE as a Cross the Street volunteer with slightly better than a Pollyannaish view of ministry and rose-colored glasses firmly secured to his face. As a middle-aged white man who sells widgets for a living, James is in many ways the last person you'd expect to see walking the streets of FPSE. If his skin color didn't make him stand out, then certainly his pocket protector did. (Yes, he actually wears a pocket protector!)

But James learned quickly that it's one thing to value community development in your mind and another entirely to value it with your feet as you walk up and down some of the most dangerous streets in the city. "James told me he was scared to death when he first began walking the streets in FPSE," says Pastor Josh. "He was afraid for his physical safety for sure, and after meeting Ben Jefferson, he was afraid for his spiritual safety," Josh laughs.

James wasn't laughing then, though. He met Ben Jefferson on one of his twice-a-week walks through the neighborhood. Ben was a formidable presence in the neighborhood. In his mid-sixties, Ben was known for his strong personality, which is a nice way of saying that Ben had the mouth of a French sailor and gave tongue-lashings to anyone who got too close to his property. Like a grumpy old centurion, Ben sat on his porch all spring and summer guarding his property, sucking down straight vodka or gin, and smoking Kools. Would-be trespassers were also kept at bay by the locked gate at the sidewalk in front of Ben's house.

As James became familiar with the neighborhood, he realized that Ben was always on his porch, no matter the day or time James walked by. He decided to strike up a conversation with Ben. "Hi there. My name's Jim. I'd like to talk to you about God," he said. It was a bold opening line that was met by an even bolder response from Ben. "You don't want to talk to me about God," roared Ben, "'cause I'm the Devil!" James nearly soiled himself, but even in that moment of fear and discomfort he knew he'd be back.

Asking others in the neighborhood for more information on Ben, James discovered that Ben's wife had recently left him. He had six or seven children and grandchildren numbering in the twenties. Ben had been addicted to crack cocaine for at least twenty-five years and was also an abuser of alcohol. He was unemployed, enslaved to bad habits and worse choices, and angry. James kept walking by Ben's house twice a week, and on every walk he tried to engage Ben in conversation about God. He was met with insults and once by an empty gin bottle hurled in his direction. Undaunted, James continued his pursuit of a meaningful conversation with this man.

Three months in, James was surprised one day when Ben actually gave him permission to open the gate and walk into his yard. James jumped at the chance. He wasn't allowed on the porch, of course, but a minor victory was still a victory in James's mind. The two men engaged in a vague conversation about James's purpose for being in the neighborhood and general topics regarding spirituality and the Bible. James left encouraged. The next visit, Ben invited James onto the porch, and as the two talked James was able to share the story of his own heart transformation upon his encounter with Jesus. Over the course of the conversation, James saw Ben's demeanor soften, and his language become more personal and vulnerable, allowing James to peek inside this cantankerous man's mess of a life. It was beautiful!

James learned that Ben was a deeply wounded man. He missed his wife. He was greatly disappointed and gravely concerned about the physical safety and health of his sons, who were mired in the drug trade. He longed to work a job again. He was tired of being a slave to crack and alcohol. In short, he was miserable. His rough exterior was the result of poor choices, rebellion, bitterness, addiction, anger, skepticism, and hopelessness, and the more he talked, the more James realized that Ben needed more than just a friend, good advice, and a listening ear. Those things were important, but what Ben needed was a rescue. More specifically, what Ben needed was a Rescuer.

So James shared the gospel—the true gospel of grace. He talked about how we can experience freedom from our sin and bad choices because of what Jesus did on the cross. He explained that Christianity is not about how much good we can muster up in order to please God; rather, it is about the One who lived a perfectly obedient life because of our inability to do so, the One who died a death on our behalf so we could objectively know God's love for us and subjectively experience forgiveness.

In the midst of the conversation, somewhere deep in his mind and even deeper in his heart, Ben gave up. He was brought to an end of himself. Ben got off the treadmill of self-effort, owned up to his wickedness, and like a child who needs comforting when he scrapes his knee, Ben accepted the comforting bear hug of his Father.

Things began to change rapidly for Ben. Not only did the gospel flame spark in his head and heart, but it actually lit his bones. Like Jeremiah, Ben was called to do something with the salvation he'd experienced. Within four months, Ben was completely sober (and still is!), his wife had moved back in, he was employed, he was attending The

Journey weekly, and he was reading his Bible voraciously. "I've heard of Genesis and Revelation," Ben said with a smile, "but none of the stuff in between!"

Ben also made an immediate connection with his new love for Jesus and his longtime love for his neighborhood. Ben approached Mission: St. Louis with an idea. "We need to move this Bible study into my house," he said very matter-of-factly one day to Josh. So that's what happened. An indigenous leader was born, and he hosted ten people every Tuesday for a Bible study at his house. It started with Ben, a couple of neighbors, and a whole bunch of young white kids from seminary. One night, after a few more new FPSE neighbors had accepted Ben's invitation, Ben spoke like a fiery prophet to the group. "What we're doing here doesn't make any sense if these white people keep coming in here and hitting the streets, meeting people if we aren't gonna do the same thing." He'd laid down the gauntlet. And the neighborhood responded. The Bible study grew. Within a few months Ben's house could no longer hold all those who were attending on Monday nights. "We had people standing on the porch, listening and looking through the open windows," describes Pastor Josh. "It was a beautiful thing." At the time of writing this, the Bible study in FPSE has seventy-five attendees on Monday and Tuesday nights.

Since his conversion, life for Ben hasn't been easy. His departure from the kingdom of death into the kingdom of light has not resulted in a tidy, comfortable life. Marriage is still a struggle at times. He's still sober, but his kids haven't necessarily laid down their addictions. Ben was even called to account by fellow Mission: St. Louis volunteers for coming down too hard on some of the neighborhood thugs he's trying to reach—how's that for irony! Life isn't perfect for Ben. But it is *life*. Real life, with purpose, meaningful relationships, freedom and forgiveness from sin, and contentment that comes with the realization that his bad choices, and even his good deeds, don't have the final word on how it all turns out. The final word belongs to Jesus. And Ben belongs to him.

17
The Hope of Mission: City Transformation

My friend Matt Carter[1] and I often talk about our desire to be "good preachers in great churches" rather than just being "great preachers in a good church." This distinction is the heart's desire of the men in Acts 29: to show the beauty of the gospel through the church, not just the communication gifts of the pastor.[2] In the same vein, we desire not just to have great churches but to have better cities. "Would your city weep if your church did not exist?" This is one of the most haunting and challenging questions that I have processed over the last few years. Many of our churches indicate in their mission statements that their desire is to be a church not just *in* the city but *for* the city.

The reality is that some in our cities would weep if our churches weren't there—they would weep tears of joy! They do not see the church, even in its purest form, as a blessing to their city but rather as a curse in their city. This is the reality Paul and Silas faced when they came to Thessalonica. To the Jews who had gathered at the synagogue, Paul preached the Old Testament's central focus—the suffering and resurrection of Christ.[3] Many came to faith that day because of Paul's gospel-centered exegesis from the Scriptures, which regularly happens when Christ is expounded as the hero of the Bible. Another consequence of this clear gospel-centered preaching, however, was that a riot ensued and several people in that great city wanted to kill Paul and Silas.[4]

I certainly acknowledge that when the church clearly proclaims the truth of God's Word, many in our great cities will hate us and desire

---

[1]Matt is the pastor of an Acts 29 church called Austin Stone Community Church; http://www.austinstone.org.
[2]Cf. Ephesians 3:10: "so that through the church the manifold wisdom of God might now be made known to the rulers and authorities in the heavenly places."
[3]Acts 17:1–4.
[4]Acts 17:5–10.

our demise because of our declaration of the gospel. My purpose in this chapter is to talk about the other side of the equation: although our declaration of the gospel by proclamation might incite a riot in our city, our declaration of the gospel by demonstration might actually endear people to the gospel.

City Realities

Let's look at some facts about how cities function today across the globe. The growth of cities is one of the most noteworthy changes in the last few hundred years.

About half of the world's population currently lives in cities. In 1800 only 3 percent of the world's population lived in urban areas.[5] More than 160,000 people move to cities every day.[6]

Just two centuries ago, there were only two "million cities" worldwide (that is, cities with one million or more inhabitants)—London and Beijing (Peking). By 1950 there were eighty; today there are over three hundred. Most of these million cities are in Africa, Asia, and Latin America, and many have populations that have grown more than tenfold since 1950. Brasilia, the capital of Brazil, did not exist in 1950 and now has more than two million inhabitants.

Mega-cities, having ten or more million inhabitants, are a new phenomenon. The first city to reach this size was New York City around 1940. There were twelve mega-cities by 1990, and as of this printing there are twenty-five. By 2015 experts expect the number of global mega-cities to be nearly forty, twenty-three of which will be in Asia. By contrast, in 1800 the average size of the world's hundred largest cities was fewer than two hundred thousand inhabitants, but now it is over five million.[7]

While some people see this trend toward urbanization as a bad thing, and cities as inherently dirty and dangerous, the migration to cities is actually a positive feature of globalization. The concentration of people in cities provides opportunities for improving health and

---

[5] See http://www.prb.org/Educators/TeachersGuides/HumanPopulation/Urbanization.aspx.
[6] See http://www.unep.org/geo2000/english/0049.htm.
[7] See http://www.ippnw.org/Resources/MGS/V6N2Schubel.html.

environmental quality. Urbanization is much more environmentally and economically efficient.[8]

City Posture

When God's people found themselves in a foreign land because of their sin, they were tempted to avoid getting involved in the city, to avoid contagion by removing themselves from the culture and from the people in the city.

> Thus says the LORD of hosts, the God of Israel, to all the exiles whom I have sent into exile from Jerusalem to Babylon: Build houses and live in them; plant gardens and eat their produce. Take wives and have sons and daughters; take wives for your sons, and give your daughters in marriage, that they may bear sons and daughters; multiply there, and do not decrease. But seek the welfare of the city where I have sent you into exile, and pray to the LORD on its behalf, for in its welfare you will find your welfare. (Jeremiah 29:4–7)

From this passage, I think we can glean a few principles that will help us as we seek to bring the gospel to our respective cities.

Plant Yourself Deep in Your City

God, through the prophets, instructs his people in a foreign city to construct houses that they will live in, to plant gardens, and to eat its harvest. It takes time to build a house. It takes time to plant and tend a garden. It seems to me that God is commanding his people to sink themselves deep into the fabric of that wicked city.

To build a house is to choose to be a neighbor to people in the city. One of the most tragic things I have repeatedly heard is that Christians are bad tippers. I have talked to numerous waiters and waitresses over the years who have confirmed that their least favorite people are Christians because they tend to be rude, demanding, and stingy. If this is true of us when we eat for two hours in a restaurant, what must we be like in the place where we reside for most of the hours of our days? If we are bad tippers, what kind of neighbors are we?

---

[8]See http://www.pubmedcentral.nih.gov/articlerender.fcgi?artid=1118907.

It is strange the way many Christians give so much money every year to foreign mission efforts without ever considering the need to be a missionary right in their own neighborhoods. What would happen if we actually started seeing ourselves as missionaries to the people who live around us by being good neighbors? What would it be like if everyone in the neighborhood knew that if there was a need for peacemaking, kindness, hospitality, or refuge, they could come to our residence to find it? What would happen if we really tried to be like salt and light[9] to the people living around us?

The instruction to plant a garden could be applied to our need to participate in "producing" for the city. An application of this is that we can actually contribute to the cultural goods of the city by involving ourselves in the soil of what makes the city the city. As Richard Mouw notes, "the directive to 'fill the earth' (Genesis 1:28) is not primarily a reproductive command. The 'filling' of the earth is a cultural activity."[10] We are directed by this mandate to cultivate the raw materials of the earth and to subdue and exercise dominion over it by developing a God-glorifying culture. This is the heart of what it means to be a Christian in culture: to participate in the creation and development of God-glorifying relationships, organizations, academies, guilds, and businesses.

Consider the implications of this. As Christians start businesses, they are able to provide jobs for people in the city as well as provide needed goods and services that enable people in the city to enjoy life. As Christians work in academia, we are able to influence the young men and women who will be the movers and shakers of the city in the coming generations. As Christians work in corporations and media, we are able to be at the center of that which exerts an inordinate amount of influence on our cities. Cultural production equals cultural influence. "Culture, then, is any and all human effort and labor expended upon the cosmos to unearth its treasures and its riches and bring them into the service of man for the enrichment of human existence unto the glory of God."[11]

We have an opportunity to get into the very soil that grows the cul-

---

[9]Cf. Matthew 5:13–16.
[10]Quoted in Henry R. Van Til, *The Calvinistic Concept of Culture* (Grand Rapids: Baker, 1972), xiii.
[11]Van Til, *The Calvinistic Concept of Culture*, 29–30.

tural catalysts of our cities by being involved in all the various fields of culture. This means that people in our churches should be professors in local universities, researchers and physicians in our local hospitals, musicians in local bands, artists in local galleries, writers in local media, and politicians in local government. As we participate in culture, we will gain the cultural power now enjoyed by many who are hostile to the church. Many in the city will be more likely to listen to the message of the church because the members have invested themselves so deeply in the city. We can go from simply protesting all that is wrong in the city to actually bringing righteousness to the city. We can move from being among the many who are recognized as problem-finders in the city to being the ones who are recognized as problem-solvers in the city.

Multiply in the City

In what has been called the cultural mandate, Adam and Eve were called to "be fruitful and multiply and fill the earth" to have kids who loved God and to develop a God-glorifying culture.[12] Certainly this command was unique in some ways to Adam and Eve as the first parents of the human race and should not be taken to imply that every family should be large. However, it is interesting that God instructs his people through Jeremiah to have children in a hostile city as a way of influencing it for good. Could it be that one of the main ways we could influence our city is by having more kids? And not just more kids, but God-loving and city-serving kids?[13]

Previously Ethan Burmeister, the father of two, would have said the latter, but two years after a "procedure," God spoke to him about the blessings of children, and he now celebrates with his wife and their *four* children the joy of God's blessing. Here is his story:

The Bible says children are a blessing. I acknowledged that fact intellectually and theologically after having two children, but I didn't really believe it. The way I acted, my fundamental belief structure and core functional patterns showed that I really was a secularist and believed that

---

[12]Genesis 1:28.

[13]I am not saying that everyone should have a certain number of children or that you are more spiritual if you have kids. For a good discussion on the question of birth control see Question 9 of Mark Driscoll's *Religion Saves* (Wheaton, IL: Crossway, 2009).

children were a curse. I had two great kids. Beautiful blue eyes, blond curls, and spunky. That was enough. The American Dream. Why have more? If you analyzed the practical reasons I could give, like time and money, it sounded fine. I had, however, a lens that was really based on personal convenience, ease, and I frankly wanted to limit my hassles.

I had been married four years to a beautiful wife, we had two children, a mortgage, had recently planted a new church, and we were busy. When my wife asked how many more children I wanted, I turned the question back on her. She said she wanted to adopt someday, but felt very satisfied in where we were. I asked myself, "We were still under the health care plan from our former church, so why not get 'it' done?" I had friends say it was the key to good sex. No more worries, hassles, questions, protections . . . but it all seemed so permanent.

I called for an appointment. They told me it was a quick procedure. You come in like you are, forty-five minutes later you're shaved, shorn, lacerated, packed in ice and on your way . . . with a limp. The morning of the event my wife said, "Are you sure? I'm having second thoughts." Wives can be so temperamental. She was obviously having an emotional reaction, and we should go with the sane decision we had made weeks earlier.

Accidentally getting tagged in the genitals during a sporting event is one thing. Every man knows what I mean: the pass bearing down on you by surprise—way too low—the impact. Then—wait for it, not yet, NOW—the shooting pain rocketing through your nervous system, the involuntary reflex of covering up seconds too late, and the residue of a gnawing feeling of nausea as your vision goes gray and you wonder if you're going to black out. Accidents are one thing, they sneak up on you, you don't see them coming. Voluntarily going in for a massive groin shot with knives is another. I'm the kind of guy who doesn't even like car keys in my pocket because of the proximity. I remember pulling into the parking lot not only *knowing* what was coming but *asking* them to do it to me and paying them for it. Was I out of my mind? "I really love my wife," I said to myself as I stepped foot into the clinic.

I was led into a room bathed in white light. It was like a dinner party at Hannibal Lecter's house. A stainless-steel table covered in white linen especially for me, the guest, was laid out with the utensils of the meal ready to go. The nurse frightened me. She was old enough to be my grandmother. She walked with a swagger like Steve McQueen in *The Magnificent Seven*. In my memory, her face had a snarl. "Get on the table," she said. I hoped she would treat me favorably. She did the "preparation work" thoroughly. Fear gripped me as I was tempted to make a break for it, and they began to aim all the lights at my midsection. I began my cold sweat.

I honestly prayed in that moment for protection from evil forces. I had a sinking feeling as it all began, but I rolled over like a deer surrendering to its pack of hunters as they dig into its flesh. The nurses could sense my apprehension and began to make chitchat about the weather and other pleasantries. Why do they do that? Does some class on patient care cover that? Newsflash: talking about weather or golf doesn't make an operation on your privates go better. The doctor even began telling jokes as he cauterized the tubes and the smoke began to roll up into the air. Were my eyes deceiving me? Was it the medication? My crotch was on fire! I esteemed myself as a good lover to my wife, but nothing ever like this. Afterward I hobbled out to the car and gently, with a capital G, sat down.

I was sitting in my study two years later studying the Genesis account of creation. God created the world in splendor and majesty. He placed our father Adam in the garden with all of the animals, but no suitable helper was found. God gave his son a beautiful wife. He commissioned the couple and issued the cultural mandate to mankind, commanding that they would be fruitful and multiply. The word "fruitful" leapt off the page. Times like this in their clarity and power don't happen every day. But I sensed a personal address in the thoughts that came to my head. "I care about children. They are a blessing and not a curse. The decision you made was not out of prayer and faith but out of convenience. You have severed one of the primary means for my blessing on your life." I don't think this is the application for every couple or every situation, and life is not handed to us in a box with an instruction manual—God was speaking to me personally. I was gripped with shame and hope at the same time. When I told my wife what I had sensed, she cried and said, "I've been feeling the same way for months, but I was waiting for God to tell you, because you needed to hear it from him."

It's one thing to repent and admit when you've made a mistake, and it's another to have to pay thousands of dollars and be operated on in your most vulnerable area to show the fruit of your repentance. We got exactly the amount we needed for the reversal on our tax return that year, and we found a world-renowned specialist who "just happened" to practice a few blocks away from our home.

When I dedicated our daughter Anna at church a year later, I explained that Anna means "God is gracious." We also have a son named Samuel, which means "God hears."

Four children are a lot to handle in an urban context, and life hasn't gotten easier, but I'm filled with an inexpressible joy for the decision we've made and for God's blessings on us as we follow him. The missionary and martyr Jim Elliot said that children are arrows in a quiver, and they are to be trained as missionaries and shot at the Devil. My hope is that my two boys and two girls will be great for God as extensions of the kingdom to a lost and dying world.

Be a Blessing in the City

"But seek the welfare of the city where I have sent you into exile, and pray to the LORD on its behalf, for in its welfare you will find your welfare" (Jeremiah 29:7).

Peter, in his first epistle, challenged his readers who were being persecuted for their faith to embrace the reality that they were resident aliens, visitors in the hostile city of Rome. They were "sojourners and exiles," which meant they were to hold onto their faith distinctives in the context of the culture in which they found themselves. They were to remain faithful to the truth but focus on good for the city. We see this paradox here:

> Beloved, I urge you as sojourners and exiles to abstain from the passions of the flesh, which wage war against your soul. Keep your conduct among the Gentiles honorable, so that when they speak against

you as evildoers, they may see your good deeds and glorify God on the day of visitation. (1 Peter 2:11–12)

Peter is telling the church to abstain from the desires of the flesh (no doubt aroused and encouraged by the city) by keeping their behavior holy among the people in the city. He is challenging the church not to assimilate into the culture but to be countercultural and distinct in all of its behavior. As the church is living a distinctly Christian lifestyle, it will be persecuted like the one whom they are trying to emulate. No matter how pure our motivations, no matter how much good we do, no matter how kind and compassionate our service, the church will be persecuted just as its Savior was.[14]

Peter is also saying that one of the ways the gospel moves forward in a hostile city is when the church does "good deeds." In context, "good deeds" seems to refer to being a good citizen in the city. Peter is saying that when the church lives courageous, generous, and virtuous kingdom lives, the citizens of the city may want to know the King who has inspired such deeds.[15] This means that when we encounter culture, we seek to be a blessing to the people in the culture. We have a unique and distinct identity as those who have been showered by grace; therefore we will seek to shower the city with grace as we sacrificially serve and work in it.

Jeremiah seems to be saying that as God's people seek the welfare or *shalom* of the city, they will be benefited by the city. This almost certainly refers to social and economic benefits. So Jeremiah is not just saying that we should seek the spiritual welfare of the city, but also the financial and social welfare of the city. What Jeremiah and Peter seem to be saying is that God's people should be great citizens of their wicked cities. They can be this because they are aliens—distinct and separate from the unbiblical values of the city, but engaged and connected to the common grace elements within the city, hoping to make the city a great place to live for all peoples.

Being a blessing to the city means that we don't adopt the culture and simply resemble the city lifestyle. This was the Babylonian plan for

---

[14]For more info on the persecuted church, see http://www.persecution.com.
[15]Richard Mouw notes that because of common grace even the unredeemed have "impulses toward justice and efforts for the common good." Quoted in Van Til, *The Calvinistic Concept of Culture*, xiii.

God's exiled people. Their plan is best seen with Daniel and his friends. The Babylonians tried to get Daniel and his friends to adopt their culture by giving them fine food and by indoctrinating them in their philosophy and religion.[16] The Babylonians changed the names of Daniel and his three friends.

Figure 17-1

Daniel: God is my judge	Belteshazzar: keeper of the treasures of Bel
Hananiah: Yahweh is God	Shadrach: inspiration of the sun (sun worship)
Mishael: who belongs to God	Meshach: of the goddess Shaca (Venus worship)
Azariah: Yahweh helps	Abednego: servant of the fire

Not only were the names of these young men of God changed, but they were changed to the names of Babylonian gods. This was no doubt a tactic to get them to lose their spiritual identity as worshippers of the one, true God and to begin building their identity on pagan deities. In a very similar manner, the city will press us to adopt its culture, its doctrines, and its gods. The good news of the gospel is that we do not have to compromise biblical truth to be a blessing to the city.

Being a blessing to the city doesn't mean that we form an enclave and withdraw from the city in order to be pure. This was the false prophets' plan for God's exiled people in Jeremiah 28, when Hananiah falsely prophesied that the exile would only last two years (not seventy as Jeremiah prophesied). This false prophecy would discourage God's people from sinking roots deep into the city as God commanded. Likewise, there will be tremendous pressure on us to simply create a subculture in the city and thus avoid the pain and the problems of the city. The good news of the gospel is that we can enter into the culture of the city and become agents of transformation.

Being a blessing to the city means we take seriously the problems of the city. The gospel does not just need to be in word but also in deed.[17] We most certainly need to be faithful to creeds that define historical orthodoxy, but we also need gospel-motivated deeds if we are to faith-

---

[16]Daniel 1–2.
[17]2 John 3:18.

fully proclaim the gospel. Richard Stearns argues that when Jesus rein-
terpreted the messianic prophecy of Isaiah 61 in Luke 4:18–19 he was
saying that the message of the kingdom wasn't less that the proclamation
of the good news for personal conversion but that it was much more. It
involves helping the sick, "recovering of sight to the blind," bringing justice, "set[ting] at liberty those who are oppressed." Stearns, the president
of World Vision, says it this way:

> Proclaiming the whole gospel . . . encompasses tangible compassion
> for the sick and the poor, as well as biblical justice, efforts to right the
> wrongs that are so prevalent in our world. God is concerned about
> the spiritual, physical, and social dimensions of our being. The whole
> gospel is truly good news for the poor, and it is the foundation for a
> social revolution that has the power to change the world. And if this
> was Jesus' mission, it is also the mission of all who claim to follow
> him. It is my mission, it is your mission, and it is the mission of the
> church.[18]

The basis for the Christian's desire for the city to be renewed
culturally, socially, and spiritually is rooted in the past through the
resurrection of Jesus Christ and in the future rising of all believers
in Christ. The resurrection is a foretaste of what God wants to do.
He doesn't simply throw out the old and bring in something new. He
makes something new by restoring the old. Jesus didn't shed his body
and believers won't shed their bodies in favor of something new, but
the old body is restored and made better. Likewise with this material
world. "God doesn't plan to utterly destroy this present world and
build a brand-new world from scratch. Instead he plans a radical
renovation project for the world we live in today. The Bible never says
that everything will be burned up and replaced. Rather, it says that
everything will be purged with fire and restored."[19] Therefore, when
we demonstrate mercy and justice we not only testify to our changed
lives because of the resurrection, we are pointing people to the con-
summation of the resurrection, which is the renewal of this material

---

[18]Richard Stearns, *The Hole in Our Gospel: What Does God Expect of Us? The Answer that Changed My Life and Might Just Change the World* (Nashville, TN: Thomas Nelson, 2009), 22.
[19]Tullian Tchividjian, *Unfashionable: Making a Difference in the World by Being Different* (Sisters, OR: Multnomah, 2009), 52. Tullian sources Thomas Schreiner's study on 2 Peter 3:10 in Crossway's *ESV Study Bible*, 2422–2423 for the foundation of this point.

world. By living distinct, generous lives we testify that Jesus rose in the past but is continually at work in the world, which can be seen in our deeds as the church of God.

The three parts of this book are titled "The Man," "The Message," and "The Mission." And we have carefully gone through what each of these sections means to those of us brave enough (or crazy enough) to face the challenges of ministry, strong enough not to quit, and weak enough to know we can't possibly do it without the absolute power of God working in and through us. But as we close, it is important to consider another meaning for these section titles.

Jesus is "The Man." The ability for us to change into the men God has called us to be is dependent upon our surrender to the Man who has perfect character. All of what we hope for in the men who lead our churches is found in the perfect life of our Lord.

Jesus is "The Message." The power for others to change is rooted in the gospel, which both rescues the sinner and grows the saint. All that we need to know, experience, and proclaim is found in the person and work of Christ.

Jesus is "The Mission." The hope we have for this world to change is rooted in the resurrection, which both empowers the church to live and proclaim the gospel but also previews to the world how God makes all things new. Our only hope for a broken, jacked-up world is restoration, and our only hope for restoration is found in the One who forever conquered the radical effects of sin through his resurrection.

The apostle Paul says it so well in his encouraging letter to the Philippian church. His whole goal in life and his whole purpose for mission rested in the resurrection: "that I may know him and the power of his resurrection, and may share his sufferings, becoming like him in his death, that by any means possible I may attain the resurrection from the dead" (Philippians 3:10–11).

The resurrection enables the man to be qualified, it authenticates the message, and through the resurrection it previews the hope that this world can be renewed and will be restored.

City Dreaming

What if our cities were littered with new churches in every neighborhood? What if pastors actually put the gospel and the church above their comfort, ego, and preferences? What would happen if we spent less energy trying to make people feel comfortable and more energy making the gospel clear? What would happen if strong godly men and women were emboldened to use their gifts in the church, knowing that God is able to draw straight lines with crooked sticks? What if pastors were actually qualified in their character? What would happen if God's people actually had someone to look at and imitate? What if God's people realized that the role of the pastor is to equip them to do ministry instead of doing ministry for them? How many nonprofits would be started by God's people to address the broken areas of the city? How many at-risk children would be tutored, and how many fatherless teens would be mentored? How many single moms would be supported? How many immigrants would look to the church as a place of help and hope? How much more of God's grace would we understand if we sacrificially served the poor and the marginalized? How many lost, broken people would cease being their own savior and trust in Jesus?

I'll leave you with a story I heard from a friend of mine, Dave Ferguson, who pastors Christ Community Church in Chicago. At a conference where we spoke together, he shared with me a humbling conversation he had with famed church-growth guru Lyle Schaller. Dave was (as a smart pastor should) gleaning wisdom from the older and more experienced Schaller about how his church could better reach Chicago with the gospel. As Dave was articulating his vision, Schaller interrupted him. "Dave," he asked, "why do I have a bigger dream for the church in your city than you do?"

Much like Dave, my heart was stabbed with conviction at hearing Schaller's question. It was crystal-clear for me. Somehow, through fear or insecurity, I had let my dreams for our church shrink. I had stopped thinking about the limitless things God could do and had been distracted by my own limitations. I prayed right there that God would forgive me of my small-mindedness. I asked God to forgive my lack of faith that God could use a man like me to bring the message of the gospel through our missionary church to our lost city. I begged God to renew my heart and mind with a vision for our city that was more like Christ's.

If you're reading this, you may be in the same boat. Whether you've pastored a church for years or whether you are a future church planter looking at a city in need of the gospel, we can all learn from Schaller's challenge. Join me in prayers of repentance and renewal so that the gospel is preached and lived out in our cities through our churches. Amen.

RE:LIT

Resurgence Literature (Re:Lit) is a ministry of the Resurgence. At www.theResurgence.com you will find free theological resources in blog, audio, video, and print forms, along with information on forthcoming conferences, to help Christians contend for and contextualize Jesus' gospel. At www.ReLit.org you will also find the full lineup of Resurgence books for sale. The elders of Mars Hill Church have generously agreed to support Resurgence and the Acts 29 Church Planting Network in an effort to serve the entire church.

FOR MORE RESOURCES

Re:Lit – www.ReLit.org
Resurgence – www.theResurgence.com
Re:Sound – www.resound.org
Mars Hill Church – www.marshillchurch.org
Acts 29 – www.acts29network.org

Other Re:Lit Books:

Doctrine, Mark Driscoll and Gerry Breshears
Leaders Who Last, Dave Kraft
Scandalous, D. A. Carson
Vintage Church Team Study Pack, Mark Driscoll and Gerry Breshears
Religion Saves, Mark Driscoll
Vintage Church, Mark Driscoll and Gerry Breshears
Vintage Jesus Curriculum, Mark Driscoll and Gerry Breshears
Death By Love, Mark Driscoll and Gerry Breshears
Total Church, Tim Chester and Steve Timmis
Practical Theology for Women, Wendy Horger Alsup
Vintage Jesus, Mark Driscoll and Gerry Breshears

Re:Lit: A Book You'll Actually Read

On Who Is God?, Mark Driscoll
On the New Testament, Mark Driscoll
On the Old Testament, Mark Driscoll
On Church Leadership, Mark Driscoll